*Warwick Studies in Philosophy and Literature*
GENERAL EDITOR: ANDREW BENJAMIN

It used to be a commonplace to insist on the elimination of the 'literary' dimension from philosophy. This was particularly true for a philosophical tradition inspired by the possibilities of formalization and by the success of the natural sciences. And yet even in the most rigorous instances of such philosophy we find demands for 'clarity', for 'tight' argument, and distinctions between 'strong' and 'weak' proofs which call out for a rhetorical reading. Equally, modern literary theory, quite as much as literature itself, is increasingly looking to philosophy (and other theoretical disciplines such as linguistics) for its inspiration. After a wave of structuralist analysis, the growing influence of deconstructive and hermeneutic readings continues to bear witness to this. While philosophy and literature are not to be identified, even if philosophy is thought of as 'a kind of writing', much of the most exciting theoretical work being done today, in Britain, Europe and America, exploits their tensions and intertwinings. When one recalls that Plato, who wished to keep philosophy and poetry apart, actually unified the two in his own writing, it is clear that the current upsurge of interest in this field is only re-engaging with the questions alive in the broader tradition.

The University of Warwick pioneered the undergraduate study of the theoretical coition of Philosophy and Literature, and its recently established Centre for Research in Philosophy and Literature has won wide acclaim for its adventurous and dynamic programme of conferences and research. With this Series the work of the Centre is opened to a wider public. Each volume aims to bring the best scholarship to bear on topical themes in an atmosphere of intellectual excitement.

# WARWICK STUDIES IN PHILOSOPHY AND LITERATURE

*General editor*: David Wood

Books in the series include:

EXCEEDINGLY NIETZSCHE
Edited by David Farrell Krell and David Wood

POST-STRUCTURALIST CLASSICS
Edited by Andrew Benjamin

THE PROVOCATION OF LEVINAS
Edited by Robert Bernasconi and David Wood

THE PROBLEMS OF MODERNITY: Adorno and Benjamin
Edited by Andrew Benjamin

NARRATIVE IN CULTURE
Edited by Cristopher Nash

ABJECTION, MELANCHOLIA AND LOVE: The work of
Julia Kristeva
Edited by John Fletcher and Andrew Benjamin

THE BIBLE AS RHETORIC
Edited by Martin Warner

WRITING THE FUTURE
Edited by David Wood

Forthcoming:

JUDGING LYOTARD
Edited by Andrew Benjamin

NARRATIVE AND INTERPRETATION: The recent work of
Paul Ricoeur
Edited by David Wood

# PHILOSOPHERS' POETS

*Edited by*

## DAVID WOOD

**ROUTLEDGE**
London and New York

*First published 1990*
*by Routledge*
*11 New Fetter Lane, London EC4P 4EE*

*Simultaneously published in the USA and Canada*
*by Routledge*
*a division of Routledge, Chapman and Hall, Inc.*
*29 West 35th Street, New York, NY 10001*

© *1990 University of Warwick*

*Typeset by BookEns, Saffron Walden, Essex*
*Printed in Great Britain by Biddles Ltd, Guildford*

British Library Cataloguing in Publication Data
*Philosophers' poets.*
*1. Philosophy and literature*
*I. Wood, David,*
*100*

Library of Congress Cataloging in Publication Data
*Philosophers' poets/edited by David Wood.*
*p.   cm. — (Warwick studies in philosophy and literature)*
*1. Literature—Philosophy. 2. Philosophy in literature.*
*3. Criticism. I. Wood, David (David C.) II. Series.*
*PN49.P44   1990*
*809'.93384—dc20   89-27433*

*ISBN 0-415-04501-0*

# Contents

# Contents

# Notes on the Contributors

ROBERT BERNASCONI is Moss Professor of Philosophy at Memphis State University. He is the author of *The Question of Language in Heidegger's History of Being* (1985), editor of *The Relevance of the Beautiful: Essays by Hans-Georg Gadamer* (1986), and co-editor with David Wood of *Time and Metaphysics* (1982), *Derrida and Différance* (1985), and *The Provocation of Levinas: Rethinking the Other* (1989).

JAY BERNSTEIN is Senior Lecturer in Philosophy at the University of Essex. He is the author of *The Philosophy of the Novel: Lukacs, Marxism and the Dialectics of Form* (1984) and *Beauty Bereaved: Aesthetic Alienation from Kant to Derrida and Adorno* (forthcoming).

PAUL DAVIES is Assistant Professor of Philosophy at Loyola University of Chicago. He is the author of a forthcoming book on Heidegger, Blanchot, and Levinas, and has written several articles on recent French and German philosophy. He is currently editing a volume of essays on the work of Maurice Blanchot.

MARIAN HOBSON is a Fellow of Trinity College, Cambridge. She is the author of *The Object of Art: The Theory of Illusion in Eighteenth-century France* (1982) and is completing a book on Jacques Derrida.

CHRISTINA HOWELLS is Fellow and Tutor in French at Wadham College, Oxford. She teaches modern French literature and some Continental Philosophy, and is the author of *Sartre's Theory of Literature* and *Sartre: the Necessity of Freedom* (1987).

NICK LAND teaches philosophy at the University of Warwick. His PhD was based on Heidegger's 1953 Trakl reading and his current interests lie in post-Kantian materialism and insurrectionary libido theory. He is currently writing a book called *The Thirst for Annihilation: Georges Bataille and Virulent Pessimism*.

JOHN LLEWELYN recently retired as Reader in Philosophy at the University of Edinburgh. He is the author of *Beyond Metaphysics? The Hermeneutic Circle in Contemporary Continental Philosophy* (1985) and *Derrida on the Threshold of Sense* (1986).

MARY McALLESTER JONES teaches French at the University of Strathclyde, Glasgow. She has published widely on Bachelard, co-edited *The Philosophy and Poetics of Gaston Bachelard* (1989), and is the author of *Gaston Bachelard: Subversive Humanist* (1990).

DAVID WOOD is Senior Lecturer in Philosophy at the University of Warwick, and has held visiting appointments at Yale, Berkeley, and Duquesne. His recent books include *The Deconstruction of Time* (1988), *Writing the Future* (1990), and *Philosophy of the Limit* (1990). He was Programme Director of Warwick's Centre for Research in Philosophy and Literature (1987-9).

# Introduction:
# Thinking Poetic Writing

Ever since Plato banished the poets from his Republic, while he himself continued to write with such artistry, philosophy has had a troubled relationship with literature. At one extreme, philosophers imbued with scientific aspirations (Kant, Husserl, Carnap) have attempted to exclude all such arts from their own discourse on the grounds that literary language, no less than everyday language, is a dangerous source of vagueness and confusion, and that its association with rhetoric is inappropriate to a discipline committed to rational argument. At the other extreme, philosophers have more or less explicitly crossed the boundary and either made a certain style of writing a feature of their philosophizing (Nietzsche, Kierkegaard), or they have tried their hand at literature themselves (Sartre). There are, however, difficulties with each of these extremes.

The attempt to exclude the literary from philosophical writing is represented as a credible goal even if it cannot be fully completed. But some would argue that the intertwining of the literal and the metaphorical is such that even the project of cleaning up language is deeply flawed – that it cannot be seriously begun, let alone completed. Moreover, it is at least arguable that the kind of discourse we call scientific is not so much free of rhetoric, as another rhetoric competing for our allegiance.

On the other hand, those philosophers who consciously adopt literary techniques in their philosophy run the risk of being classified as merely *edifying* thinkers, who may be able to shake us out of our complacencies but cannot offer us any substantial alternative vision. Those who actually write novels, plays, or poems with a philosophical intent can never resolve the problem of exemplarity – of making the transition from the concretely imagined instance to a philosophical generalization – without reverting to philosophy of a more standard sort.

However, this problem of generalization can be reversed so as to capture a central problem for philosophy: its application to the concrete. While literature may not allow us to adjudicate on philosophical claims, there is every reason to think that the possibilities of imaginative description offered by literature can help us grasp what, in practice, certain philosophical claims might come to. If literature is or can be something of an experimental exploration of the ramifications of a philosophical position, and if that process is an essential dimension to the consideration one gives to a philosophical claim, then a philosophy that did not have its literary enactments or corollaries would be radically deficient. It is true that philosophical claims are usually asserted as the result of arguments, but not only do examples figure in the stages of such arguments, the fact that some philosophical proposition has been *proved* only alerts us to the need to begin our assessment of its scope and significance. And while further discussion and the private exercise of imagination have their place, literature is surely the most powerful exploratory tool.

There is another general direction and thrust of philosophers' interest in poetic writing. Without necessarily having an account of why or how it occurs, philosophers have often run up against the limits of what can be said. For Kierkegaard, there were matters which he called subjective and which were to him all-important, which simply could not be said directly, and for which indirect communication was the only remedy. He describes this in his *Concluding Unscientific Postscript* as a mode of communication in which the writer uses all the artistic means at his disposal to awaken the reader to what can only be indicated, not stated. For Wittgenstein, we inevitably run up against the limits of language, and contrary to positivism, what cannot be said – the ethical – is all-important. And it is Heidegger, that adept advocate of *thinking*, who reminds us at the end of his celebrated if barely understood *Time and Being* that the propositional form in which he has been writing, is not really adequate to capture his thought. It is the same Heidegger who finds the essence of language best revealed in poetry, particularly that of philosophical German poets (such as Rilke, Hölderlin, Georg, and Trakl), and for whom poetry and thinking occupy twin peaks. The point is that poetic discourse may be able to say what philosophy can know it cannot. If the limits of language were always the limits of a particular use of language, then it would matter enormously for philosophy if poetry could reach the parts that eluded a theoretical discourse.

The role of the poetic here derives from a consideration of the limits of traditional philosophical discourse. However, another dimension to this relationship has become apparent after Derrida's recent deployment of deconstructive strategies. It would be wrong to follow Rorty in thinking that philosophy is *just* a kind of writing, but after Nietzsche, Heidegger, and Derrida something has happened to our perception of the medium of philosophy. Not only does it, less contentiously, take a linguistic form, but it corrodes any idealistic account of what 'taking a linguistic form' might mean. Philosophy may typically suppose, indeed demand, that it is articulating *concepts* rather than the contingent terminological deposits of history, but such demands carry no guarantees of satisfaction. Philosophy is not just *any* kind of writing, but writing it is, even if it is distinctively a writing that would dissemble its own status. This designation does not so much mark a discovery as license a certain style of self-scrutiny. While philosophy was able to understand itself in its own terms, in conceptual terms, it was never vulnerable to the radical reflection that flows from the loss of that assured mirror. Once philosophy comes to see itself as one textual articulation of traces or differences among others, then it will have to capture its own distinctness in contrast to other forms of writing without any assured mastery over them. This does not make philosophy just another voice in the conversation of the West. Or rather the perspective from which that jaded judgment is made could never be that of philosophy. But if the distinctiveness of philosophy is understood in terms of its difference from other modes of writing, its relation to poetic and other literary texts will become central, and more interestingly problematic than ever. What we can expect is that the borderlines will be recast – not just moved, but rethought. More structural parallels will become visible, more mutual incursions and transgressions, at the same time as the boundary is maintained. (It is, of course, a myth of misreading – largely of his *White Mythology* – that Derrida reduces philosophy to literature.)

The essays in this volume are united in their careful focus on concrete instances of philosophers probing poets and other writers. The first three papers can be grouped around the figure of Heidegger, for whom the relation between philosophy and poetry came to be central. Robert Bernasconi excavates from a footnote in *Being and Time* Heidegger's treatment of Tolstoy's 'The Death of Ivan Ilyich'. The difficulty in interpreting Heidegger here bears on the crucial question in Heidegger's work of the relationship between theoretical (existential) inquiry, and everyday (existentiell) description. Through this example, Bernasconi unfolds with exquisite analytical care the levels and layers of Heidegger's project in *Being and Time*, showing how this concrete instance – Tolstoy's treatment of a socially inconvenient death – leads to a breakdown of Heidegger's key distinction, and teaches us of the destructive effect of all literary examples on the autonomy and integrity of the philosophical text. In Paul Davies' essay Heidegger is a key player in a tug of war with Levinas over the reading of Blanchot. Blanchot's crediting of the poem with the power to open on to the future seems to echo Heidegger unproblematically. Yet Levinas sees in Blanchot a break with Heidegger. He reads Blanchot as denying that the dialogue with poetry can give thinking a future. Rather poetry (and even the *récit* in the form of Blanchot's *Thomas the Obscure*) reveals the *il y a* – 'the mute and terrifying presence of existence' – that can only ruin ontology. For Levinas, Blanchot's *récits* force a transformation of the critical space that would read them, and his understanding of the poetic can be seen as inaugurating a stage beyond any dialogue of the Heideggerean sort. However, by looking at Blanchot's readings of Hölderlin and Char, Davies shows that his differences with Heidegger have to be more subtly gauged. With Blanchot, the distinctive disruption of thought by the advent of poetry is given the most radical expression. Nick Land's paper is more sharply focused on Heidegger's reading of Georg Trakl. Land, following in the wake of Derrida's discussion of Heidegger's treatment of *Geschlecht*, brilliantly and polemically marks the point at which Heidegger refuses the truly destructive and incendiary import of Trakl's poetry, and how he finally succumbs to 'a grotesque recapitulation of Kant's compromise with the ontotheological tradition'.

In the first of two papers on Derrida, John Llewelyn deploys an almost Joycean scholarship in discussing the importance for Mallarmé's writing of the death of his son Anatole at the age of eight: 'Derrida elicits from Mallarmé . . . why the project for an orphic explication of the earth was bound to fall short . . . and hence why no book could be a spiritual instrument in which the soul of the departed could be safely entombed.' And no more can a poem ever be completed. In the second, Marian Hobson intriguingly discusses one of those places ('La dissémination') in which Derrida does not so much write *on* another text, as write *in* it. Many generalizations about deconstruction ignore these kinds of text. Sollers had written a 'novel' – *Nombres* – organized around a principle of nominal, syntactic, citational, and general textual dispersion dubbed *dissemination*. Derrida's lengthy response mimics this same form, reproducing much of Sollers' own text, sometimes creatively deformed in the process, and, as Hobson shows, weaves together four different kinds of textual reflexivity. Derrida finds in Sollers' novel a guide to the production of the illusion of the Subject, and of the experience or value of Presence. Hobson discusses Mallarmé, compares Derrida's position to Kristeva's, and reminds us of the connection with Derrida's *Limited Inc abc* (on John Searle) in which the same textual dispersion of the Subject is articulated.

The final three papers are devoted to Sartre (on Flaubert, Mallarmé, Genet, and Baudelaire), Bachelard (on Shelley), and Adorno (in Beckett). Those whose view of Sartre's understanding of language is moulded on the prosaic narrowness of his *What is Literature?*, will be astonished by the Sartre unveiled by Christina Howells, a Sartre who came to acknowledge the importance of what Kierkegaard called the indirect use of language. She shows that even in that early work (in footnotes), Sartre anticipated the suggestion he worked out later (*L'Idiot . . .*) that poets' failure to communicate conceptually marks a distance, albeit negatively, from bourgeois ideology. Failure escapes totalization. With characteristic clarity, Howells traces the complex development of Sartre's position through his treatment of Mallarmé, Baudelaire, Genet, and Flaubert, and her closing remarks offer us a vision of a Sartre not only fascinated with the devices of other writers, but quite often practising them himself. This is a Sartre far more *indécidable* and far more interesting than some (such as Derrida) have made him out to be.

Mary McAllester Jones' paper deals with the poetic reflections of that most idiosyncratic of twentieth-century French thinkers, Gaston Bachelard. Bachelard was essentially a philosopher of science drawn to poetry in the course of writing his *Psychoanalysis of Fire* in 1938, seeing its importance for 'a complete theory of human imagination'. McAllester Jones shows the connections between his theory of poetry and his philosophy of science, which is based on the idea of a polemical and speculative relationship between thought and reality. While he tends to read only bits of poems – trawling for images – Shelley engages his fuller attention. Shelley is for Bachelard exemplary in his deployment of aerial images, images of lightness and elevation – essentially images of human transcendence. Shelley is 'a poet of the aerial substance'. And Bachelard exemplifies in his often impressionistic readings a response to poetry which acknowledges by trying to continue it, an encounter with 'an explosion of language', with new unexpected language. Finally, and in a very different vein, Jay Bernstein shows us how and why Beckett was so important for Adorno in the course of offering a view of why art is so important for philosophy. He begins by a remarkably succinct presentation of Adorno's aesthetics within a post-Kantian problematic. Art, through its non-conceptual form, embodies a resistance to the ideology of domination, to totalization, to identity-thinking, even if the very idea of this autonomy is drawn from the society against which art stands out. And the transformative power of art depends critically on its reception. Beckett's *Endgame* assumes a recent disaster. If this is the consequence of unending totalization, 'Beckett's artistic problem [is] to authenticate alterity, excess, the non-identical in such a way that recuperating . . . it is impossible.' Adorno is silent about the overall meaning of the play because it is its positive absence of meaning that 'puts meaning on the agenda'. Art cannot explain its determinate negation of existence without ceasing to be art. Philosophy cannot continue without ceasing to be philosophy. Adorno's *Aesthetic Theory* is perhaps a synthesis of these two moments.

Each of these papers is a major contribution to our understanding of philosophy's relation to non-philosophy, and to literature and poetry in particular. It is to be hoped that the success of the various approaches tried out here will inspire imitation.

David Wood

## · 1 ·

# Literary Attestation in Philosophy: Heidegger's Footnote on Tolstoy's 'The Death of Ivan Ilyich'

## ROBERT BERNASCONI

Tolstoy's name appears only once in Heidegger's published writings. He is named in a footnote to the discussion of Being-towards-death to be found in the first chapter of the second division of *Being and Time*. The footnote reads, 'L.N. Tolstoi hat in seiner Erzählung "Der Tod des Iwan Iljitsch" das Phänomen der Erschütterung und des Zusammenbruchs dieses "man stirbt" dargestellt.' Macquarrie and Robinson provide the following translation: 'In his story "The Death of Ivan Ilyitch" Leo Tolstoi has presented the phenomenon of the disruption and breakdown of having "someone die" ' (*SZ*, p. 254). The footnote seems straightforward enough. It would appear to invite a reading of Tolstoy's story which would serve to illustrate Heidegger's account of the phenomenon of everyday Being-towards-death.

The context in which the footnote appears, helps to confirm this meaning. The footnote is to be found in section 51 of *Being and Time*, a section entitled 'Being-towards-death and the Everydayness of Dasein'. The previous section had provided a preliminary sketch of the existential-ontological structure of death in an effort to show how Dasein's existence, facticity, and falling reveal themselves in the phenomenon of death. But in the same place Heidegger acknowledged that a *formal* sketch of this kind was insufficient on its own.

Being-towards-death must be exhibited in everydayness; the connection between Being-towards-death and care must be given phenomenal confirmation. Hence section 50, which provided a *formal* sketch of the ontological structure of death guided by the account of care arrived at in the final chapter of the First Division of *Being and Time*, was followed by section 51, which provided a *concrete* analysis of everyday Being-towards-death with the aim of confirming the formal sketch. However, insofar as the analysis was limited to the everyday, it remained essentially incomplete. For that reason, in section 52, the exposition went into reverse (*Umkehr*) and the interpretation of everyday Being-towards-death was interrogated in preparation for the introduction of authentic Being-towards-death. The latter was supposed to complete or supplement the former with a view to forming the 'full existential concept of death'.

This programme is not unproblematic. How are formal structures to be provided with concrete confirmation? In the Introduction to *Being and Time* Heidegger had employed a distinction between the existential and the existentiell in order to address the problem of our access to these structures and he returned to it whenever their basis was in question. The distinction operated in the following way. 'The question of existence is an ontical "affair" of Dasein' (*SZ*, p. 12). That is to say, it is a question which can only be 'cleared up', or 'brought to order' through existing. Heidegger gave the name *existentiell* to the kind of understanding which arises in this way. It was specifically divorced by him from the theoretical transparency of the ontological analysis of existence which he described as *existential*. Heidegger returned to the question of theoretical research, its praxis and its source in authentic existence in the second part of section 69, but only to postpone a full discussion of these questions to a part of *Being and Time* which was never written. Nevertheless, enough was said there to indicate that this cluster of problems had widespread implications, even for the conception of phenomenology set out in the Introduction. I will not pursue these questions here. I shall on this occasion set artificial limits around the question of the ontic foundation of ontology – the question of so-called metontology – in order to focus on some preliminary issues suggested by the chapter on Being-towards-death.

In spite of the attention that chapter has received, commentators have tended to ignore the fact that, far from being a self-contained unit, it leaves authentic Being-towards-death without ontic attestation. This can be shown simply by observing the structure of the chapter. Section 53 provided only the existential projection of an authentic Being-towards-death. It explored the existential conditions of the existentiell possibility of authentic Being-towards-death, but without offering a sketch of the existentiell possibility itself. That is to say, it was directed to the formal structures of existence insofar as they condition this ontical potentiality-for-Being. But the chapter ended without the addition of a concrete analysis which would serve to confirm these structures in the way that section 51 had supported the formal sketch found in section 50. The omission governs the next two chapters of *Being and Time*. The existentiell possibility of authentic Being-towards-death had been elucidated in its existential conditions in the course of the first chapter of the Second Division. Ontic attestation of this existentiell possibility remained to be established.

I have suggested that Heidegger employed the distinction between the existential and existentiell in order to describe how the ontological analysis of Dasein was supported at the ontic level. But existentiell descriptions, which are supposed to help confirm the existential analysis, can also serve to compromise the latter. At the end of section 49 Heidegger observed that from an ontic perspective, ontological characterization is liable to appear formalistic to the point of emptiness (*SZ*, p. 248). The concrete analyses of everyday Being-towards-death were supposed to compensate for this. All existentiell possibilities of Being-towards-death must be consistent with the ontological structures. Indeed the latter would provide the basis for the former. But the reverse cannot be countenanced. 'The existential definition of concepts must be unaccompanied by any existentiell commitments' (*SZ*, p. 248). This requirement had already been stated in section 9 and had necessitated the adoption of Dasein's average everydayness as the starting-point of the inquiry. This was to avoid construing Dasein 'in terms of some concrete possible idea of existence' (*SZ*, p. 43).

In the context of section 49 this meant that the existential analysis of death had to be kept rigorously separated from other interpretations. So, for example, all 'ontic other-worldly speculation' about an after-life must be rigorously excluded. The ontological interpretation of death is characterized as 'this-worldly'. Not, as Heidegger made clear in one of his lecture-courses, that this prejudges the traditional questions of immortality and resurrection.[1] It is rather the precondition for posing such questions in a legitimate manner. But can existentiell commitments and ideals ever be excluded? Heidegger is unambiguous in the answer that he gives at the end of the chapter.

The ontological investigation has, he says, taken place 'without holding up to Dasein an ideal of existence with any special "content", or forcing any such ideal upon it "from outside" ' (*SZ*, p. 266). One can legitimately ask whether this answer would have been quite so persuasive had the elucidation of the existentiell possibility of authentic Being-towards-death not been postponed to a later chapter. Of course, its omission from this chapter does nothing of itself to secure the purity of the analysis. The absence of an explicit account of authentic Being-towards-death at the ontic level is no guarantee of the lack of an ideal of existence operating implicitly within the analysis. But this consideration turns out to be unimportant anyway. Heidegger was to undercut this line of questioning later in the book when he conceded after all that there had indeed been 'a definite ontical way of taking authentic existence, a factical ideal of Dasein, underlying our ontological interpretation of Dasein's existence' (*SZ*, p. 310). I shall return to this point later. I mention it now only as some indication of how serious the question of the relation between the existential and the existentiell will prove for the analysis. It is not too much to say that what is at stake is the very possibility of fundamental ontology as usually conceived. The purpose of this essay is to suggest that Heidegger's brief reference to Tolstoy's story plays a more intimate role in this drama than might at first be imagined. But first the footnote itself must be submitted to a more careful examination.

The footnote is, as I have already said, to be found in section 51. The section takes up the phrase 'one dies' (*man stirbt*). This 'one' is the 'they' (*das Man*) of everydayness, the nobody (*das Niemand*), and the phrase gives rise to an analysis of three kinds of fleeing in the face of death. The three – temptation, tranquillizing, and alienation – are drawn from the four phenomena used in section 38 to characterize falling. The fourth, entanglement or *Verfängnis* in the sense of exaggerated self-dissection, is omitted from section 51, although later 'the fetters of a weary "inactive thinking about death" ' (*SZ*, p. 258) and 'brooding over death' (*SZ*, p. 261) gain Heidegger's attention. Here the temptation is said to be that people try to persuade the 'dying person' that he or she is not dying; tranquillization takes the form that even when someone dies the tranquillity and carefreeness of the public is not to be disturbed; and finally the alienation of Dasein from its ownmost non-relational potentiality-for-Being occurs when anxiety in the face of death comes to be regarded as fear and passed off as weakness. The reference to Tolstoy is appended to the discussion of the second of these, tranquillization or *Beruhigung*. Specifically, it is attached to the sentence which reads, 'Indeed the dying of Others is seen often enough as social inconvenience, if not even a downright tactlessness, against which the public is to be guarded' (*SZ*, p. 254).

No reader of Tolstoy's story would have any difficulty in recognizing how it illustrates the phenomenon in question. From the first chapter, which opens with the announcement of the death of Ivan Ilyich, Tolstoy is concerned with 'the exceedingly tiresome demands of propriety'. These are exhibited in the context of both the requiem service (T, p. 102) and the issuing of condolences to the widow. Both interrupt 'the recognized order of things' – namely, a regular game of cards such as Ivan himself used to play (T, p. 104). The expression on the face of the dead man serves as 'a reminder to the living', but one they prefer to ignore as having nothing to do with them (T, p. 104). Similarly, it is remarked later in the story that Ivan's daughter was 'impatient with illness, suffering and death because they interfered with her happiness' (T, p. 149). So Tolstoy's story illustrates what Heidegger calls the social inconvenience of death. It also provides examples of the other kinds of fleeing in the face of death. The temptation to talk 'the "dying person" into the belief that he will escape death' (*SZ*, p. 253) is exhibited by a belief both in wonder-working icons (T, p. 130) and in the curative powers of medicine: 'Stimulate the sluggish organ, check the activity of another – secretion ensues, and everything would come right' (T, p. 134). Other people – with the exception of the young peasant Gerassim – come to mean falsity (T, p. 151): 'Gerassim alone told no lies' (T, p. 143). And finally, Ivan Ilyich exhibits his alienation – which is the third form of fleeing in the face of death – not only by his fear of death, but also by the way he goes along with the attempts of people around him to persuade him that he is getting better. It would even be possible to illustrate the fourth phenomenon of falling by pointing to the entanglement in the frenzied self-dissection which Ivan engages in as part of his revolt against death and his attempt to find a moral explanation of why he must die.

Details such as these, as well as the placing of the footnote within section 51 of *Being and Time*, no doubt encouraged Macquarrie and Robinson to offer the translation of it which they did: 'In his story "The Death of Ivan Ilyitch" Leo Tolstoi has presented the phenomenon of the disruption and breakdown of having "someone die".' The disruption and breakdown is the social inconvenience (*gesellschaftliche Unannehmlichkeit*) which the illness and death of someone causes for those in the immediate vicinity. That this is the interpretation underlying the translation receives partial confirmation in Macquarrie's book on *Existentialism* where he himself draws on Tolstoy's story to 'illustrate' Heidegger's account. 'For everyone except Ivan (and even for him up till the moment when he becomes aware that he is mortally ill) death is a most inconvenient and disagreeable subject, not to be thought about or talked about. For Ivan, it becomes a theme of engrossing importance, colouring everything else.'[2] Macquarrie, doubtless recalling the description of the phenomenon of entanglement, denies that Heidegger is recommending morbid brooding over death: 'He explicitly rejects such brooding.' But Macquarrie does not look to Tolstoy's story for a concretization of anything but the everyday attitude to death.

Nevertheless, Heidegger's footnote permits another reading, a reading which corresponds more closely to the German. It would run: 'L.N. Tolstoy, in his story "The Death of Ivan Ilyitch" has presented the phenomenon of the shattering and the collapse of this "one dies" .' On this reading Heidegger's point would not be that Tolstoy's story exhibits the everyday attitude to death, or at least not that only. The story would also be called upon to show the shattering of the everyday attitude. Tolstoy, having presented the way we for the most part refer death away from ourselves to everyone else, shows how one individual, Ivan Ilyich, comes to confront his own death. But at what point in the story does this happen? How might the everyday attitude be brought to a point of collapse? And would that mean that Tolstoy's story was cited in preparation for the analysis of authentic Being-towards-death?

The shattering and breakdown of the 'one dies' takes place in the first instance as the recognition that I myself am going to die. This is something certain. Not in the everyday manner of being certain, which is a question of the kind of certainty we can have about beings as we encounter them. The certainty which belongs to anticipation – or rather 'running ahead' (*Vorlaufen*) – is somewhat different (*SZ*, p. 265). In the story we read that Ivan comes to realize that the textbook syllogism 'Caius is a man, men are mortal, Caius is mortal' does apply to him after all. 'If I had to die like Caius I should have known it was so, some inner voice would have told me. But there was nothing of the sort in me, and I and all my friends, we knew that it was quite different in our case. And now here it is!' (T, p. 137). Tolstoy comments, 'Strangely enough all that used to cover up, obscure and obliterate the feeling of death no longer had the same effect' (T, p. 138). This is registered in the sixth of the twelve chapters. And in the seventh chapter, the pretence, the lie, the temptation to believe that he would get better is less a comfort than a torment to Ivan (T, p. 142). At these moments everyday evasion of death is no longer effective. But does it amount to a 'shattering and collapse of the "one dies" '?

From chapter six through chapter eleven, Ivan Ilyich's attitude to death fluctuates. Even at the beginning of the last chapter, we can still read that Ivan's doubts remain unresolved (T, p. 159). Ivan had already begun to entertain the suspicion that his life had in some way been mis-spent, but as the final chapter opens, he may still be found maintaining that he had led a proper life. Because he appears to believe that the nature of his death should be in some way related to the quality of his life, he continues his revolt against death. 'That very justification of his life held him fast and prevented him from advancing, and caused him more agony than anything else' (T, p. 159). Ivan Ilyich is still caught up with himself, as is illustrated by the way he wants to be pitied. Has the inauthentic evasion of death been shattered so long as Ivan Ilyich is still in this frame of mind?

Authenticity is not to be understood as a simple alternative to inauthenticity. It is true that at the beginning of the existential analysis, and when he is rehearsing that beginning as in section 45, Heidegger gives the impression that authenticity, inauthenticity, and indifference are formally equivalent modes. But Heidegger makes few attempts to maintain this impression. The inauthentic and the indifference of averageness frequently merge in everydayness and the fallenness of the 'they'. And as soon as Heidegger had posed the question of the who of Dasein in its everydayness, another tendency emerged. It came to be recognized that '*Authentic Being-one's-Self* does not rest upon an exceptional condition of the subject, a condition that has been detached from the "they"; *it is rather an existentiell modification of the "they" – of the "they" as an essential existentiale*' (*SZ*, p. 130). That is why Heidegger can ask whether Dasein can maintain itself in an authentic Being-towards-its end: 'How is the ontological possibility of an *authentic* Being-towards-death to be characterized "Objectively", if, in the end, Dasein never comports itself authentically towards its end . . .?' (*SZ*, p. 260. Cf. also *SZ*, p. 169). His answer – which is that Dasein cannot be said to *be* authentic in the same manner in which Dasein *is* inauthentic – returns us to the question of attestation: 'The question of Dasein's authentic Being-a-whole and of its existential constitution . . . can be put on a phenomenal basis which will stand the test only if it can maintain a possible authenticity of its Being which is attested by Dasein itself' (*SZ*, p. 267). The sentence should be read with the emphasis on possibility. It is the possibility of authenticity which is crucial and indeed it is this focus on possibility which enables Heidegger to reverse the alleged priority of the 'they' to say that the they-self is an existentiell modification of the authentic self (*SZ*, pp. 317–18). Or, as was already said in section 52, 'inauthenticity is based on possible authenticity' (*SZ*, p. 259). So if there was a shattering of the everyday in Ivan's case, this means not that he was held in authenticity as some kind of constant state, but in its possibility. It is hard to see, even on these terms, that there was such a shattering prior to the brief last chapter of 'The Death of Ivan Ilyich'. This is the centre of gravity of most readings of Tolstoy's story anyway. Examining now two very different attempts to relate Tolstoy's story to Heidegger's account of death, it will be no surprise to find that they both also come to focus on this final chapter.

The most extravagant claims have been made by Walter Kaufmann, who provided the alternative, more literal, translation of Heidegger's footnote that I quoted above. He insisted that 'Heidegger on death is for the most part an unacknowledged commentary on "The Death of Ivan Ilyitch" ',[3] an uncritical repetition of 'Christian commonplaces in secularized form'.[4] Kaufmann maintained this thesis by emphasizing Ivan Ilyich's courage, specifically his having the courage at the end to defy propriety and shriek.[5] Kaufmann appears to have understood this moment as a passage from an evasive fear of death to anxiety or dread in the face of death. It was, in other words, an overcoming of the alienation of Dasein from its ownmost non-relational potentiality-for-Being. But Kaufmann did not explain the significance of the fact that in Tolstoy's story, Ivan Ilyich subsequently becomes quiet. Kaufmann emphasizes Ivan Ilyich's anxiety before death as expressed in the scream, but he says nothing about the moment when it seems that there is neither fear, nor the shock of anxiety, because, in Ivan Ilyich's own words, 'death is over' (T, p. 161). This suggests that one cannot identify Heidegger with Tolstoy, at least on the basis of the minimal and highly selective reading that Kaufmann offered.

William Spanos has written on the relation between Heidegger and Tolstoy's story in more detail and with much greater sensitivity than Kaufmann. And yet Spanos's reading is also in certain respects one-sided. Whereas Kaufmann selected only those passages from the story which assist him in his attempt to reduce Heidegger to Tolstoy, Spanos was inclined to see only those aspects of Tolstoy's story which are in conformity with his picture of Heidegger. So, for example, Spanos focused on the image of the black sack which Tolstoy introduces in chapter nine to show Ivan resisting his death. Spanos understood this resistance as having its source in Ivan's dread (*Angst*). It is Ivan's dread or anxiety in the face of death which prevents him from 'perceiving anything positive in the weak impulse to assist the process of dying'. But that left Spanos in difficulty when it comes to providing an interpretation of the passage in the last chapter where Tolstoy has Ivan entering the black sack, now described as a hole, and finding light within it (T, p. 159). Spanos confronted this problem by leaving behind the language of *Angst* from *Being and Time* and turning instead to the later Heidegger's notion of releasement (*Gelassenheit*) (S, p. 31). That Tolstoy wrote 'Let the pain be' (T, p. 160) might seem to provide some justification for this reference to *Gelassenheit*. But what is the relation between Ivan's *Angst* and his *Gelassenheit*? It is hardly surprising that Spanos avoided this question. It goes far beyond the question of the relation of the early and the late Heidegger. It might perhaps be conceded that *Angst* is not wholly lacking from the later Heidegger and that *Gelassenheit* is not altogether absent from *Being and Time*. But to establish a proximity between *Angst* and *Gelassenheit* would only serve to suggest that if Ivan exhibited *Gelassenheit* in his last moments when accepting death, then his earlier resistance of death should have been construed by Spanos, in terms of Heidegger's well-known distinction, as fear rather than dread. Spanos identified certain 'Heideggerian' moments in 'The Death of Ivan Ilyich' but it is at best unclear whether he succeeded in giving a coherent reading of Tolstoy's story in terms of Heidegger.

Spanos understood his treatment of the story as an attempt 'to get below the exclusively socio-moral readings that interpret death as merely a judgement against the hollowness of his life'. He believed that Tolstoy's ultimate point was not simply a moralistic or ontic one, 'but rather, or at least primarily, an ontological one' (S, p. 34). With his introduction of this distinction Spanos touched on the central problem of the relation between the existential and the existentiell outlined above, even if he did not seem fully aware of its contours as a problem. Spanos joined with Kaufmann in identifying Tolstoy's moralizing as the major obstacle to securing some form of unity which would join Tolstoy and Heidegger. This is hardly surprising, given Heidegger's frequent renunciation of the moralizing tone which his language tends to evoke. But the fact that Heidegger's language evokes this tone in spite of his expressed intentions cannot be dismissed so quickly, as I shall try to show later.

The strength of Spanos's reading of Tolstoy's story lies in his treatment of its temporality. The ever-quickening tempo of the story corresponds with a transformation in Ivan's temporality. The weakness of Spanos's essay, on the other hand, is to be found in his failure to confront the difficulties of giving a reading of the end of the story which would be consistent with a Heideggerian intention. As to the first, Ivan's encounter with death is, for Spanos, an encounter with temporality (S, p. 17). Spanos was right to observe that Ivan's confrontation with death was not something sudden, reserved until the end of his life: 'the process is not abrupt'. He situated in Book Six Ivan's 'first positive intimation' of the imminence of death, 'faint and brief though it is' (S, p. 19). But this qualification is perhaps not readily reconcilable with a rather bolder claim made by Spanos also about Book Six. Referring to Ivan's crucial encounter with the 'my-ownness of death', Spanos wrote that 'He has been driven out of the refuge provided by the public spatial structure of *das Man* into authenticity' (S, p. 17). The difference in emphasis between these two judgments is not a simple consequence of indecision on the part of Spanos. The tension in Spanos should be referred to the tension within Heidegger's own treatment of authenticity. Heidegger, I noted earlier, ultimately seems to focus on possible authenticity and not on the sense in which one might *be* authentic as one might *be* inauthentic. The question has further ramifications beyond those I have introduced here. I mention it now largely in order to be able to indicate the depth of Spanos's understanding of the last chapter. There, at the 'instant of surrender', Ivan 'dis-covers "the right thing": that life is *relationship* and . . . redemption is never lost to the past, but is *always* a possibility of the future' (S, p. 32). In this way, Spanos seems to opt for an understanding of authenticity as *possibility*.

Nevertheless, it is at this same point that the difficult passage from *Angst* to *Gelassenheit* is situated. Spanos presented Ivan's last words – 'death is finished' – as meaning that death has undergone a paradoxical metamorphosis: 'death, in the courageous act of confrontation, undergoes a paradoxical metamorphosis: *It* becomes a benign agent, a *Thou*'. Spanos called this a 'de-structed sense' (S, p. 33). His references to Greek and Hebraic archetypes at this point are not, however, sufficient to clarify precisely what he meant. The *It* belongs to Book Six, where, Spanos told us, it occurs over a dozen times. But there is some difficulty explaining the source of the *Thou*, without having recourse to Buber's famous and, in this context, somewhat inappropriate dichotomy.

Spanos's introduction of the *Thou* does, if only unwittingly, alert us to the fact that if the familiar characterization of Heideggerian Being-towards-death is followed, the last pages of Tolstoy's story seem to represent an almost unambiguous collapse into the inauthentic. Is Ivan's exclamation of joy not the denial of anxiety in the face of death? Are not his final words – 'Death is over. It is no more' – inserted into the novel as 'a way of escape, fabricated for the "overcoming of death" ' (*SZ*, p. 310)? Is not their echo of the final words of Jesus Christ suggestive of an unwarranted introduction of 'ontical other-worldly speculation' (*SZ*, p. 248)? Is not Ivan's recourse to his wife and son in his final hours, having neglected them throughout his life, a pathetic failure to acknowledge that he must die alone? Does not the conclusion of Tolstoy's story slide into inauthenticity with its proposal of what amounts to 'norms and rules for composing oneself towards death . . . for "edification" ' (*SZ*, p. 248)? And is not the story simply propaganda for Tolstoy's own unsubstantiated idea that 'the better a man's life the less dreadful death is to him and the easier it is for him to die'[6] – a view which represents a temptation for the dying person no less inauthentic than that of a hope in doctors or icons? It would appear that a Heideggerian reading of the story must stop short of the last moments of Ivan's life for good reason. It runs completely counter to the *existentialist* picture of man dying alone which has been drawn from Heidegger's discussion of death by critics from Sartre onwards. That would help explain – without legitimating – Spanos's sudden shift of gear, whereby his references to *Being and Time* gave way to talk of *Gelassenheit*.

Both the existentialist approach to death and that represented by

Tolstoy's moralizing would, insofar as they come into conflict, have to be characterized as existentiell. Spanos sought, by contrast, to give an ontological reading of the story. He explicitly opposed his reading both to Kaufmann's existentialist interpretation and to what he regarded as the more conventional literary interpretation, which treats the story as 'essentially a *vehicle* for a moral (ontic) assertion' (S, p. 3). Nevertheless, it may prove as hard to reduce the moralizing weight of Tolstoy's 'The Death of Ivan Ilyich' as it has proved difficult for Heidegger to convince his readers that his own discussion was, as he claimed, 'far removed from any moralizing critique of everyday Dasein' (*SZ*, p. 167).

At this point it is tempting to have recourse to another reading of Tolstoy's story, one which would be less intent on diminishing the moral basis of the story, but which at the same time would secure its philosophical significance. A reading inspired by the ethical philosophy of Emmanuel Levinas might well meet these requirements.[7] Certain parallels would quickly emerge between Tolstoy's story and Levinas's discussion of death, a discussion developed in specific contrast to Heidegger's account in *Being and Time*. So, for example, Levinas insists that death has the temporality of a perpetual postponement. Death is always 'ever future', leaving time 'to be for the Other' (*TeI*, pp. 212–13; *TI*, pp. 235–6). Ivan's discovery that 'It was still possible to put it right' (T, p. 160), evokes Levinas's insistence that 'There is before a death a last chance that heroes seize, which is not death.'[8] Does that mean that, insofar as Heidegger uses Tolstoy's story as evidence for his own analysis, the evidence in fact goes against him? According to Heidegger, it is the 'they', not the hero or the authentic Dasein, who has more time (*SZ*, p. 425). Other details could be used to support a Levinasian reading. The important question – 'What if in reality my whole life has been wrong?' – arises when Ivan Ilyich was looking at 'Gerassim's sleepy, good-natured face' (T, p. 157), thereby recalling Levinas's claim that it is the face of the Other which puts me into question. And, above all, do not the concluding pages of Tolstoy's story suit very well Levinas's description, where 'Death source of all myths, is *present* only in the Other, and only in him does it summon me urgently to my final essence, to my responsibility' (*TeI*, pp. 153–4; *TI*, p. 178)? So, according to Levinas, the relation with death maintains the social conjuncture. The doctor is regarded by him as an *a priori* principle of human mortality, so that death approaches accompanied by hope in someone

(*TeI*, p. 210; *TI*, p. 234). And the crucial transformation in Ivan's relation to his own death comes when he is, in Levinas's phrase, 'liberated from the egoist gravitation' (*TeI*, p. 213; *TI*, p. 236). But decisions for and against rival philosophical interpretations of a story cannot be made on the basis of a few details. It would be necessary to attempt a sustained Levinas's reading of 'The Death of Ivan Ilyich'. But to what purpose? And what does it mean to call a reading of a story after the name of a philosopher? Valuable though it might be to explore such a reading on some other occasion, in the present context it would distract from the question of the character and legitimacy of philosophical readings of literature.

What is the role of literary examples within philosophy texts? What is literary attestation? Is an attestation such that it could not only fail to attest, but in certain cases actually refute what it was introduced to support? Or must formal structures always govern the consideration of concrete possibilities? In this essay I can provide no more than a prolegomenon to a serious consideration of such questions. It is undertaken in the conviction that, by appealing to Heidegger's language of the existential and the existentiell, the question may be put in a particularly forceful way. The difficulties that accumulate around Heidegger's distinction, such that it sometimes seems appropriate to talk of the collapse of the distinction and thus the breakdown of the very project of fundamental ontology, do not count against this. They are rather to be considered as evidence of the power of the terms themselves. Nobody has yet shown that subsequent philosophy, including that of the later Heidegger, is better able to answer these questions simply because it has turned away from the difficult – perhaps impossible – distinction between the existential and the existentiell.[9]

It should be recalled that Heidegger introduced the footnote on Tolstoy in a section on the everyday attitude to death. This concrete treatment was introduced as a response to the 'peculiar *formality* and emptiness of any ontological characterization' (*SZ*, p. 248). But the problem extended further than that. So long as the account was formal, it was in danger of being arbitrary. It needed confirmation. Heidegger had already encountered a similar problem in the course of his presentation of care as 'a basic existential-ontological phenomenon' (*SZ*, p. 196). In order to defend himself against the charge of arbitrariness, Heidegger had felt obliged to show that there was a prior ontico-existentiell basis for this ontological interpretation. 'In explicating Dasein's Being-as-care, we are not forcing it under an idea of our own contriving, but we are conceptualizing existentially what has already been disclosed in an ontico-existentiell manner' (*SZ*, p. 196). It is for this reason that Heidegger in section 42 cited one of the ancient fables of Hyginus on care. Heidegger described the document as 'pre-ontological'. It was, he said, a primordial expression of Dasein, 'unaffected by any theoretical interpretation and without aiming to propose any' (*SZ*, p. 197). This claim was somewhat compromised when Heidegger conceded that the priority of care maintained by the fable arose in the context of the familiar interpretation of man as a compound of body and mind or spirit (*Geist*) (*SZ*, p. 198). Furthermore, Heidegger in a lecture-course acknowledged that he was in the first instance drawn to the phenomenon of care not by the fable, which he noticed only subsequently, but in the course of his reading of Augustine and Christian anthropology in general.[10] But the primary question here is not that of whether we find Heidegger's justification of his selection of the phenomenon of care convincing. The question is why he should have recourse to a so-called 'pre-ontological' document to justify the existential-ontological interpretation. His answer reversed familiar categories. 'The testimony which we are about to cite should make plain that our existential interpretation is not a fabrication (*Erfindung*), but that as an ontological "construction" it has a basis which has been sketched out beforehand in an elemental way' (*SZ*, p. 197). In other words, the suspicion is less that the fable is a fabrication or a fiction, than that without its testimony, the existential interpretation itself would have to be regarded as one.

The same issues are at stake in the course of the chapter on Being-towards-death. The task is that of providing phenomenal confirmation for the ontological status accorded to care understood as the totality of Being-a-whole (*SZ*, p. 252). The danger is that the attempt to provide an existential projection of an authentic Being-towards-death would result in no more than '*a fanciful undertaking*' (*ein phantastisches Unterfangen*) and '*a merely fictitious arbitrary construction*' (*eine nur dichtende, willkürliche Konstruktion*) (*SZ*, p. 260). At the end of the first chapter of the Second Division, Heidegger confirmed that authentic Being-towards-death, although now shown to be *existentially* possible, still had the status of a fanciful or fantastical exaction (*eine phantastische Zumutung*) at the *existentiell* level (*SZ*, p. 266). The implication is that fundamental ontology would lose its scientific credentials and be reduced to the status of mere literature, a work of fiction. For, as Heidegger has already warned, the character of an arbitrary fiction (*willkürliche Erdichtung*) is that it lacks the testimony of the thing at issue, which alone is the proper basis of conviction (*SZ*, p. 256). The problem is not resolved in the course of the chapter on Being-towards-death. Heidegger chose to emphasize the problems of a characterization of authentic Being-towards-death. Was it because the presentation of everyday Being-towards-death in section 51 was relatively unproblematic, being a simple application of the structures already outlined in chapter five of the First Division? Or was it not because, from the outset and *contrary to the order of presentation* the possibility of authenticity had underpinned the analysis so that all doubts must ultimately come to be directed to it? This latter hypothesis is partially confirmed by the way in which the 'obviousness' of the analyses in Division One are put in question in the course of Division Two (*SZ*, p. 332). Division One does not provide a secure foundation for Division Two.

The hypothesis under examination, based on the revised translation of Heidegger's footnote, is that Heidegger's reference to 'The Death of Ivan Ilyich' serves not only to confirm the account of everyday Being-towards-death, but also to mark a place where the factical idea of authentic existence intervenes. As Heidegger subsequently admitted, such ideas had inevitably determined the formal analysis from the outset. To put it another way, Heidegger would subsequently attempt an existentiell confirmation of the existential structures in an effort to save fundamental ontology from being reduced to the status of an arbitrary fiction. Meanwhile, this footnote reference to Tolstoy's story was a kind of holding operation, a temporary measure, although perhaps not without permanent consequences for the meaning of *Being and Time*.

The language to which Heidegger has recourse in the face of the difficulties threatening to overwhelm the quest for fundamental ontology gives a centrality to the question of the relation of philosophy and literature that readers of *Being and Time* seem not to have observed. The rhetoric implies that fiction is outside the truth. Were the ontological analysis to prove a fiction, it would no longer be philosophy. But Heidegger's own practice belies that rhetoric, even on the restricted reading of the footnote provided by Macquarrie and Robinson. The analysis of everyday Being-towards-death was supported, not by the evidence of direct observation, but by a work of

ROBERT BERNASCONI

fiction. This is not accidental. If we could readily face up to this evasion as a matter of course, if it was obvious to us, if we only need to have it drawn to our attention for us to be able to acknowledge it, then Heidegger's account of everydayness would have to undergo radical revision. Rather than confirming Dasein's fallenness, all claims about the predominance of fallenness would have been compromised. And yet Heidegger began with everydayness on the grounds that it is ontically closest to us, notwithstanding that it is also ontologically the furthest. Under what circumstances does the inauthentic show itself as such? What is the point of access to Dasein in all its modes – authentic, inauthentic, and undifferentiated between the two? I shall not rehearse that controversy here.[11] There is some suggestion in section 9 that Heidegger looked to averageness as the everyday undifferentiated character of Dasein in order to circumvent the difficulty that Dasein might be construed in terms of some possible concrete idea of existence (SZ, p. 43). However, the difficulty of situating the everyday in relation to the inauthentic and the undifferentiated makes this interpretation far from easy to sustain. There is also some difficulty in correlating it with Heidegger's explicit references both to anxiety as that which makes the authentic and inauthentic manifest to Dasein as possibilities (SZ, p. 191) and to conscience as revealing Dasein's lostness in the 'they' (SZ, p. 307). These seem to point to authenticity as performing the role of providing this access. In that case, Tolstoy's story must itself in some way share in authenticity. For even on the minimal reading of the footnote, 'The Death of Ivan Ilyich' is required to reveal Dasein in its inauthenticity.

I shall not here try to follow Heidegger through all the stages of the second chapter of the Second Division during his search for testimony of authentic existence as an existentiell possibility. Nor shall I repeat the analysis in chapter three where he attempted to secure an essential connection between this existentiell possibility and the ontological possibility already projected in the course of the chapter on Being-towards-death. Nevertheless it can briefly be indicated that the subsequent analysis took the form it did precisely because Heidegger kept separate two questions. First, there was the question of existentiell attestation of Dasein's authentic potentiality-for-Being. Secondly, there was the question of correlating this existentiell attestation with the existential structures already arrived at in the chapter on Being-towards-death, that is to say, with Dasein's authentic potentiality-for-Being-a-whole. The first question pointed to resoluteness, through a discussion of what the everyday interpretation of Dasein calls 'the voice of conscience' (*SZ*, p. 268). The second question was that of how resoluteness as an existentiell tendency could be brought – or even 'welded' (*SZ*, p. 305) – together with 'running ahead' (*vorlaufen*) as the existential structure of Being-towards-death (*SZ*, p. 302). The minute care with which Heidegger charted his course is some indication of the importance he attached to these questions.

It was thus not until chapter three that Heidegger attempted to address directly the question already raised in the course of chapter one of the Second Division as to whether the existential conception of death is possible in an existentiell way or whether it is an arbitrary fiction (*SZ*, p. 303). And, on the basis of a repetition of section 53 now rethought in terms of resoluteness, the answer soon follows that this conception is not just a fictional possibility forced upon Dasein, but is a mode of an existentiell potentiality-for-Being attested by Dasein (*SZ*, p. 309).

This reconstruction of Heidegger's attempted resolution will have to suffice for the present purpose. Heidegger was well aware of how far his discussion fell short of fundamental ontology, if it were to be regarded, in Husserl's phrase, as a rigorous science. The lecture-courses of the Marburg period show this most clearly, but it is apparent from *Being and Time* itself. For example, at the beginning of the third chapter Heidegger asked if the attempt to bring together resoluteness and running ahead did not amount to an 'unphenomenological construction' (*SZ*, p. 302). Heidegger's rejection of this proposal rendered inevitable a revision of the concept of phenomenology of the kind he called for in the fourth chapter of *Being and Time*. He had by then already conceded that it would be mistaken to conceive Dasein's authentic potentiality-for-Being-a-whole in terms of proof: 'It would be a misunderstanding to shove this existentiell possibility aside as "unproved" or to want to "prove" it theoretically' (*SZ*, pp. 309–10). Three times in the course of as many pages, Heidegger insisted that the formal idea of existence which he had elucidated was not binding on his readers in an existentiell way (*SZ*, pp. 312–14). He warned that the phenomenon needed to be 'protected against the grossest perversions' (*SZ*, p. 310), but did not indicate how this might be done. If as a first step one might try to make the concrete ideal of existence as explicit as possible, it has to be said that Heidegger did not accomplish very much in this direction. There is a sentence which helps to explain why. 'Philosophy will never seek to deny its "presuppositions", but neither may it simply admit (*zugeben*) them' (*SZ*, p. 310). Philosophy cannot admit its presuppositions in the sense of granting them or acceding to them. It must constantly fight against these ontic presuppositions, even if it can never be presuppositionless. But for that very reason, a philosophy will often give the illusion of being more rigorous or compelling to the extent that it fails to acknowledge its presuppositions and simply keeps silent about them.

It is with this in mind that I return now to Heidegger's footnote on 'The Death of Ivan Ilyich'. We were left with the choice between, on the one hand, the translation by Macquarrie and Robinson which restricted the significance of the reference to the everyday and, on the other hand, the alternative translation which left the problem of interpreting the final chapter of Tolstoy's story in an effort to find there the shattering of the 'they', the shattering of the 'one dies'. Because the first alternative adopts a somewhat forced reading of Heidegger's footnote, it is important to pursue the second route.

Literary texts have a certain autonomy, but what happens to them when they are submitted to philosophically inspired readings? How does a literary example function within a philosophical text? Heidegger says that 'The ontological "truth" of the existential analysis is developed on the ground of the primordial existentiell truth. However, the latter does not necessarily need the former' (*SZ*, p. 316). We may not be able to decide for sure whether Tolstoy's story does indeed provide the existentiell basis for Heidegger's existential analysis, but Heidegger eventually admits that he cannot do without some such existentiell ideal. And novels are peculiarly effective at this level. Just as the Greeks recognized that only the poetic could preserve *praxis*, so we need literary texts to show resoluteness and Being-towards-death. Authentic Being remains hidden from others (*SZ*, p. 260). Tolstoy has his own way of telling us this by means of the story itself. The first chapter – first in order of presentation, but last according to the internal time story – shows us very clearly that Ivan Ilyich's wife had not understood his deathbed experience. Nor can we read such an understanding into the bloodshot eyes and morose look of his son. Even Gerassim, who it will subsequently emerge is not to be condemned, appears in the first chapter to be part of the conspiracy: ' "It's God's will. We shall all come to it some day," said Gerassim, showing the even white teeth of a peasant – and like a man in the thick of urgent work he briskly opened the front door . . .' (T, p.109).

In the context of Book One, when Gerassim responds to one of the departing guests that 'It's God's will. We shall all come to it some day' (T, p. 109), he could readily have been taken to exhibit a further form of the inauthentic attitude to death, one which refers it to an external power. Only retrospectively do we recognize that Gerassim understood more of death than the others, so that his words – 'We shall all come to it some day' – are not another form of the 'one dies', but an expression of Being-towards-death. Only subsequently does it emerge that he alone is capable of exhibiting the pity which acts, until in his last moments Ivan too learns it. In this way, Tolstoy's reserved introduction of Gerassim serves to confirm the same point that Heidegger made when he suggests that 'in accordance with its very meaning, this authentic Being must remain hidden from the Others' (*SZ*, p. 260). It is not only that Ivan's death remains unintelligible to the everyday common-sense approach of Ivan's wife (cf. *SZ*, p. 309). Until informed by the narrator, the reader is no more able to understand Gerassim than the characters in the story. The novelist as narrator alone can penetrate the veil which conceals a person's attitude towards death. This power on the part of the story-teller to reveal aspects of the fictional characters which in real life nobody could ever know with certainty about even their most intimate friends is just one of the ways in which literature threatens to mislead us in the course of its very attempt to instruct us. As we shall see, when it comes to the more extravagant example of what Ivan is thinking at the moment of his death, Tolstoy exhibits a certain reticence.

Close examination of the last chapter shows that Tolstoy offers alongside each other two accounts of Ivan Ilyich's death. In one version, death is the key and, in the second, the emphasis is placed on the Other. The different versions are not offered to the reader as alternatives, but that is not to say that they can immediately be dissolved into one. And yet Tolstoy's doubling of his text at this point has, so far as I am aware, provoked no comment in the vast extensive secondary literature on the story.[12]

The first version is given with reference to the image of a black sack. Tolstoy had introduced it in chapter nine at the point where Ivan had sent his wife away and had gone to sleep with his legs resting on Gerassim's shoulders. It seemed to Ivan that he was being thrust into a narrow, deep black sack. He had both co-operated with and resisted this agonizing process, until at the moment when he burst out of the sack he regained consciousness. He awoke to find Gerassim still attending him, but he too was now sent away. Alone Ivan cursed God and questioned his life. In the face of his pain he declared, 'Here's my sentence. But I am not guilty' (T, p. 153). The sack has been variously interpreted.[13] It is most likely that it represents death or, more precisely, the dying person's acceptance or refusal of death. What we find is that so long as Ivan insists that his life has been good, he is unable to accept his death and, in terms of the image, is unable to enter the sack. In chapter twelve, the final chapter, Ivan Ilyich is again found resisting being forced into the black sack or black hole: 'That very justification of his life held him fast and prevented him from advancing' (T, p. 159). But the obstacle disappears and death is no longer regarded as an enemy force. 'Suddenly some force smote him in the chest and side, making it still harder to breathe; he sank through the hole and there at the bottom was a light.'[14] Tolstoy is making the point that Ivan has at last recognized his guilt which he had previously refused to do.

I have tried to show above that Heidegger's account of Being-towards-death cannot be treated in isolation, as has been done all too often. The first chapter of the Second Division of *Being and Time* leads into a discussion of the connection betwen Being-guilty and Being-towards-death. This connection, which according to Heidegger must 'be elucidated phenomenally' (SZ, p. 305), is well illustrated by Tolstoy's story. The shattering of Ivan's everyday attitude takes place in guilt. Not that the guilt arises from the failure to perform some long-recognized duty. Ivan Ilyich at this point ceases to look for past failures or omissions which would serve to explain to him why he had to suffer this pain. It is at least plausible that his guilt is detached from relationship to any law or 'ought' (SZ, p. 283), leaving the possibility open that Ivan is guilty *authentically* (SZ, p. 287). In order to act, Ivan has to stop being preoccupied with the question of what he had specifically done to make him guilty, just as Heidegger in section 59 passed from this everyday conception of guilt to a formal conception of it (SZ, p. 283). ' "No, it was all wrong," he said to himself, "but no matter." He could, he could do the right thing. "But what *is* the right thing?" he asked himself, and abruptly grew quiet' (T, p. 159). This quiet cannot be understood as a quietening of the screaming which had continued for three long days, for Tolstoy records in the next paragraph that 'the dying man was still shrieking desperately' (T, p. 160). It is a quietening of the internal soliloquy brought on by uncertainty as to what might be the right thing to do. It is the silence of conscience.

However, at this point Tolstoy interrupts the narrative and subjects it to a form of repetition. The details of Ivan's self-questioning are repeated and the questioning is again apparently resolved in a quietening of his thoughts. The transition between the two accounts is marked by the phrase 'It was at this very same moment . . .' Here is the text.

This was at the end of the third day, an hour [*sic*] before his death. At that very moment his schoolboy son had crept into the room and gone up to his father's bedside. The dying man was still shrieking desperately and waving his arms. His hand fell on the child's head. The boy seized it, pressed it to his lips and burst into tears.

It was at this very same moment that Ivan Ilyich had fallen through the hole and caught sight of the light, and it was revealed to him that his life had not been what it ought to have been but that it was still possible to put it right. He asked himself: 'But what *is* the right thing?' and grew still, listening. Then he felt that someone was kissing his hand. He opened his eyes and looked at his son. (T, p. 160)

The same recognition, 'It was all wrong', followed by the same question, 'But what *is* the right thing?' The same silence and then the discovery of his son. Up to this point there are no important differences between the two accounts, even if some of the details raise the question of whether Tolstoy might have added to the text at some later stage. For example, in the passage just quoted Tolstoy says that these events took place one hour before Ivan's death, but a little later we read that 'For those present his agony lasted another two hours' (T, p. 161).[15] These two unreconcilable accounts of objective time make it tempting to attach the statement that it was one hour before his death to the passage that immediately precedes it and the statement that it was two hours to the description of his final encounter with his son and his wife. Not that anything is resolved thereby. Both take place 'at this very same moment'.[16] But it is as if, by what was perhaps no more than a slip of Tolstoy's pen, we can all the more readily separate two different descriptions of Ivan's changing relation to his own death. One simply marks the transformation of his guilt, while the other seems to refer that transformation to an encounter with his son and his wife. That separation might have been used to mark the difference between what might be called a standardly Heideggerian interpretation from a Levinasian one, had I not earlier renounced using Tolstoy's text to stage a confrontation between these two philosophers. Instead I shall focus on further levels of indeterminacy in the story.

The difference between the two different versions of the events one or two hours before Ivan's death lies in the fact that whereas the first version offers only an external account of Ivan's recognition of his son at his bedside, the second version goes further by telling the reader what Ivan felt and thought, albeit with a certain reticence on Tolstoy's part. In the second version, Ivan's quietness is only temporary. He finds an answer to the question 'But what *is* the right thing?' and he appears to find it by looking at his son and looking at his wife and feeling sorry for them both. Ivan comes to the conclusion that 'It will be better for them when I die.' He wants to say this but does not have the strength. Instead he sends his son away and apologizes. ' "Take him away . . . sorry for him . . . sorry for you too . . . " He tried to add "Forgive me" but said "Forego" and, too weak to correct himself, waved his hand, knowing that whoever was concerned would understand.'

Ivan had already come to the conclusion that action was at this point more important than words. ' "Besides, why speak, I must act." ' Perhaps the suggestion is that, by apologizing and by asking his son to be taken away, he had in fact acted. Had Ivan simply told those around him what the reader is told about how he felt – that he knew he was a misery to them and that he knew it would be better for them were he to die – he would by contrast have relied only on words. Ivan does not try to explain himself. He tries to do something to make it less painful for them. He is not asking to be understood and in that sense he has chosen solitude.

This concern for action marks a change. Ivan has now learned the lesson that Gerassim seemed to know instinctively: for each person the recognition of mortality – Being-towards-death – should guide his or her actions. The young peasant had earlier given his own death as a reason for going to the assistance of his master: 'We shall all of us die, so what's a little trouble?' (T, p. 143). But Ivan's concern that his son should be spared seeing him in his pain and Ivan's words of apology to both his son and his wife did not satisfy his concern to act. The unease recurred: 'He felt full of pity for them, he must do something to make it less painful' (T, p. 160). The word for pity is *zhalet*. The same word was prominent at the end of chapter seven when Ivan Ilyich wanted to be pitied, as he was pitied when he was ill as a child. Now he feels pity not for himself, but for others.[17] The first thought of those around him at his death was for themselves (T, p. 101). Ivan's last thought was not of himself, but of them. He had at the last chosen to live for Others and this meant, in the situation in which he found himself, the acceptance of his own death.

Ivan no longer answered his own question 'what *is* the right thing?' by reference to a conception of his duties, as he had once done (T, p. 111 and p. 116). He now finds the answer in the situation which confronts him. He sees his son and wife and responds to them. In responding to their faces he finds his responsibility (cf. *SZ*, p. 288). And this is the approach which Heidegger also adopted in *Being and Time*, following Aristotle from whom Heidegger's account of conscience, resoluteness, action, and situation in large part derives. The situation as Ivan now saw it, having looked at his wife and his son, was that he must do something for them: 'release them and release himself from this suffering' (T, p. 160). By focusing on them as well as on himself, his own pain does not disappear, but he is able to *let it be*. And at the same time his habitual fear of death also dis-appears. It is then that Ivan discovers light in place of death (T, p. 160), a light which corresponds to that he found at the bottom of the hole in the first account of his recognition and acknowledgement that his life had been wrong (T, p. 159). In this way the hole is passed through.

This indeterminacy of the second account in spite of the greater detail Tolstoy provides is highlighted by the confusion which arises when Ivan means to say '*prosti*' (forgive), but only succeeds in uttering the word '*propusti*' (let [me] pass through). Ivan does not even try to correct himself, but he is said to be content in the knowledge that 'whoever was concerned would understand' (T, p. 160). If Ivan was asking for forgiveness from those around him, then he was deceived in thinking he was understood.[18] There is no indication that anyone was aware of Ivan's change of heart. Hence it is more likely that the reader will think of God at this point, although to do so might simply be another example of what Heidegger called 'ontical other-worldly speculation' (*SZ*, p. 248). If Tolstoy does not make the reference more explicit, it is for a reason. Literature too can be more persuasive to the degree that it does not admit its presuppositions.

Many of the problems of interpretation which arise in reading Tolstoy's story lie in the indeterminacy of the final lines of the story. Some of the difficulties already emerged in the examination of the obstacles to Spanos's attempt to establish a correlation between Heidegger's existential account of Being-towards-death and Tolstoy's story. For example, there is the difficulty that Ivan's fear gives way ultimately to joy, not anxiety. That difficulty can perhaps be addressed by observing that Heidegger does indeed give a place to joy: 'Along with the sober anxiety which brings us face to face with our individualised potentiality-for-Being, there goes an unshakeable joy in this possibility' (*SZ*, p. 310). Similarly, the fact that in response to a bystander's comment that 'it is all over', Ivan utters 'in his soul' the words 'Death is over. It is no more' (T, p. 161) need not prove a stumbling-block. What is striking is that although it lends itself to a religious reading – in which case it is taken as a reference to the last words of Christ, *consummatum est*[19] – no single interpretation is forced on the reader. Does it indicate an 'overcoming of death' of the kind which Heidegger condemns as a perversion (*SZ*, p. 310)? Or could it be Tolstoy's way of remarking the impossibility of experiencing death?

So long as our focus is on the story as a work of literature, it is not obvious that this question must be decided. Tolstoy raises the question, leads the reader towards an answer, but holds back from giving an unambiguous answer. The reader has shared in Ivan's preparation for death, but is excluded from his final moments. One of the more striking features of the traditional treatment of literary and philosophical texts is that ambiguity or undecidability is not only tolerated, but often admired in art. By contrast, it has not been acceptable in philosophy, at least for long periods. It might even be suggested that the religious reading of the phrase 'death is over' belongs to the second more concrete account of Ivan's last moments. Similar problems of interpretation arise in connection with the phrase 'whoever was concerned would understand' as applied to Ivan's failed attempt to say 'forgive' or even 'goodbye'. It presumably refers to either God or the son, but by virtue of its indeterminacy the way is open for it to be included in a more open reading of the final pages of the book. 'The Death of Ivan Ilyich' was the first story Tolstoy published after his conversion. [20] As such, one might have expected it to be more specific in its Christian message, although in that case Heidegger would have had to have renounced the story as an example of inauthentic otherworldly speculation.

But why does Tolstoy give what looks like two accounts of the same event? Tolstoy describes the scene and then repeats it in what can most readily be understood as a flashback. [21] If the second account, the flashback, offers a more concrete account this is because it encapsulates certain existentiell commitments, whereas the earlier more reticent version is, by contrast, to be understood as an attempt to withdraw from those ideals of existence. More specifically, the flashback provides the sketch of an answer to the question of why Ivan grows quiet and is able to find light in place of dark. And it seems that such an answer can only be given at the concrete or existentiell level. There is thus a remarkable appropriateness to Heidegger's reference to 'The Death of Ivan Ilych' because the final pages of Tolstoy's story struggle in their own way with a similar problem of reticence that faced Heidegger.

Heidegger cannot simply underwrite Tolstoy's account: 'The idea of existence which we have posited gives us an outline of the formal structure of the understanding of Dasein and does so in a way which is not binding from an existentiell point of view' (*SZ*, p. 313). Heidegger cannot avoid existentiell commitments, but nor is his formal analysis reducible to the one which is operative through his text. It is not a matter of indifference or irrelevance which existentiell ideals have influenced his thought and presentation of the existential. And yet Heidegger's reticence about the ideals of existence governing his analysis serves to protect the reduction of the formal existential analysis to the existentiell level. Nevertheless, this silence left the way open for another ideal – for convenience, I might call it the existentialist ideal – to serve in its place and dominate the reading of his text. Is it a failing on the part of Heidegger's readers that they have inserted an existentiell to mask the existential? Or is it not the case that it is impossible to maintain the formalization of the existential without concretization? And, just as the distinction between existential and existentiell cannot ultimately be maintained, neither can the distinction between philosophy and literature. On a number of occasions Heidegger comments on how an existential analysis does violence to the everyday and its tranquillized obviousness (*SZ*, p. 311). Is there not here also a basis for an understanding of the violence literary examples perform within philosophy? Such examples – and all examples are in a sense literary – destroy the autonomy and integrity of the philosophical text.

## Abbreviations

S William V. Spanos, 'Leo Tolstoy's "The Death of Ivan Ilych":
A Temporal Interpretation' in *De-Structing the Novel: Essays in Applied Postmodern Hermeneutics*, edited by Leo Orr, Troy: New York, The Whitson Publishing Company, 1982.

SZ M. Heidegger, *Sein und Zeit*, Tübingen, Niemeyer, 1967; translated by J. Macquarrie and E. Robinson in *Being and Time*, Oxford, Basil Blackwell, 1962. All references will be to the German text, the page numbers of which can be found in the margins of the English translation.

T L. Tolstoy, *The Death of Ivan Ilyich*, translated by Rosemary Edmonds, Harmondsworth, Penguin, 1983.

Tel E. Levinas, *Totalité et infini*, The Hague, Martinus Nijhoff, 1974.

TI *Totality and Infinity*, translated by A. Lingis, Pittsburgh, Duquesne University Press, 1969.

## Notes

1 M. Heidegger, *Prolegomena zur Geschichte des Zeitbegriffs*, herausgegeben von Petra Jaeger, Gesamtausgabe Band 20, Frankfurt, Klostermann, 1979, p. 434; *History of the Concept of Time*, translated by T. Kisiel, Bloomington, Indiana University Press, 1985, p. 314.

2 John Macquarie, *Existentialism*, Harmondsworth, Penguin, 1973, p. 153.

3 Walter Kaufmann, 'Existentialism and Death' in *Existentialism, Religion and Death*, New York, New American Library, 1976, p. 198. The first version of this essay was published in the *Chicago Review* in 1959.

4 Walter Kaufmann, *Discovering the Mind*, vol. 2, New York, McGraw-Hill, 1980, p. 214.

5 *Existentialism, Religion and Death*, p. 199. Also *Discovering the Mind*, vol. 2, p. 213.

6 Quoted by Temira Pachmuss in 'The Theme of Love and Death in Tolstoy's "The Death of Ivan Ilyich" ', *The American Slavic and East European Review*, vol. 20, no. 1, 1961, pp. 76–7.

7 Levinas does not, to the best of my knowledge, discuss Tolstoy's 'The Death of Ivan Ilyich', but in *Otherwise than Being or Beyond Essence* he does take up another of Tolstoy's stories about death. There he refers to 'Tolstoy's tale where an order for enough boots for 25 years is sent by one that will die that very evening he gives the order'. *Autrement qu'être ou au-delà de l'essence*, The Hague; Marinus Nijhoff, 1974, p. 165; *Otherwise than Being or Beyond Essence*, translated by Alphonso Lingis, The Hague,

Martinus Nijhoff, 1981, p. 129. This seems to be a reference to Tolstoy's 'What Men Live By', although in that story the man makes provision for only one year, not twenty-five. *Twenty-Three Tales*, translated by Louise and Aylmer Maude, London, Oxford University Press, 1919, p. 72.

8   E. Levinas, *Le temps et l'autre*, Montpellier, Fata Morgana, 1979, p. 61.

9   Heidegger does take up the existentiell again in an historical context in *Nietzsche 2*, Pfullingen, Neske, 1961, pp. 477–80; translated by Joan Stambaugh in *The End of Philosophy*, New York, Harper & Row, 1973, pp. 71–4.

10  *Prolegomena zur Geschichte des Xeitbegriffs*, p. 418; *History of the Concept of Time*, p. 302.

11  For a discussion of these issues, see among others: Klaus Hartmann, 'The Logic of Deficient and Eminent Modes in Heidegger', *Journal of the British Society for Phenomenology*, vol. 5, no. 2, 1974, pp. 118–34; Joan Stambaugh, 'An Inquiry into Authenticity and Inauthenticity in *Being and Time*', in *Radical Phenomenology*, edited by John Sallis, Atlantic Highlands, Humanities Press, 1978, pp. 153–61; Robert J. Dostal, 'The Problem of "Indifferenz" in *Sein und Zeit*', *Philosophy and Phenomenological Research*, vol. 43, no. 1, 1982, pp. 43–58; Charles B. Guignon, 'Heidegger's "Authenticity" Revisited', *Review of Metaphysics*, vol. 38, 1984, pp. 321–39; Jay A. Ciaffa, 'Toward an Understanding of Heidegger's Conception of Inter-relation between Authentic and Inauthentic Existence', *Journal of the British Society for Phenomenology*, vol. 18, no. 1, 1987, pp. 49–59; and William McNeill, 'Heidegger and the Modification of *Being and Time*', Ph.D. Dissertation, Essex University, 1986.

12  I have here provided a list of works consulted in an appendix and it will be seen that for the most part I have confined myself to secondary literature in English. Two essays stand out as being particularly relevant for the reading I have given. John Wiltshire claims that Tolstoy 'seems to work with two different and logically contradictory accounts of Ivan Ilyich's life and death, and to work with them simultaneously'. Nevertheless, he denies that there are two accounts in the last chapter, which he seems to regard as a failure. This is because he regards the contradictory strands of the story to be, first, that current which leads to conversation and, secondly, a sub-current which gives a sense of the arbitrary and senseless aspect of Ivan's life-history. Wiltshire is dissatisfied with the last chapter because Tolstoy immediately converts the relinquishing of the ego or dissolution of the will into a 'conduct-morality' which requires Ivan to act, 'when his power for "acting" could never have been less'. John Wiltshire, 'The Argument of Ivan Ilyich's Death', *The Critical Review*, vol. 24, 1982, pp. 53–4. Jan Van der Eng finds 'three contrastive descriptions of Ivan Il'ic's dying'. 'There is a description that registers his physical reations. It is preceded by two accounts of the exact moment of death, one rendered by Ivan Il'ich himself, the other by someone who

*33*

witnesses his dying.' 'The Death of Ivan Il'ic', *Russian Literature*, vol. 7, 1979, pp. 181–2. I am grateful to Tina Chanter for alerting me to the existence of these and a number of the other essays on 'The Death of Ivan Ilyich' which can be found appended in the bibliography.

13 Often interpreted as the womb, Boris Sorokin understands the black bag to refer to the blind gut which Ivan suspects as a cause of his illness. 'Ivan Il'ich as Jonah: A Cruel Joke', *Canadian Slavic Studies*, vol. 5, no. 4, pp. 487–507.

14 Tolstoy draws an analogy at this point between being drawn into the black sack and the experience of motion in a railway-carriage, where one thinks one is going forwards but suddenly becomes aware of the fact that one is in fact going backwards. Tolstoy is perhaps mistakenly recalling the experience when one thinks one is in a moving train, but in fact one's own is stationary and it is another train which is moving. If Tolstoy has indeed misdescribed the experience, then it is probably in his eagerness to draw a parallel between this image and another, to be found earlier in the story, where Ivan imagined he was climbing, although he was in fact going steadily downhill (T, p. 153).

15 The translation by Louise and Aylmer Maude decides in favour of concealing the inconsistency by reading at this point 'two hours before his death': *Ivan Ilych and Hadju Murad*, Oxford University Press, 1934, p. 72. I am grateful to Angela Livingstone of the Department of Literature at the University of Essex for confirming that the Penguin translation provides the correct translation of Tolstoy's Russian text.

16 If Tolstoy gives the impression of being confused about the objective time of the last events of Ivan's life, he nevertheless makes sure that the reader is well aware that Ivan experiences the temporality of his death differently from his wife and that neither of them follow clock-time: 'To him all this happened in a single instant, and the meaning of that instant suffered no change thereafter' (T, p. 161).

17 Robert Russell, 'From Individual to Universal: Tolstoy's 'Smert' Ivana Il'icha', *Modern Language Review*, vol. 76, 1981, p. 631. Perhaps the most illuminating contrast is how Ivan Ilyich had, at a time when he was looking for pity, found his son's frightened look of pity dreadful to see (T, p. 150).

18 For a reading which gives special significance to this confusion see Gary R. Jahn, 'The Role of the Ending in Leo Tolstoi's "The Death of Ivan Il'ich" ', *Revue Canadienne des Slavistes*, vol. 24, no. 3, 1982, p. 235n. However, his focus is on the way the two words unify the two themes and principles of organization of the story. Angela Livingstone suggested to me that *prosti* could in Tolstoy's time also mean 'goodbye'. In that case a further possibility is introduced arising from the fact that in the first chapter Ivan's wife tells Piotr Ivanovicsh that Ivan had 'said good-bye to us a quarter of an hour before he died, and even asked us to take Volodya away' (T, p. 107). In spite of the inconsistency about the time, the fact

that she mentions Volodya suggests that she had this incident in mind. It would mean that a further ambiguity had been introduced. If he meant 'forgive' when he meant to say *prosti* but said *propusti*, he was not understood by his wife. But if he meant 'goodbye', then he was understood. Tolstoy leaves no indication of which is the correct interpretation. Angela Livingstone has also emphasized to me the problems posed by the phrase 'whoever was concerned would understand' and suggested the more literal translation 'he to whom it was necessary [to understand] would understand'.

19 John 19, v. 30. See also Gary R. Jahn, 'The Role of the Ending in Leo Tolstoi's "The Death of Ivan Il'ich" ', *Revue Canadienne des Slavistes*, vol. 24, no. 3, 1982, p. 237.

20 Edward Wasiolek, *Tolstoy's Major Fiction*, Chicago, University of Chicago Press, 1978, p. 167.

21 I am again indebted to Angela Livingstone, this time for pointing out to me that there is no pluperfect tense in Russian so that flashbacks are not distinguished by a change in tense.

## Bibliography of Secondary Literature
## Consulted on Tolstoy's 'The Death of Ivan Ilyich'

Bartell, James, 'The Trauma of Birth in "The Death of Ivan Ilych": A Therapeutic Reading', *Psychocultural Review*, vol. 2, no. 2, 1978, pp. 97–117.

Donnelly, John, 'Death and Ivan Ilych', *Language, Metaphysics, and Death*, edited by John Donnelly, New York: Fordham University, 1978, pp. 116–30.

Jahn, Gary R., 'The Role of the Ending in Leo Tolstoi's "The Death of Ivan Il'ich" ', *Revue Canadienne des Slavistes*, vol. 24, no. 3, 1982, pp. 228–38.

Jankelevitch, Vladimir, 'Tolstoi et la mort', in *Sources*, Paris: Le Seuil, 1984, pp. 23–31.

Kaufmann, Walter, 'Existentialism and Death', in *Existentialism, Religion and Death*, New York: New American Library, 1976, pp. 192–218.

Kaufmann, Walter, *Discovering the Mind Volume 2*, New York: McGraw-Hill, 1980, pp. 209–16.

Kulenkampff, Jens, ' "Der Tod des Iwan Iljitsch". Sterblichkeit und Ethik bei Heidegger und Tolstoi'. A paper delivered in Duisburg on 29 November 1985 to a Colloquium in honour of Werner Marx. To be published in *Sterblichkeitserfahrung und Ethikbegründung*, edited by Walter Brüstle and Ludwig Siep, Essen: Verlag Die Blaue Eule.

Matual, David, 'The Confession as Subtext in "The Death of Ivan Il'ich" ', *International Fiction Review*, vol. 8, no. 2, 1981, pp. 124–8.

Olney, James, 'Experience, Metaphor, and Meaning: "The Death of Ivan Ilych" ', *The Journal of Aesthetics and Art Criticism*, vol. 31, no. 1, 1972, pp. 101–14.

Ovsyaniko-Kulikovsky, D.N., 'On Ivan Ilich', in *Tolstoy: The Critical Heritage*, edited by A.V. Knowles, London: Routledge & Kegan Paul, 1978, pp. 419–24.

Pachmuss, Tamira, 'The Theme of Love and Death in Tolstoy's "The Death of Ivan Ilyich" ', *The American Slavic and East European Review*, vol. 20, no. 1, 1961, pp. 72–83.

Paskow, Alan, 'What do I fear in facing my death?', *Man and World*, vol. 8, 1975, pp. 146–56.

Perrett, Roy W., 'Tolstoy, Death and the Meaning of Life', *Philosophy*, vol. 60, 1985, pp. 231–45.

Rohde, Eric, 'Death in Twentieth-century Fiction', in *Man's Concern with Death*, London: Hodder & Stoughton, 1968, pp. 160–76.

Russell, Robert, 'From Individual to Universal: Tolstoy's 'Smert' Ivana Il'icha', *Modern Language Review*, vol. 76, 1981, pp. 629–42.

Smyrniw, Walter, 'Tolstoy's Depiction of Death in the Context of Recent Studies of the "Experience of Dying" ', *Canadian Slavonic Papers*, vol. 21, 1979, pp. 367–79.

Spanos, William V., 'Leo Tolstoy's "The Death of Ivan Ilych": A Temporal Interpretation', in *De-Structing the Novel: Essays in Applied Postmodern Hermeneutics*, edited by Leo Orr, Troy: New York: The Whitson Publishing Company, 1982, pp. 1–64.

Turner, C.J.G., 'The Language of Fiction: Word-clusters in Tolstoy's "The Death of Ivan Ilyich" ', *The Modern Language Review*, vol. 65, 1970, pp. 116–21.

Van der Eng, Jan, 'The Death of Ivan Il'ic', *Russian Literature*, vol. 7, 1979, pp. 159–92.

Wasiolek, Edward, 'Tolstoy's "The Death of Ivan Ilyich" and the Jamesian Fictional Imperatives', *Modern Fiction Studies*, vol. 6, no. 4, 1960–1, pp. 314–24.

Wasiolek, Edward, *Tolstoy's Major Fiction*, Chicago: University of Chicago Press, 1978, pp. 165–79.

Wexelblatt, Robert, 'The Higher Parody: Ivan Ilych's Metamorphosis and the Death of Gregor Samsa', *Massachusetts Review*, vol. 21, 1980, pp. 601–28.

Williams, Michael V., 'Tolstoy's "The Death of Ivan Ilych": After the Fall', *Studies in Short Fiction*, vol. 21, 1984, pp. 229–34.

Wiltshire, John, 'The Argument of Ivan Ilyich's Death', *The Critical Review*, vol. 24, 1982, pp. 46–54.

# · 2 ·

# A Linear Narrative?
# Blanchot with Heidegger in
# the Work of Levinas

## PAUL DAVIES

*Levinas se méfie des poèmes et de l'activité poétique . . .*
Blanchot[1]

*Le poète, devant le 'ruissellement eternel du dehors',
n'entend-il pas les voix qui appellent hors du monde
heideggerien?*
Levinas[2]

Following some introductory remarks and as a preliminary exploration into the nature of the *entretien* between them, the first part of
this essay calls attention to the uniqueness of Blanchot's text *as* it is
encountered inside Levinas's. The second part, by way of conclusion,
tries to say something about the beginnings of Blanchot's reading of
Heidegger. Two comments or provisos: (1) In the first part,
Heidegger is presented very much in the terms that Levinas adopts
when speaking of him and no attempt is made there to complicate the
issue. This allows us to see more clearly the effects of Levinas's reading of Blanchot. The second part, in some respects, hopefully makes
up for such reticence. (2) Throughout the essay, there is no real distinguishing between 'poetry' and 'literature'. I am aware that
recently much has been made of Heidegger's supposed privileging of
poetry as the essence of art over and against literature, and the ensu-
ing debate can be seen to have owed much to Blanchot or at least to a
reading of Blanchot. Here, because the aim is to try and describe the

scene of an initial encounter, such issues and questions have been deferred.

## Introduction

In that part of his commentary on Heidegger given over specifically to the question of the poet's *task*,[3] Arion Kelkel recounts how the poet is alone capable of experiencing the 'absence of the gods' and the 'world's night' as a time of beginning, as an origin. That moment of the most extreme oblivion, when it is impossible to think of what is to come, is also the time when the future can be most genuinely addressed. The absence or default of the gods comes to the poet's aid.

Reading through these well-known expressions, we come across several that are maybe less familiar. The poet lives in a time which is *this side*, the *hither side*, of time ('le temps en deçà du temps'). We are directed to a saying of Hölderlin's not used by Heidegger in which the poet is linked to a 'double infidelity' of gods and men: the poet speaks from 'under the form of infidelity where there is forgetting of everything'. Is this infidelity synonymous with what Heidegger says about the 'gedoppelten Mangel und Nicht'[4] (the double lack and not) in 'Hölderlin and the essence of poetry'? Kelkel, who would have us think so, writes that 'the poet enters into a dialogue with the god who turns away'.[5] A sentence that reminds us of the passage in 'Wozu Dichter?' where Heidegger describes the 'holy' as the trace of the absent gods.[6] The trace that is nonetheless older than both gods and mortals; the most ancient, an absolute anteriority. It is the trace to which the poet must attend and, in so doing, lead the rest of us ('we others') toward the turning itself, that point where thinking, open to the very essence of poetry, might finally become *another* thinking, a thinking other than metaphysics.

A footnote, however, refers us to *L'Espace littéraire* and to Blanchot's reading of the 'Anmerkungen zum Oedipus', where Hölderlin speaks of the 'allvergessenden Form der Untreue'.[7] And it is *L'Espace littéraire*, although another chapter, which is quoted as Kelkel continues:

The poet thus experiences the poverty of solitude, which is 'an understanding (entente) of the future, but a powerless understanding: prophetic isolation which this side of time (en deçà du temps) always announces the beginning', so writes Maurice Blanchot for his part (de son côté) meditating on the original experience of the poet (p. 604).

It is not made clear that 'the poverty of solitude' (la pauvreté de la solitude) is also Blanchot's phrase.[8]

In the next paragraph, Kelkel deals with the accusation that Heidegger's adoption of Hölderlin's language constitutes a 'godless mysticism', and the commentary slowly moves away from this topic (the poet's task) and this 'myth' (the naming of the holy) back to their applications, to what they mean for the development of Heidegger's work. The ease with which the summary slides into Blanchot's writing and then, having partly acknowledged it, leaves it, is puzzling. As though with this sort of language and this way of encountering poetry it cannot be a matter of differences, of degrees, or of wholly other readings.

Yet Blanchot's text runs so close to Heidegger's, although rarely naming it, moving with it in its responses to Hölderlin's words and in its sense that 'forgetfulness, error, the unhappiness of erring can be linked to an historical time, the time of distress' (die dürftiger Zeit, le temps de la détresse).[9] For Blanchot as well as for Heidegger, to think the essence of poetry is to think from out of that time. Such thinking *is* historical and for it 'essence' is never a general term designating a universal; *P*oetry, *L*iterature. It is rather the singular poem or work itself; the space of the work. It is what *happens* in the work. Like Heidegger, Blanchot will insist on an enquiry into the art work that radically displaces the projects of aesthetics and the traditional interpretations of the thing. When, for example, Blanchot and Heidegger recall Hölderlin's question 'What are poets for . . .?', they do so not for the sake of commentary or criticism but in order to pose it for themselves. This moment (this 'now') in which the poet's question becomes its reader's is the occasion of the most tentative of encounters, an encounter that must also become a matter for thinking. In Heidegger's case, it leads – and has already led – to his attempting to describe the requisite unobtrusiveness of the nature of 'commentary': most famously, in the foreword to *Erläuterungen zu Hölderlin's Dichtung*, as snow falling onto a bell, a non-poetic writing that lets the language of the poem ring out. Blanchot, too, alongside his incorporating and reading of the poet's words seeks ever subtler ways of saying what such a reading (a 'criticism' that uniquely marks the uniqueness of the work) entails, and in the preface to the 1963 edition of his *Lautréamont et Sade* – entitled 'Qu'en est-il de la critique?' – he does so with reference to Heidegger's foreword. It is not just that Blanchot and Heidegger *read* a poem or poet, it is that they raise perpetually and of necessity the question of the *time* of that reading.

However unfamiliar Blanchot's terms might be (an impoverished, prophetic isolation; a powerless grasping of the future), they still surely fall under the headings and themes of 'expectation' and 'forgetfulness' that, for Heidegger, uniquely turn the poet to the future and require of thinking that it enter into a dialogue with poetry. Recall the final page of 'Wozu Dichter?' In the time of distress, the future is present *only* with the arrival of the poet's words. An essay of Blanchot's on 'René Char', for the first time bring together each of the terms later developed in the passage used by Kelkel. It concludes with what appears to be an identical statement to Heidegger's. If the poet seems capable of the future, and if poetry can overcome (dépasser) time and exist prophetically, it is because the essence of the poem is an awaiting of itself and of power. 'It is only because there is the poem that the future is possible.'[10] Perhaps, then, it is not surprising that Blanchot, *de son coté*, should be so easily assimilated.

But Levinas, in his review of *L'Espace littéraire*, will claim to find in the work as a whole and on the very page that Kelkel cites in particular, an invitation 'to leave the Heideggerian world'.[11] He will drive a wedge between these two investigations into the essence of the work and testify to Blanchot's importance for the encounters between philosophy and art, poetry, literature. But to what end and for what purpose? At times it seems as though Levinas's whole project could be described precisely as an attempt to retrieve philosophy from these encounters and to give it another sense and task. What is the nature of the role Levinas would have Blanchot play, a role in which it seems he is to be thought continually *with* and continually *against* Heidegger?

'Does the poet before the "eternal rustling of the outside" hear the voices which call from outside of the Heideggerian world?': a question posed by Levinas at the close of 'Maurice Blanchot et le regard du poète'. Given the confidence of many of the statements made in that essay, the expressed aim of which is to explicate the new 'category' and new 'mode of knowledge' (mode de connaissance) that Blanchot – not a philosopher – supposedly brings to philosophy, the question carries a surprisingly cautious tone, a caution that might well amount to a 'distrust'. Left unanswered in that essay, could the question not be extended across each of Levinas's occasional writings on poetry and literature, and to it could they not be seen to offer differing responses. The paper on Celan,[12] for instance, would seem to suggest that *yes* there is such a poetic hearing. The paper on Laporte[13] would perhaps suggest the contrary. But this is to proceed too quickly and to overlook everything that is odd in the question's being asked at all. It is by no means incidental that it first arises from a reading of Blanchot. To be precise, it is the second of two questions. The first asks whether or not Blanchot gives to art 'the function of uprooting (deraciner) the Heideggerian universe'.[14]

This interjection of Levinas's name into the beginnings of a comparative study of Heidegger and Blanchot might seem curious, perhaps even a little irritating. But what is most puzzling in Blanchot's proximity to Levinas might actually help us in setting up such a study. And what is most puzzling in that proximity can be very easily obscured by having the two stand in a linear relation, the latter incorporating the former and setting him to work in the transition from 'ontology' to 'ethics' and so in the 'break' from Heidegger. Levinas, as we shall see, frequently encourages such a view and thus draws our attention away from the relation. I would suggest that the complexities of this relation, this proximity, underlie and effect much of Blanchot's more recent writing, a writing that since the gathering together and publishing of the pieces that make up *L'Entretien infini* (1969) has refused, or further complicated, the distinction between 'fiction' and 'non-fiction'.[15] Levinas will make use of this distinction.

Four texts, all written in 1946, announce from the outset the themes and tensions of our discussion. In two essays, one on Char (already mentioned) and the other on Hölderlin (alluded to but not named),[16] Blanchot poses a series of questions to Heidegger's conception of a dialogue between poetizing and thinking, questions that seem to conceal themselves. This conception of a dialogue is at the same time being complicated and extended, although not unproblematically, in 'Wozu Dichter?' Ten years later, Levinas comments on the experience of reading the 'later Heidegger' after and alongside reading Blanchot. Here, Blanchot's questions have produced results. Everything seems decided and the matter settled:

for Heidegger, art beyond all aesthetic signification made the truth of Being shine, yet it had this in common with other forms of existence. For Blanchot, however, the vocation of art is unique, incomparable (hors pair) . . . to write does not lead to the truth of Being. One may say that it leads to the error of Being, to Being as a place of *errance*, to the uninhabitable.[17]

Levinas believes, let us say, that Blanchot shows the impossibility of a dialogue between thinking and poetizing ever securing a future for thinking. The erring onto which it necessarily opens is sometimes thought by Levinas as the 'nocturnal dimension of the future' and it is described and disclosed under the aegis of the *il y a* (the 'there is'), a notion first introduced by Levinas in a paper of 1946 and reprinted the following year as a section of *Existence and Existents* (chapter iv, part 2, 'Existence without existents', trans. A. Lingis, The Hague, Martinus Nijhoff, 1978). This is where we must begin.

# I

The *il y a* designates the mute and terrifying presence of existence, the sound heard when one hears nothing. It is always spoken of as an incessant and interminable shuddering, rustling, murmuring, and these words and others like them imply the continuing of signification beyond the domains of 'sense'. That 'non-sense' signifies, this is the thought that, from the first, so intrigues Levinas. Introduced explicitly as something untouched by the existential analytic of Dasein, the *il y a* is the *impossibility* of not being that comes to trouble and to disturb a thought that would seize on death as man's utmost *possibility*. In testifying to a passivity that is never yet extinction but that always overruns any formulation of a 'proper end', the *il y a* can be seen as a contribution to ontology that thereby ruins it, an idealist reduction rendering all idealism unfeasible. For Levinas, it turns us towards a thinking that is beyond idealism and other than ontology.

What are its sources? In conversation with Phillipe Nemo, Levinas speaks of it in opposition to Apollinaire's work of the same title, a work of which he was unaware. He also says that it is a theme found in Blanchot where it is called the *neuter* (le neutre) or the *outside* (le dehors).[18] But neither of these words can be said to play a part in Blanchot's earlier writing and he himself, in a text of the time, cites the *il y a* as Levinas's phrase.[19] Later he will call it 'one of Levinas' most fascinating propositions',[20] but he will not acknowledge an easy synonymity.

Levinas describes the *il y a* in terms of the night and insomnia, themes that also preoccupy Blanchot. Insomnia denotes a constant vigilance to the night in the night. It is not explained by talk about the cares of the day. The night in the night (Blanchot's 'other night') has no relation to the day. Always prior to the day (*this side of* [*en deçà de*] the day), the night in the night is incommensurable with it. Insomnia is exposure to impersonality. It is not *I* but one who does not sleep, just as it is not *I* but *one* who dies. I become, Levinas says, the object of an anonymous thought. Blanchot's text 'Le Dehors, la nuit', part of *L'Espace littéraire*, only appeared in 1953, six years after *Existence and Existents*.

A footnote in part two of the fourth chapter of *Existence and Existents* does, however, refer us to Blanchot, and more specifically to his 'roman' or 'récit', *Thomas the Obscure*. That book, we are told, 'opens with the description of the *il y a*. The presence of absence, the night, the dissolution of the subject in the night . . . the reality of irreality are there all admirably expressed' (pp. 103, 63). It is not that Blanchot's story illustrates the point Levinas is trying to make, nor is it in any way an aid to the argument. The status of the work, the fact of its being literature, is central to the footnote. When Thomas's body is enveloped and invaded by what is *outside* it, without the outside's ever becoming inside, and when 'his thought, mingled with the night, (keeps) watch'[21] anonymously, it is true that we are close to Levinas's phenomenological descriptions of sleeplessness. But, more importantly, as readers in front of the work, we are 'suddenly somewhere other than we expected to be'.[22] Just as for Heidegger the art work reveals the being of the thing as 'zuhanden' without rendering it simply there ('vorhanden'), so Blanchot's work constitutes a genuine showing of the *il y a* without thereby thematizing or representing it.

In the first part of the fourth chapter ('Exoticism'), the work of art is thought of as a withdrawing from the world and as already the dispossessing of a subject. Art is not the representation of the thing, but that into which the thing falls back: the image preceding the thing as both its absence and its condition. As a strangeness signifying through the absence of things, art *is* the opening out onto the *il y a*. It is also, however, the substitution of an image for the 'nowhere'[23] from which things come. As such, we might say, art can function as a distraction from the *interminable*, denying it in order to sustain a certain order and possibility: art as protection.[24]

In Levinas's noting of it, Blanchot's art is one that has realized the *image* as anarchic origin, an art that in its self-manifestation has lost all protective naïveté. 'Writing' will henceforth be known as the insomnia of the day: endlessly vigilant, endlessly beginning, but never bringing anything about. Blanchot's is a literature become the 'recherche de l'irréel'. In such a guise, it is for Levinas exemplary:

Poetic language which has set aside (a écarté) the world allows the incessant murmur of this distancing (éloignement) to reappear, like a night revealing itself within the night. This is not the impersonality of eternity (and this means for Levinas the impersonality of ontology) but the incessant, the interminable, beginning again from under the attempt to negate it (sous la négation qu'on puisse en tenter).[25]

The *il y a*, existence without existents, is in some way present with this existent. The work of art is the thing that names the most radical absence of things. An idea central to Blanchot's writings from the 1950s onwards is that of the work as its own absence. The word 'désoeuvrement' will name, amongst so much else, both the absence of the work (as thing, as *existent*) and the inertia, the passivity, that accompanies the existence and the coming into existence of this absence.

(Perhaps, though, the work names the *il y a* in a more literal sense as well. In 1947, Blanchot publishes 'Le dernier mot', written originally in 1935–6. Walking past a pack of guard dogs in the night, the narrator notes their silence:

It was only after my passing that they began to howl again: trembling howls, muffled, which at this hour of the day resounded like the echo of the word *il y a*. 'There without doubt is the last word', I thought listening to them.

Both the source and not the source, for the narrative continues:

But the word *il y a* still sufficed to reveal the things in this distant quarter . . .)[26]

Regarding the *il y a*, one commentator writes 'here the thinker must make way for the poet'.[27] Others, too, will see the *il y a* and this encounter between philosophy and literature as a marginal issue, as no more than a necessary (and polemical) moment in the development of Levinas's work. If this is where poetry must take over, it is also, presumably, where poetry can be left. Does Levinas not imply as much himself in the preface to the second edition of *Existence and Existents*? There, he seeks to situate the discussion of the *il y a*. He comments on its perhaps premature outcome in the analysis of the 'hypostasis' with which the book ends: the coming about of the existent that is the overcoming or vanquishing of this existence without existents. Yet he does so because the analysis is not to be read as a securing of the existent, in the sense of showing it, in all its aspects, as reducible to thematization. For Levinas's work since then has shown that the existent is open to another 'defection' and another incommensurability: defection that does not return it to the *il y a*. Thought from out of this an-archic, neutral existence, the existent (consciousness) lives in *separation* and is found in a relation that neither violates nor subordinates that separation. The relation with the other (*Autrui*) that Levinas calls 'proximity'. Would Levinas's work not present itself then in the form of a philosophical narrative, a logical and chronological chain of concepts or phrases: Heidegger's existential analytic – an existence without existents – an existent in separation – the proximity of *Autrui*? Levinas, in conversation, often seems to map out just such a path.

The movement, in *Existence and Existents*, from the discussion of art in general to the citing of the particular can be seen as a movement from an art about which philosophy can still theorize (in the first part of chapter iv, Levinas does propound a philosophy *of* art) to one which presents itself at a point where no further theorizing is possible. That is to say, when the *il y a* is introduced, when the radical and dissembling neutrality that characterizes poetic or literary language shows itself as such, philosophy no longer knows how to respond. And yet, the poem (the tale) continues to call for a response, for another response.

Levinas seems to insist on there being a fundamental distinction between Blanchot's 'fictional' and 'non-fictional' ('critical') writings. If the former names or shows the *il y a*, then the latter enquires into this naming or showing. It asks to paraphrase just one of the many formulations, about what is brought into play by the fact that something like poetry or literature can exist at all. It is there, in the 'criticism', that a notion such as 'désoeuvrement' can be developed and articulated. It is worth noting the care with which Levinas follows Blanchot from the encounter with the *work* to the question of the implications of that encounter.

He has dedicated two texts to readings of what he takes to be 'fictional' works. In his essay on *l'Attente, l'oubli* (1966), before embarking on a discussion of its 'theme', Levinas notes the tentativeness of such an endeavour. One can only ever speak of a theme with which the work is *perhaps* (*peut-être*) concerned and an experience onto which the work *perhaps* opens.[28] This seems to be no more than an expression of the modesty presumed by any literary hermeneutics. But Levinas pauses over this 'peut-être' and deems it worthy of a fairly extensive footnote.[29]

In Blanchot's tale (*L'Attente, l'oubli*), we are not confronted with personalities, allegorical or non-allegorical. Figures stripped of all possessions and so made wholly abstract nonetheless occur as a sensible plenitude. They acquire weight and substance as if from nothing and nowhere. (All of Levinas's words here recall everything he has said about the *il y a*.) The oppression of this plenitude can hardly be communicated save in the way one speaks of a delirium once the fever has subsided or of night once the day has risen. That the fever has not fallen and the day not risen and that *there is* communication, 'this is the literary space of Maurice Blanchot'. It is the signification of this space that interests Levinas. It is that there is signification here. But how is one to say it without making of it an interpretation, one that the work must always refuse? As though the critic were to say that one way of reading it is to see it in terms of this oppressiveness but another way etc. . . . It is not a matter, then, of a plurality of interpretations where the reader's 'perhaps' simply acknowledges those other possibilities.

Remaining with the footnote: imagine the significations of Blanchot's stories as reflections which disappear as soon as one leans across the page. One cannot approach them from another more appropriate direction for what they reflect does not stand in line with them. Their signification is incommensurable with any expression of it. The footnote concludes by asking: 'May one try to fix each of these *miroitements* (brilliant, reflected gleamings) without fear of extinguishing them?' And Levinas answers: 'Everything must be said here under the modality of the 'perhaps' just as Blanchot himself does when he wants to explicate what is in his books.'[30] And yet why *must* anything be said at all? Why can't the thinker simply make way for the poet?

For Levinas, Blanchot's 'tales' become an issue for thinking and continue to implicate the thinker precisely because they refuse the traditional and hermeneutical responses: responses to determined types of writing; responses guaranteed by a method, a critical distance, a horizonal schema, etc. Because they cannot be responded to, Blanchot's tales call for another response, one that Levinas admits unfolds as 'commentary' and within 'criticism', but one that is transformed by a new understanding of both the 'space' of the tale and the nature of literary language. The encounter between thinking (philosophy) and poetizing (literature) comes about for Levinas, just as it does for Blanchot and Heidegger, of necessity and at a particular moment.

Levinas and Blanchot would come together then as readers of Blanchot's work. But Levinas's explications increasingly depend upon his reading of Blanchot's. Our interest is with what Levinas says about Blanchot's explications. This is the topic of 'Maurice Blanchot et le regard du poète' and it is here with respect to Blanchot as a reader of his own and others' work that Levinas enacts a confrontation with the 'later Heidegger'. What does Blanchot, in his non-fiction, give to Levinas? An answer lies in the very title of the essay.

'Does Blanchot give to art the function of uprooting the Heideggerian universe?' This asks whether a polemic against Heidegger underlies or is implied in Blanchot's investigations into the work of art. What we find in those investigations, Levinas says, is the idea that literature and poetry presuppose the 'gaze of the poet'. The phrase recalls the title of the essay that Blanchot designates as the 'centre' of *L'Espace littéraire*, 'Le regard d'Orphée'. There we read that to look at Eurydice in the night is to lose 'the welcoming intimacy of the first night', the night that belongs to day. It is to look at the 'instant when the essence of night appears as the other night',[31] the night in the night. The gaze of the poet is the gesture by which *essence* becomes *other*. Essence continues as other, as the inessential. It is, Levinas adds, 'an original experience in the two senses of the adjective: fundamental experience and experience of the origin'.[32] This *regard* is the new 'category' and new 'mode of knowledge' that Levinas wishes to define. It names a way of revealing, a bringing to revelation, of 'that which remains other in spite of its revelation'. In naming such a showing, Blanchot declares that it belongs '*not to thought (la pensée) but to the language of the poem*'.[33]

There are two senses in which Levinas can be said to read the 'gaze of the poet' as a statement against Heidegger and we shall try to illustrate both. First, the experience of the work as an origin shows itself to be ruinous of philosophy ('ontology'). It comes to such thought as though it were the 'very extreme of nihilism'. Second, the saying of this experience belongs to the work itself (to the language of the poem) and thus evades philosophy, at least philosophy as 'ontology'.

Ontology, for Levinas, always values and presumes the potency of the *neutral*, the *impersonal*, the *in-different*. Neutrality, neither one thing nor the other but their *ground*, the guarantor of their commensurability, is marked by its generosity and benevolence. It is what makes ontology possible. With respect to poetic language and to the work of art, this neutrality has ensured that philosophy has always had the last word. The essence of the poem is thought away from the poem, to the poet, say, or to the nature of poetry. When there is no last word and when criticism experiences the absence of the authority under which it has operated for so long, attention is drawn to the poem itself and to the language of the poem as the essence of the poem. This is a language that neutralizes all thought of a potent neutrality. Here, ontology is exposed to a *neutrality* that it can only think by 'domesticating' it: the history of ontology being nothing less than the history of that process of *domestication*. Blanchot, we are told, 'shows how the *impersonality of the work* is that of the silence which follows the departure of the gods, a silence inextinguishable as a murmur'.[34]

Why is it, Blanchot asks in *L'Espace littéraire*, that when history contests it, art becomes an 'essential presence'? It is tempting to see Blanchot's account of the work in and from this history as adding a final, catastrophic stage to and beyond Heidegger's.

It is in the nature of the work of art to survive its original context, meaning and function, terms that already stand witness to this survival. Only when the gods have fled does the temple show itself as a work of art and the work of art as a matter for philosophy. And it is only with the ending of aesthetics that this situation – the withdrawing absence – comes to light. For Heidegger, the propensity of the work to live in and from this withdrawing absence means that through it alone the absence can speak. The 'world's night' is the time of deepest forgetfulness because even the absence of the gods is no longer noticed. The poet's task is to recall that absence and to bring it to utterance *as* something strange and distressful.

For Blanchot, we might say, what speaks in the work is *no longer* gods nor men, *no longer* their presence nor their absence. It is the movement of the survival of the work itself, living on after every theme has been forgotten and after the forgetting itself has been forgotten. When we name the work as this *surviving*, we name it as the interminable *not yet*. This is why we can speak of there being a poetic grasp of the future, but a powerless one, for it is a grasping from a time that is never in time, a time *en deçà de* time. Levinas is right to say that the absence of a conjunction in the title of *L'Attente, l'oubli* stops the words from becoming themes and from naming states *in* time. We hear instead a waiting, an expecting, that becomes a forgetting of what is expected and so an expectation of expectation ('l'attente de l'attente').

Everything Heidegger would say about a 'dialogue' with poetry, indeed the whole Heideggerian encounter with art, must for Levinas fall short of this most disturbing 'space'. Even the way in which 'ontology' relinquishes its claim to have the final word with respect to the poem in Heidegger constitutes a final word. Levinas would still detect here the sense of something being possible for an impersonal, neutral thinking, the sense of a future that might be activated and brought about. Blanchot, with 'the gaze of the poet' says as a non-securing revelation what the ontologist cannot say. It constitutes an experience of the limits of ontology. The saying of these limits comes as an extreme nihilism, ontology's only future and the future's 'nocturnal dimension'.

The time in which the work shows itself as an origin is, for Heidegger, the time of the end of metaphysics, the 'between' (das Zwischen): the time when thinking and poetizing (no longer secured by a method or direction) are turned in on themselves and experience the absence of a *word* and a *god* respectively. In and from such a 'context', the poet's naming of the *holy* as what is anterior to both gods and mortals at the time when the work is no longer the voice of either, is heard by the thinker as something positive, as evidence of a possibility *for* thinking.

For Blanchot as well, poetry always inaugurates something. And if the poem 'says beginning' then it belongs to what does not begin. But, here, when language becomes poetic language (when language turns into literature), what Blanchot will call the 'neuter' and Levinas hear as the *il y a* comes into play. The language of the poem shows itself as the interminable, the incessant. At the moment when the poem is experienced as an origin, it carries in its wake and at its centre the question of the most radical anteriority. An anteriority that renders nothing possible, not even the thought of *nothing*. The time of this encounter with the work is indeed the time of a 'between', the *no longer* and the *not yet*, but it is a 'between' that is somehow 'outside'; the time and the space of exile.

If Blanchot's 'critical' writing, falling between philosophy and poetry, shows the impossibility of their 'Heideggerian' encounter, we must turn now to consider the *status* of that writing itself: a writing 'under the modality of a *perhaps*', a writing which declares that a 'revelation' belongs 'not to thought but to the language of the poem'. The 'theme' of anteriority will be a useful starting point.

There has always been an anteriority proper to the work of art and one immediately intelligible to the discourses on art. For example, the writer knows that what is written will only acquire its true significance in the hands of the one who will read it. He knows too that those hands will not be his. But it is Blanchot, especially in his responses to Kafka, who takes this very familiar experience and who investigates it until the anteriority in question (so easily justified by referring to the nature of 'Literature', 'Poetry', etc.) seems to become more and more impossible, unthinkable and unthematizable. Irreducible to a particular field of philosophy or criticism and to a particular type of aesthetic experience, it will in Blanchot's work come to testify to an *impossibility* at the heart of all communication.

To take another instance or aspect, artistic activity, Levinas reminds us, has always given to the artist 'the experience of not being the author of his works'.[35] This 'strange inmixing in human causality' goes by the name of *inspiration*. It is the experience of inspiration onto which Levinas says *L'Attente, l'oubli* 'perhaps' opens, an experience – in Blanchot's words – 'kept hidden by a name in the time of the gods'.[36] It is a crucial word in Blanchot's texts where it both denotes and undergoes a transformation.

Retrieved in the 1946 essay on René Char from what Blanchot calls 'une analyse bâtarde', inspiration means nothing other than the 'anteriority of the poem in its rapport with the poet'.[37] The movement from the poet to the poem is reversed. No longer the overwhelming moment when a word or message (a secret) is imparted to an *existing* someone – its meaning in the time of the gods – inspiration is rather 'the granting of existence to someone who does not yet exist',[38] to someone whose time is *not yet*. This is the thought around which the Char essay revolves.

Traditionally, then, inspiration guarantees the movement from poet to poem: inspiration–poet–poem. It serves as the euphemism for anything that provokes or brings about the work, anything that gives a reason for an existing someone's writing something. In the time of the gods, inspiration is made to denote the relation between the poet and a named sender (the one who imparts) where that name might be a concept (Poetry), an experience, a need, a feeling, or whatever. Inspiration, or what has passed for inspiration, would thus draw attention away from the work (the poem) itself. It makes sure that something can always be said by naming that outside of the work to which the work can be referred.

The reversal occurs where and when these names are lacking. But it cannot be said as the movement from inspiration to the poem: inspiration–poem–poet. This would still ensure a critical circumscribing of the process. The poet would come to exist as an outcome of the inspired creation of the poem. We could speak of the poet as an 'effect' of the poem. At any time it could be said that there will be a time in which the poet will exist and will be present. Blanchot says that the inspiration does not lead to the work, rather 'the work is the road to inspiration'. The work leads to the granting of existence, it does not grant that existence itself. In short, for Blanchot, the poet cannot be represented in any account of the movement from the poem to inspiration. The poet is twice removed from himself, firstly with respect to the poem and secondly with respect to inspiration as the time of the poem. Inspiration, which has hitherto named a controllable anteriority, the sense of something beginning, comes to signify the experience of what is always still to come, of what is always yet to begin.

What does this mean? Poetic speech addresses the future. It speaks of the future. It is 'prophetic'. But 'prophetic', here, does not imply the dictating or determining of future events. The word affirms that the language of the poem does not depend upon anything *present*. There is no 'truth' contemporaneous with it that might one day verify what it says. With the word 'prophetic', Blanchot wishes us to hear in the phrase 'the speech *of* the future', a double genitive. The poem speaks of the future but it is also the future's speech. It opens us to a future in which it *will* speak. Char's poetry consists of poems in which in each instance the poem is still to be. They have 'said nothing yet', but they call to and 'indicate' (*indiquer*)[39] the only future in which anything will be said. This is what the poem's being an origin entails.

The future is rare, and not every day is a day of beginning. Even rarer is the word (*parole*) whose silence holds in reserve a word (still) to come . . .[40]

The effect of inspiration as the time of the poem is ruinous both on any attempt to fit the poem into a context and on the poet's relation to the language of the world. In *L'Espace littéraire*, the gaze of the poet is described as an 'inspired gaze'.[41] Inspiration is the moment when the first night becomes the other night. It is the approach of the uninterrupted, an approach forever accumulating. But now these words have begun to resound differently.

The *space* of the poem is the place of the most patient call to the future. Again, noting the genitive, we might say – and Blanchot often does – that the call to the future is a call to the call of the future. Blanchot obliges us to think of such a call as a *welcoming* that does not *domesticate*. He recalls Char's 'A une sérénité crispée', where the poet speaks of and to a 'promise of a future which does not belong to me'.[42]

A future which is not mine, a future which is not rooted in the present and in the actions of a present subject, is indicated (albeit differently and uniquely) for Blanchot, in the poetry of Mallarmé.

In one of his essays on the poet ('Le livre à venir'), Blanchot is intrigued by the way in which Mallarmé speaks of poetry as 'endow(ing) our sojourn with authenticity' and then, with 'Un coup de dés', creates a work in which the present is robbed of all content save the turning of the work itself towards the future.

Alongside Mallarmé's words on 'authentic dwelling', Blanchot cites Hölderlin's 'poetically man dwells (demeure)'. He quotes, too, the saying that 'what remains (demeure) is founded by the poets'. He then adds:

> Maybe the significance I give to these words does not conform pecisely to Heidegger's interpretation. Because, according to Mallarmé, what poets found, space – the abyss and the foundation of language – is what does not remain (ne demeure pas), and man's authentic sojourn is not the shelter where he seeks protection, but corresponds to the reef, the shipwreck (perdition), and the gulf . . .[43]

I apologize for moving so clumsily into such a difficult reading (Blanchot's!) of such a difficult poet, as though anything here could be summarized. The point is simply to begin to hear in Blanchot's 'literary space' that which compels Levinas to speak of its 'inviting us to leave' Heidegger. And there is a sense here of the oppositions of which Levinas is so fond: an 'authenticity' 'outside the truth of being', an 'authenticity' of erring. . . .

It might be the case, as some have suggested, that Levinas places undue emphasis on the relatively few occasions Blanchot speaks of 'authenticity'. Certainly, he rejoices in these lines where Blanchot writes of the poet and the artist as '*seeming* to have received the mission':

to recall us obstinately to error, to turn us toward that space where everything we propose, everything we have acquired, everything we are, everything that is opened on the earth and in the sky, returns to insignificance, where what approaches is the non-serious and the non-true, *as if* perhaps from there sprang forth the source of all authenticity.[44]

We would stress, however, the irony in that 'seeming' and that 'as if' and suggest that, on this point, the relation with Heidegger cannot be the one of simple opposition – one authenticity against another – that Levinas sometimes, but not always, seems to want. Much later, in *L'Écriture du désastre*, in the context of another reading of Heidegger, Blanchot will write that 'it is certain that one weakens Heidegger's thought when one interprets "being-for-death" as the search for authenticity through death (and so as a) vision of a persevering humanism'.[45] There, too, we will read that if there is one inauthentic word 'it is the word "authentic" '.[46] Even more importantly, and as a way of compounding Levinas's 'distrust', we should record Blanchot's words immediately after he has asked whether or not the non-true might be 'an essential form of authenticity': 'To this question there can be no response. *The poem is the answer's absence*'[47] (my emphases). In this context, it is useful as well to recall Derrida's comment concerning *l'attente de l'attente*: 'Levinas has begun to hear a response.'[48] Blanchot, himself, never says this so explicitly.

To return for one more, highly condensed, passage from 'Le livre à venir', again concerning 'Un coup de dés':

the whole poem is traversed . . . by the echoing, unwavering dominant (*neutral* PD) voice that expresses the future; an ever negative future ('never shall abolish') that nonetheless is dually extended; in a past future-perfect cancelling action even in its apparent failure ('will not have taken place') . . .

(The 'line' Blanchot cites – 'N'aura eu lieu' – is untranslatable. It is read under the cover of the 'Rien' on the far left of the page, cf. *Oeuvres complètes*, pp. 474–5.)

and in a new possibility towards which, beyond negations and supported by negations, the poem leaps – the time of exception in the height of a 'perhaps'.[49]

And the essay closes with these words from the poem: 'EXCEPT at the height PERHAPS . . .' ('EXCEPTÉ *à l'altitude* PEUT-ÊTRE . . .'). A speech which empties the present, guaranteeing it no secure link to a future, confronts itself – at the point of greatest passivity –

as the call to another future, a future which will never be present. The only true rapport with such a future is that of the *attente*.

It is no doubt too fanciful to suggest that Levinas had *this* 'perhaps' in mind, not least because of his having used the word in 'Énigme et Phénomène',[50] and yet might it not have been there as an echo or an encouragement? Either way it enables us to see the extent to which the 'perhaps' is not, here, in any sense primarily the reader's. The poem does not, any longer if it ever did, just give itself under the guidance of a particular word or gesture. Rather, it also and primarily gives the word or gesture under which it lets itself be read. In Blanchot's reading of it – that is, in his reading of both the poem and the poem's giving of itself – he never leaves its vicinity. He reads and writes his reading in and around this 'space': a space which can only be thought in terms of a perpetual approach, the approach of the guiding word which gives the work. The 'perhaps' will thus be a particular 'perhaps' (Mallarmé's). Cited elsewhere by Blanchot, it would denote the way in which the work (that of Mallarmé's being a crucial and historical instance) now gives itself to us differently. Blanchot's fidelity to the poem and to this extraordinary 'space' accounts for Levinas's giving to Blanchot's 'non-fiction' such a curious status. Yet, at the same time, Levinas does abstract from the work. He does derive something like a general principle from the 'perhaps'. That word, in Levinas's essay, both acknowledges the necessity and the fragility of the encounter with the work (the poem) and it enables Levinas to uphold the distinction between 'fiction' and 'non-fiction' and so to move slowly away from the tale – the neutral space of the tale – itself.

We can consider another text, one in which Blanchot is not mentioned but which seems to adhibit the terms of our discussion so far. In a section of 'La Trace de l'Autre' entitled 'movement without return', Levinas employs the notion of the 'Oeuvre' to designate an 'activity', a 'production', which eludes the economy of the *same* and which requires the utmost patience (passivity) on the part of the self. This 'Work' is not an acquisition, it does not leave its producer with a sense of his having achieved something. There is no increase. But nor is the 'Work' to be conceived as a simple nihilism, an ultimate devaluing of the self. Levinas writes that 'the future for which the work is undertaken must be posed, from the very outset, as being indifferent to my death'.[51] The 'Oeuvre', in 'The Trace of the Other', constitutes the 'space' of the transition from 'being-for-death' to 'being for-beyond-my-death' ('to be for a time which will be without me'). If the work requires my patience ('Be patient!'), it is because I no longer have any time to call my own, and the movement it marks is that from my self to the other, a movement without return.

Blanchot's 'criticism' will not speak of a 'nocturnal dimension of the future', for there is not simply *a* poetic grasping of the future amongst others. As we said earlier, Blanchot's 'insomnia' and 'gaze of the poet' will not provide synonyms for the *il y a*. Nonetheless, in Levinas's reading of them, those terms and that 'criticism' will *both* frustrate ontology and open up a future which will be other than ontology's. So said, it comes as no surprise to read the following difficult but not untypical sentence from *Otherwise than Being . . .*:

The rumbling (bourdonnement) of the *il y a* is the non-sense in which essence turns and in which thus turns the justice issued out of signification.[52]

This 'thus' (ainsi) and this twofold turning (tournant) are hints – already heard in the *Oeuvre* – that the move into what Levinas calls 'ethics' cannot simply be thought to involve two or more discrete moments, the first negative (the frustrating of essence and the projects of essentialism, the neutralizing of being, the most violent indifference) and the second or others positive (the naming of the beyond essence, a de-neutralizing, 'non-indifference'). Certainly ontology and ethics are two and are separate, but the ontological frustrating or ruining of ontology already comes from elsewhere and is already the turning of and into this *elsewhere*.

Using Levinas's characterization of Heidegger's thought as 'ontology', can we not distinguish between the following three moments, or better, the following three ways in which thought is exposed and vulnerable?

to the Nothing (to nothingness).

to the *il y a* (to the impossibility of nothingness).

to alterity, to the Other.

If the second names the turning of the first (ontology) into the third (ethics), then it seems that we cannot speak of there being a gap between the second and the third, but only of a *turning*.

It is in that part of 'The Trace of the Other' dealing with the 'Work' that we find one of the clearest and most familiar expressions of an opposition to Heidegger: *exile* (Abraham forever leaving his fatherland) over and against *return* (Odysseus' homecoming), the former being the 'site' of another 'authenticity'. If the 'Oeuvre' shows the movement from one to the other, can we simply introduce Blanchot's name and his 'criticism' into the account of that movement? With respect to the question of both the work of art and the encounter with poetry, can we not re-write our three moments so as to incorporate Blanchot's 'contribution', his 'invitation'? Thought exposed:

to the 'Nothing of the (world's) night':[53] ontology positing a future as thinking in a dialogue with poetizing.

to the 'impersonality of the work' and thus to the impossibility of the dialogue.

to alterity, to the Other.

The dialogue between thinker and poet like 'ontology' and 'idealism' would falter before the *il y a*. This seems to hold things together very well. Levinas always reads the 'later Heidegger' through what we might call the 'results' of Blanchot's enquiry into the work of art. But it doesn't take long to realize that, said like this, there is something very strange about Blanchot's 'contribution', a strangeness echoed in that opening question.

'Does the poet before the "eternal rustling of the outside" hear the voices which call from beyond the Heideggerian world?' Does the poet, disclosing and naming the *il y a*, hear the call to 'ethics' that is the beyond essence? Would it not seem that here the transition from the second 'exposure' to the third is not so inevitable? Either the poet in Blanchot's work and that work itself remain at the second 'moment' or they do not. But what would remaining there mean? How could it be possible save by our having recourse to a linear narrative: Levinas taking leave of the 'later Heidegger' by way of Blanchot. This linearity conceals both the awkwardness of the *place* accorded to poetry (literature) in Levinas and the anxiety of that question to the poet, a question that Blanchot's 'explications' must always provoke.

Towards the end of his 1972 interview with André Dalmas, Levinas speaks of the two ways in which Blanchot's work *simultaneously* presents itself to the reader. First, it 'announces a loss of meaning and a dissemination of discourse'. This is when we confront it as if it were the 'very extreme of nihilism'. Here we would be 'doomed to the inhuman' and to the 'fearfulness of the Neuter'. Second, however, 'Blanchot's literary space recalls that the "world of totality" is not total and that there is another discourse that it cannot silence.'[54] Our question is to the place of this doubleness of Blanchot's text in Levinas's twofold turning of 'ontology' into 'ethics'. It cannot be the doubleness accruing to those moments in the history of philosophy when Levinas believes that the *ethical relation* has been named against the dominance of 'ontology', because this would be to lose the difference between *philosophy* and *poetry* (literature), the difference which draws Levinas to Blanchot in the first place.

If we want to close down the discussion, deny that there is any real ambiguity here, and say that Levinas clearly envisages a movement 'beyond' Blanchot, perhaps we are forgetting what it would be to invoke such a metaphorics. Let us look at one example. We would need to give a detailed reading of Girard's *Mensonge romantique et vérité romanesque* in order to show exactly how Blanchot's 'literary space' is being employed. But towards the end of the book, following the suggestion that the conclusion of a work be considered as a successful attempt to overcome the inability to conclude, we read:

The impossible conclusion defines a 'literary space' which is not beyond this side of (en deçà de) reconciliation. The fact that this space is the only one accessible to our own time of anguish is disquieting but not surprising to anyone who bears in mind the evolution of the structure of the novel. . . . The great novelists cross the literary space defined by Blanchot but they do not stay there. They push beyond that space toward the infinity of a liberating death.[55]

So many of the themes here – 'reconciliation', another 'objective' history, a 'liberating death' beyond the *not yet* – are no longer available to Levinas. His reading of Blanchot, even at its most questionable is not reducible to these (one would have to say) pre-Heideggerian formulations. Levinas knows that Blanchot's work will not *let itself* be read like this. The *en deçà* opens out onto the space of exile.

We began by showing how Blanchot's writing on the *experience* of the poet and the question of the future was deemed similar enough to serve as its commentary. Levinas, insisting on the differences between them, sees Blanchot's text as an arraignment of Heidegger's, showing it to be subservient to the *il y a* as the 'nocturnal dimension of the future', a dimension that Heidegger's text cannot think or name as such. The naming of the *il y a*, the only mode of revelation appropriate to it, is poetry. For Levinas, Blanchot's fiction says the *il y a*, and his non-fiction says that the *il y a* is said without being thematized. Do we not see here one unfurling of the 'dire' (the saying), which will – in *Otherwise than Being* . . . – 'expose in essence even what is on *this side*, the *hither side* of ontology (*en deçà de* l'ontologie)'?[56]

On the one hand, Levinas is a careful reader of Blanchot. Even the problematic distinction between 'fiction' and 'non-fiction' actually helps to complicate the early development of the 'saying'. It certainly seems that between *Totality and Infinity* and *Otherwise than Being* . . . , Levinas searches for a subtler way of describing or performing the turning of 'ontology' into 'ethics', and the linearity that characterizes much of the earlier work diminishes. On the other hand, Blanchot's work never brings Levinas to temper or to alter his comments on Heidegger.

Blanchot's name appears just once in the main text of *Totality and Infinity*, as barely more than an aside in this summarizing section from the 'conclusions':

We have thus the conviction of having broken (avoir rompu) with the philosophy of the Neuter: with the Heideggerian Being of the being (l'être de l'étant) whose impersonal neutrality the *critical* work of Blanchot has so much contributed to bring out . . . (My emphasis.)[57]

Our question is simply to the difference between the *breaking with* and the *bringing out of* neutrality, and our argument suggests the impossibility of Levinas's ever formulating that difference. This is not a failure or inability on his part. The undecidability of the *between* that Levinas would have Blanchot be draws our attention – in a way that a text like Kelkel's never can – to that other proximity, Blanchot's *to* Heidegger.

What then is the nature of those questions that Blanchot undoubtedly does pose to Heidegger? The following remarks are necessarily tentative. We will look very briefly at a moment – from the 1946 essays on Char and Hölderlin – when Blanchot encourages us to read him *with* Heidegger. (I would argue that unless the implications of this early 'invitation' are noted then many of Blanchot's later and apparently more polemical comments concerning Heidegger are easily misconstrued.)

## II

Everything so far has been written under the sign of a 'for Levinas', and it would be very easy (and elsewhere it will be necessary) to show how, on nearly every point, Heidegger's work cannot be so constrained. We could recall the solicitude with which Heidegger marks the thinker's move towards the poem. Having posited the primacy of the poem with respect to 'poetry', he never ceases to ask about what happens when the thinker or philosopher takes a word or phrase from the poet. Clearly never a matter of usefulness, but nor is it, from the first, simply part of an historically inevitable dialogue. In 'Wozu Dichter', Heidegger seems to allude to a reading of poetry that leads thinking into a dialogue with poetry, a dialogue that is of the history of Being.[58] Prior to the dialogue with the poem, there is a reading of the poem, a reading which is nonetheless a part of this dialogue. There is something undeterminable in the time of *this* reading, something not easily dealt with.

However, in 'La parole "sacrée" de Hölderlin', Blanchot suggests that on one issue – to which we will return – Heidegger is more sensitive to the tradition than to the experience of the poet.[59] And in the Char essay, there is a hint at something apparently unavailable or unacceptable to Heidegger. Char's poetry is

a revelation of poetry, a poetry of poetry, or as Heidegger almost says of Hölderlin, his is a poem which is the essence of the poem.[60]

What is the sense of this 'almost' ('à peu près')? Let us recall that phrase from the essay in which the essence of the poem is described as 'an awaiting of itself' ('. . . l'essence du poème est d'être attente de lui-même . . .'). Presumably, we may conclude that, for Blanchot, the poetry of Char and Hölderlin is one in which, albeit in different ways, the neutral space of this *attente* is disclosed. It is a space that Heidegger 'almost' recognizes, 'almost' says, and one that evades him because of his fidelity to or concern with the tradition. If we hear in this last word, Levinas's evaluation of the tradition as 'ontology', then we sense the temptation of his reading of Blanchot with Heidegger. Away from that reading, do Blanchot's remarks allow for another interpretation?

Both the Char and the Hölderlin essays originally appeared in *Critique* as reviews of particular publications. In each case, one of these publications is a prose reading of the poet: for Char, Mounin's

*Avez-vous lu Char?*; for Hölderlin, Heidegger's commentary on 'Wie wenn am Feiertage . . .' which had just been translated and printed in *Fontaine*. Mounin's work is very quickly, although not unsympathetically, left to one side as Blanchot pursues another way of writing with and around Char's poetic writing. Heidegger's text, however, is a more abiding and provocative presence. The encounter with the language of the poem, enacted so rigorously in both essays, becomes more explicitly the topic of the second essay. It is not stretching things too far to suggest that one of the things the Hölderlin essay does is to clarify the 'almost' read in that apparently throwaway remark.

When the poet enquires into the essence of poetry, as he does in the works of Char and Hölderlin, he confronts the poem no longer as the result of action or experience, but as a beginning; a beginning always anterior to itself. The poem, we might say, is the perpetual *obfuscation* of what lies this side of beginning, this side of anything's being said. Earlier we gave as an example of this anteriority, the writer's awareness that the work will only become itself for the reader. The work will only signify in being read and, for the writer, this reader is always yet to be born. Blanchot comments on how the sense of this *powerlessness* often leads the writer to write *as though* he were the reader: the reader 'prematurely and falsely engendered'. The result of such a contrivance can be a surface eloquence, 'those fine phrases which cannot be said to have been written but to be readable'.[61] Char and Hölderlin's work never yields to such a temptation. It never so simply circumvents what is actually the opposite predicament to the one characterized above by Girard. The poem's beginning cannot really be described as the overcoming of the inability to begin because that inability is the poem's very centre. We must be wary of hearing in this distinction between the 'written' and the 'readable' a contribution to literary or philosophical 'criticism'. It arises from the work's turning in onto itself and becoming an issue for itself. An event which occurs with the departure of the gods. In such a time, the work discloses at its heart something *un-readable*. The 'peut-être' in Mallarmé's 'Un coup de dés' would be just such an 'unreadable'.

The word 'inspiration', the 'key' to the whole discussion in the Char essay, plays no part in 'La parole "sacrée" de Hölderlin', although in Blanchot's second essay on the poet ('Le Tournant' [1955] reprinted and shortened in *L'Espace littéraire* as 'Hölderlin's

Itinerary'), it will be central. In the 1946 essay, the theme of anteriority is broached differently, in Hölderlin's own terms, terms that we already know from Heidegger.

At the start of the essay Blanchot voices some vague doubts about Heidegger's reading. He asks whether there can ever be an encounter between an autonomous philosophical reflection and a poetic language that came into the world 'nearly 150 years ago'. It seems the naïvest of questions, one to which we could imagine any number of philosophical responses. For Blanchot, however, a profounder response comes from the poem itself:

> on this point the poem has responded: a poem is not without date but in spite of its date it is always to come, it is spoken in an 'à présent' which does not respond to a historical context or reference. It is *pressentiment*, and it designates itself as that which is not yet. It demands from the reader the same *pressentiment* which will make of him an existence not yet come.[62]

('Pressentiment' translates the German 'Ahnung'. The verbs 'pressentir' and 'ahnen' introduce us, from the first, to the sense of anteriority we have been considering. As a presaging, a foreboding or divining - inadequately conveyed in the use of the possessive 'having a presentiment of' - they designate, in Blanchot's reading of Hölderlin and indeed throughout Blanchot's work, the state in which the only present is this passive, patient turn towards the future. Char's poems are called 'the songs of *pressentiment* par excellence'.)

Now, if this is the response of the poem to Blanchot's question about a dialogue or encounter, it is also importantly a response echoed by Heidegger himself. At the close of his lecture on 'Wie wenn am Feiertage . . .', he raises precisely the matter of the time of the poem. In the French translation, the appropriate sentence begins: 'La poésie de Hölderlin est à présent' ('Hölderlin's Dichtung ist jetzt . . .').[63] Heidegger is referring us back to and Blanchot moving us towards these famous lines from the poem, lines which determine how this 'jetzt' is to be understood:

Jezt aber tagts! Ich harrt und sah es kommen
Und was ich sah, das Heilige sei mein Wort.
(But now day breaks! I waited and saw it come
And what I saw, the Holy be my word.)

Forgoing reading or summarizing the poem, let us note what brings Blanchot and Heidegger together and what seems to keep them apart. For both, the poet's being compelled to name the *holy* - an absolute anteriority – arises from the obligation to speak even after the fleeing of the gods, the guarantors of all communication and mediation. The *holy* is named in a way that neither thematizes nor objectifies. The waiting that precedes the naming, the 'ich harrt', is not terminated in some*thing* arriving. It is sustained as *pressentiment* in the saying of anteriority. The *holy* transforms the *now* (the 'Jezt', the 'à présent') in the poem into a *not yet*.

For Blanchot, the *holy* testifies to the way in which the condition of *pressentiment* overruns every aspect of the poem: explicitly, as the state shared by that which is to be named, 'nature', 'being', the '*Allgegenwärtig*', and by the one who is to do the naming, the poet in the poem; but also implicitly, as the poem itself – Hölderlin's poem and Hölderlin's poetry – and in the habitude (the hebetation) of the reader who in reading that poetry attends to the *holy* at its heart.

Heidegger's commentary attends to the *holy*. It identifies the *holy* as the word at the centre of the poem. In this respect Blanchot says, it is particularly '*ahnend*'. Given Blanchot's investment in this word and its translations, it would be hard to exaggerate the significance of this acknowledgement.

The essential state of the poet is not founded on the gift by which he received the god but on the holy which surrounds and seizes him.[64]

As *ahnend*, the poet exists as *not yet*, exists only by virtue of the existence to come with the poem. To be seized by the *holy* is, for Blanchot, to have a presentiment of its coming, a coming prior to all the times in which one says 'something comes'. To name the holy is to welcome the *holy*: naming as welcoming. The *holy* is the 'unreadable' at the heart of Hölderlin's work. It is the point at which the work turns itself towards a future it can neither know nor predict nor bring about. It can assure us of nothing. We might say that in the naming of the *holy*, the poet says *come* to what is without name, to what is unnameable. The *holy* – 'this' unreadable – draws everything it touches into the time and the space of an *attente*. To the extent that it is *ahnend*, Heidegger's reading, too, is drawn into that space, the space of literature.

Heidegger's commentary, we are led to infer, is however not *ahnend* – in other words, it draws back from the neutral space of the poem – in its response to the question concerning the essence of the holy and in what it takes to be the results of the poet's naming the holy. It is at this point that Blanchot begins to develop the themes and questions that constitute the major part of his subsequent discussions of Heidegger (the major part of what he says *about*, rather than *to*, Heidegger). Here, without expanding on them, we simply indicate two of these 'themes':

1) Blanchot suspects Heidegger of removing the word 'nature' from Hölderlin's poem – of not reading it within the space of the poem – and of presenting it in the context of another vocabulary, one that gives it a history and one that renders it familiar. This would be one of the luxuries a 'philosophical' reading might allow itself. Blanchot, on the contrary, has always insisted upon the poverty of poetic language when compared to the projects and the possibilities of philosophy. He questions the move Heidegger makes from the word 'nature' in the poem, where it is as fundamental or as neutral as any other, to the word 'nature' in the language of the tradition, where it might be described as derivative and secondary, and said to have already lost the force and the vitality of the Greek *physis*, the word the poet *should* have used.

(We do not want to take up this discussion here, simply to note how it begins. The issue of Heidegger's etymologies and translations is often raised in Blanchot's writings in the 1960s and 1970s. It finds its 'fullest' treatment in *L'Écriture du désastre*.)

2) The problem of how the holy is to be named, of how it is to be brought to language, is described at one point by Heidegger as the problem of thinking the most troubling *immediacy* without thereby mediating it. This immediacy registers in 'Wie wenn am Feiertage . . .' as 'chaos'. Heidegger describes 'die Erschütterung des Chaos'. The violent shaking, the originary disturbance, of chaos which offers no point of support and no foothold. In the poem, 'chaos' – that which frustrates all speech – is linked in some obscure way to the *law* that demands that the poet does speak. Blanchot disputes what he takes to be Heidegger's claim that this paradoxical *law* and this originary agitation are resolved and calmed in the naming of the holy. The disagreement here centres on Heidegger's reading of the words '*still*' (silence, stillness) and 'innigkeit' (interiority). Blanchot suggests that silence is marked by the same contradiction and laceration (*déchirement*) as language.

Heidegger often emphasizes the importance of hearing the naming of the holy together with the departure of the gods. If in singing of the gods, in naming them, the poet has always also named the holy, he has done so unknowingly. To name the holy as he does *now* is to attend to the trace of the gods. Robert Bernasconi reminds us of how Heidegger in the *Letter on Humanism* refers us to his lecture on 'Wie wenn am Feiertage . . .' for insight into the history of Being, and so into the way in which metaphysics at the time of its ending experiences itself. As Bernasconi says, it is not a matter of Heidegger's taking the idea from Hölderlin or even of his being influenced by him.[65] It is a matter rather of the dialogue, or encounter, between thought and poetry. The dialogue belongs to – is *of* – the history of Being, and 'the history of Being' is thought from out of a reading of Hölderlin. Blanchot would have us wonder whether such a circle does not detract from what is strangest in Hölderlin's poem. If the gods – the bearers and referents of the poet's speech and, as we said before, the guarantors of mediation – are fled, then the poet is faced with the full paradoxical force of the obligation that *is* poetic speech: to speak when there is nothing to say and no means by which to say it.

*Die Erschütterung des Chaos, die Schrecknis des Unmittelbaren* (the terror of the immediate): in the French translation of Heidegger's lecture, we read the following lines:

L'ébranlement est apaisé mais l'adoucissement le conserve. L'élément effrayant, atroce, du Sacré repose dans la douceur de l'âme 'du poète'. (The disturbance is calmed but the appeasing conserves it. The frightening, the atrocious, element of the holy reposes in the peacefulness of the poet's soul.)[66]

*L'ébranlement* translates *die Erschütterung*. It is also one of the words frequently used by Blanchot and Levinas to characterize the *il y a*. Might we not find here the concise form of their objections to Heidegger and the finest justification of what Levinas says about Blanchot's contribution? The lecture continues:

The holy is present as the Coming (*Kommendes*, *Venant*), this is why it is never represented or apprehended as an object.

Is what is most disturbing and difficult about this sentence not mitigated by the ones that immediately precede it?

Obviously there could be several Heideggerian replies to these questions. It would be interesting, for example, to re-examine what Heidegger says about *innigkeit* in 'Hölderlin and the Essence of Poetry', a text in which the poem's essence is described as division, opposition, and conflict, and where there are hints of an essential restlessness.

But this is not our central concern. Blanchot, in 1946, addresses the point of greatest obscurity in Heidegger's dialogue between thinker and poet, the point of its beginning. Unlike Levinas who reads that address in order to step away from the dialogue (and we have shown some of the problems that befall that step), Blanchot remains there. If Heidegger continues to clarify and to think in ever subtler terms the nature of the dialogue, it will be possible to read Blanchot alongside that development, and not necessarily because Blanchot himself wills such a reading but because of his sense of the impossibility of its being otherwise.

Blanchot begins, then, by asking about the time of an encounter with poetry and about the nature of the 'now' shared by poet and reader. With Heidegger and after Hölderlin, he will call it 'the destitute time', 'the time of distress'. But if, for Heidegger, the 'now' in which he and Hölderlin are held is that of the end of metaphysics, for Blanchot, it is the time which 'at all times is proper to art'. How, in closing, are we to understand the difference between these interpretations of the *dürftiger Zeit*? They would seem to have nothing in common. Blanchot's concern is with the demand made by the work that the writer enter a time in which there is no present (the time of writing). The time is destitute because empty. Blanchot sometimes speaks of *the absence of time*, the impossible 'now' that is the writer's solitude and distress. And yet there is a crucial historical sense in Blanchot's account. He also speaks of *the time of the absence of time*. Two questions can be teased out of Blanchot's essay on Hölderlin, the first to be posed more directly in *L'Espace littéraire*.

1) What is the time in which the poet asks 'What are poets for in the destitute time?'?

This doubling of the question is not simple. To ask about the time of the time is, for Blanchot, to ask about the time in which the absence of time is itself heard or read in the work, the time of a new understanding of literary space. Which leads to the second question:

2) What is the time in which a thinker reads the 'holy' at the heart of Hölderlin's poetry?

In Blanchot's terms, Heidegger's *reading* the holy is every bit as disturbing for thinking as the poet's naming the holy is for poetizing. The event of naming the holy leaves the poet, and poetry, forever exiled in a between (caught in 'the double lack and not'). Here we see the new understanding of literary space, the time of writing disclosed in writing. The event of reading the holy leaves the thinker, and thought, in a similar state. For both, we might say, there is an experience of the impossibility of closure, the impossibility of stepping out of, or away from, the between.

'La parole "sacrée" de Hölderlin' is the only occasion when Blanchot so explicitly organizes a text around a response to Heidegger. This response cannot be read as a criticism, nor as advocating another approach to Hölderlin. We would detect in it an identifying of what in Heidegger's work opens him to the 'space of literature'.

Blanchot's texts will hereafter let themselves run alongside Heidegger's just as they do Levinas's and neither of these proximities can be easily named, and neither one can be used to judge or to decide for the other, just as neither one can be thought as analogous to the other.

Distrustful of poetry, thinking is nonetheless obliged to entrust itself to it; in other words to read it – (a reading perhaps always marked by an *almost*). If Blanchot with Levinas shows the extent and the seriousness of that distrust, then Blanchot with Heidegger insists on the force and the weight of that obligation.

## Notes

1  Maurice Blanchot, *L'Entretien infini*, Paris, Gallimard, 1969, p. 76: 'Levinas is distrustful of poems and of poetic activity . . .'
2  Emmanuel Levinas, *Sur Maurice Blanchot*, Montpellier, Fata Morgana, 1975, pp. 25–6: 'Does the poet before the "eternal rustling of the outside", hear the voices which call from outside the Heideggerian world?'
3  Arion Kelkel, *La Légende de l'être*, Paris, Vrin, 1980, p. 603ff.
4  Martin Heidegger, *Erläuterungen zu Hölderlins Dichtung* (Gesamtausgabe Bd4), Frankfurt am Main, Klostermann, 1981, p. 44.
5  *La Légende de l'être*, p. 605.
6  Heidegger, 'Wozu Dichter?' in *Holzwege*, Frankfurt am Main, Klostermann, 1950: Trans. 'What are poets for?' in *Poetry, Language, Thought*, A. Hofstadter, New York, Harper & Row, 1971.
7  Johann Hölderlin, *Sämtliche Werke*, Stuttgart, Kohlhammer Verlag, 1952, vol. 5, p. 202; M. Blanchot, *L'Espace littéraire*, Paris, Gallimard, 1955 (Collection Idées), p. 374: Trans. *The Space of Literature*, Ann Smock, Lincoln, University of Nebraska, 1982, p. 272.

8 *L'Espace littéraire* pp. 338, 247
9 ibid., pp. 335, 246.
10 Blanchot, *La Part du feu*, Paris, Gallimard, 1949, p. 108.
11 *Sur Maurice Blanchot*, p. 20
12 Levinas, 'De l'être à l'autre' in *Noms propres*, Montpellier, Fata Morgana, 1975.
13 Levinas, 'Roger Laporte et la voix de fin silence' in *Noms propres*, Montpellier, Fata Morgana, 1975.
14 *Sur Maurice Blanchot*, p. 25.
15 The question of the ways in which Blanchot chooses to classify his texts – *récits, romans, critique*, etc. – is a complex one. *L'Attente, l'oubli*, a text that Levinas clearly reads as 'fiction' does not present itself as such. It is in *L'Entretien infini*, however, that Blanchot – referring back to his own earlier 'critical' writings *L'Espace littéraire* and *Le Livre à venir* – asks for another type of book. And although *L'Entretien infini* contains pieces from the time of those earlier writings, here they are added to and altered, accompanied by 'dialogues', by voices, by everything that up to now has been called 'fiction'.
16 'La parole "sacrée" de Hölderlin' in *La Part du feu*.
17 *Sur Maurice Blanchot*, p. 19.
18 Blanchot, *Éthique et infini*, Librairie Arthème Fayard et Radio-France, 1982, pp. 37–40.
19 *La Part du feu*, p. 320.
20 'Notre compagne clandestine', in *Textes pour Emmanuel Levinas*, édition J-M. Place, Paris, 1980, p. 86.
21 *Thomas l'Obscur* (Nouvelle Version), Paris, Gallimard, 1950, pp. 19–20: Trans. *Thomas the Obscure*, R. Lamberton, New York, David Lewis, 1973, p. 16.
22 *Holzwege*, p. 20: *Poetry, Language, Thought*, p. 35.
23 cf. *Totality and Infinity*, trans. A. Lingis, Pittsburgh, Duquesne University Press, 1969, p. 141. To help with the argument here, it would be useful to read an essay of 1948, 'La réalité et son ombre' (*Les Temps Modernes*, vol. 4, pp. 769–89): '. . . d'une doublure essentielle de la réalité par son image, d'une ambiguïté 'en deçà' . . .'
24 There are thus two notions of 'image' at work here and we would need to follow some later texts of Blanchot's (including 'The essential solitude' and 'The two versions of the imaginary' [both in *L'Espace littéraire*]) in order to appreciate the difficulties underlying them. Put (too) simply, one notion would be familiar to a certain aesthetics and so to a traditional conception of the object – as present, as re-presentable; whilst the other would arise from the movement *beyond* or the *overwhelming* of that aesthetics.

We must be wary, though, of bringing Blanchot and Heidegger together too quickly. Certainly the two senses of 'image' can be said in terms that recall Heidegger's; that is to say, as both reducible *and* irreducible to metaphysics, to the metaphysics of the *copy*. And certainly Heidegger's comments on the image (Bild) in '. . . Poetically Man Dwells . . .' (*Vorträge und Aufsätze*, Pfullingen, Neske, 1954, pp. 194–5: Trans. *Poetry, Language, Thought*, p. 226) might be thought to prove that the 'results' of his enquiries are the opposite to Blanchot's. But the relation between Blanchot's 'beyond' (always a *pas au-dela*, both a step and stop) and Heidegger's 'overcoming' is not so easily won. We want to find the right way of making it an issue, of letting it become an issue. The ambiguity that Blanchot invokes by playing on the double *pas* is also at work in the *au-dela* as *en deçá*, the unthematizable *this side*, the most troubling of proximities.

For Levinas, of course, any difference between Blanchot and Heidegger can at any moment be cited to encourage our breaking with Heidegger. Everything in this respect testifies against Heidegger. This paper is attempting to show the untenability of such a position: untenable in Levinas's own terms and untenable because of the care he brings to his reading of Blanchot. A more specific discussion around the question of the 'image' will, elsewhere, take us to a closer reading of '. . . Poetically Man Dwells . . .' and to some of Lacoue-Labarthe's work on *mimesis*, this latter being itself inspired – at least in part – by a particular reading of Blanchot (cf. Lacoue-Labarthe, 'Typographie' in *Mimesis*, Paris, Aubier-Flammarion, 1975; *L'imitation des modernes*, Paris, Galilée).

25  *Sur Maurice Blanchot*, p. 16.
26  In *Après Coup*, Paris, Éditions de Minuit, 1983, p. 66.
27  T. de Boer, 'An Ethical Transcendental Philosophy' in *Face to Face with Levinas* (ed. R. Cohen), New York, SUNY, 1986, p. 88.
28  *Sur Maurice Blanchot*, p. 30.
29  ibid., p. 78.
30  ibid.
31  *L'Espace littéraire*, pp. 227, 171.
32  *Sur Maurice Blanchot*, p. 13.
33  ibid., p. 14.
34  ibid., p. 15.
35  ibid., p. 29.
36  *L'Espace littéraire*, pp. 248, 186.
37  *La Part du feu*, p. 104.
38  ibid.
39  'La Bête de Lascaux', Cahiers de l'Herne 15, 1971, p. 73.
40  ibid., p. 74
41  *L'Espace littéraire*, pp. 231, 173–4.
42  *La Part du feu*, p. 106.
43  *Le Livre à venir*, Paris, Gallimard, 1959 (Idées), p. 349: Trans. in *The Sirens Song* (ed. G. Josipovici), Brighton, Harvester, 1982, p. 240.
44  *L'Espace littéraire*, pp. 337, 247.
45  *L'Écriture du désastre*, Paris, Gallimard, 1980, p. 180.
46  ibid., p. 98

47 *L'Espace littéraire*, pp. 337, 247.

48 *L'Écriture et la différence*, Paris, Le Seuil (Points), 1967, p. 152: Trans. *Writing and Difference*, Chicago, University of Chicago Press, p. 103.

49 *Le Livre à venir*, pp. 354–5, 243–4.

50 We should note that 'the modality of the "perhaps" ' is actually Levinas's phrase. Our interest is in his extending it to Blanchot's 'explications'. In 'Énigme et phénomène', Levinas speaks of 'a new modality' expressed by *'that* "perhaps" and *that* "if one wants" ("si l'on veut")'(*En Découvrant l'existence avec Husserl et Heidegger*, Paris, Vrin, 1967, p. 209). He does so in order to suggest the way that a meaning beyond meaning – beyond any plurality of meaning – enters into meaning. This radical *disturbance* is not contained or calmed by a rational order. But nor does it arrive as something irrational. Our concern, here, is with what happens when the event of this disturbance is discussed with reference not to Levinas's 'ethics' (the infinite approach of the neighbour) but to Blanchot's 'writing' (the infinite approach of *l'espace littéraire*). In returning to the former, is there not, in Levinas's reading of the latter, some sort of abstraction? And what of that other disturbance, the non-sense in sense, the *il y a*? The question can be answered in terms of a particular linear conception of Levinas's own project, but not so easily dealt with in terms of his relation to Blanchot and to Blanchot's 'project'.

51 ibid., p. 191.

52 *Autrement qu'être ou au-dela de l'essence*, The Hague, Nijhoff, 1974, p. 208: Trans. *Otherwise than Being or Beyond Essence*, A. Lingis, The Hague, Nijhoff, 1981, p. 163.

53 *Erläuterungen zu Hölderlins Dichtung*, p. 44.

54 *Sur Maurice Blanchot*, pp. 50–2.

55 *Mensonge romantique et vérité romanesque*, Paris, Grasset, 1961, pp. 307–8: Trans. *Deceit, Desire, and the Novel*, Y. Freccero, Baltimore, Johns Hopkins, 1965, p. 309.

56 The 'en deçà de' is used throughout *Otherwise than Being . . .*, in particular cf. pp. 63, 49.

57 *Totalité et infini*, p. 274: Trans. *Totality and Infinity*, p. 298.

58 *Holzwege*, pp. 269–70 (Trans. p. 96).

59 *La Part du feu*, p. 123.

60 ibid., p. 105.

61 *L'Espace littéraire*, pp. 268, 200.

62 *La Part du feu*, p. 116.

63 *Erläuterungen zu Hölderlins Dichtung*, p. 77 (French translation by J. Rovan in *Fontaine* No. 54, 1946, p. 234).

64 ibid., pp. 67, 226.

65 Robert Bernasconi, *The Question of Language in Heidegger's History of Being*, Atlantic Highlands, Humanities Press, 1985, p. 42.

66 *Erläuterungen zu Hölderlins Dichtung*, pp. 68–9, 228. Cf. *La Part du feu*, p. 128ff.

# Narcissism and Dispersion in Heidegger's 1953 Trakl Interpretation

## NICK LAND

Martin Heidegger's thinking continues to have a massive – and constantly growing – influence on the development of modern 'philosophy'; in the formulation of its questions, the selection of its 'objects', and the constructions of its history. Yet this in itself might not be enough to explain why his 1953 essay on the Austrian poet Georg Trakl should be of interest to us. Does Heidegger's essay perhaps represent Trakl to us in a way that is enlightening or informative? Does it tell us something about poetry, or history, or language in general? Does it, in fact, succeed in doing anything at all? In his safely vacuous text on Trakl's poetry Herbert Lindenberger writes:

> It would seem gratuitous to complain of the wrongheadedness of Heidegger's approach to Trakl, for Heidegger does not even pretend to use the poets he writes about for any purpose except the exposition of his own philosophy. But Heidegger's study of Trakl seems to me considerably less successful than his study of Hölderlin . . . (*GT*, p. 141)

Lindenberger does not ask what meaning can be given to 'success' within a history – like Heidegger's history of being – for which the proper sense of progress has always been the expansion of devastation; a history, that is, which has been perpetually deflected from thinking by a pervasive theo-technical tradition. Platonic-Christian culture has made it not only possible, but also imperative, to think of poetry as the product of a poet, and, derivatively, as something to be 'used' by a philosopher for the purpose of illustrating representational concepts. It is this tradition which directs us to ask about the usefulness and representational adequacy of Heidegger's essay. Such questions are symptoms of a profound and *positively* constituted illiteracy, whose hegemony it has been the intellectual task of the (post-)modern age to question.

As for Trakl – who failed to organize his desires according to the laws of his civilization, failed to keep a job, became addicted to opium, enmeshed in alcoholism, failed to defeat his psychosis and died of a cocaine overdose in a military pharmacy – what would we be doing to him if we said he had 'succeeded' as a poet? Appropriating his delicate, futile ardour to a society that has forgotten how to despise itself? Trakl's traces are the ruins of a miserable, even horrific, failure. A failure to adapt or conform, to repress or sublimate adequately, to produce, resolve, comfort, or conclude. This failure is not merely a default, however, but a violently traumatic condition. The evolution of his style, if it is still possible to write coherently of such a thing, is a drive towards the dissolution of every criterion for evalu-ation. It is this above all which he learns from his decisive encounters with Rimbaud and Hölderlin. The traditional aesthetics which would distinguish a traumatic content from a perfectly 'achieved' formal presentation loses all pertinence as Trakl presses language into the shadows. The last thing we should want is for Heidegger to 'master' these traumatized signs. To learn from Trakl is to write in ashes.

A long essay by Heidegger appeared in the sixty-first (1953) issue of the German literary periodical *Merkur* which discussed the work of Georg Trakl. This mysterious text, at once intensely personal and strangely detached, was entitled *Georg Trakl. Eine Erörterung seines Gedichtes* ('Georg Trakl. A situating of his poetry'). The same essay, renamed *Die Sprache im Gedicht* ('Language in the Poem'), and now subtitled *Eine Erörterung von Georg Trakls Gedicht* ('A situating of Georg Trakl's poetry'), was later published (in 1959) as the second division of Heidegger's book *Unterwegs zur Sprache* (*On the Way to Language*). The essay which precedes it in the book, *Die Sprache* ('Language'), is also concerned with Trakl, or, more precisely, with the reading of a single Trakl poem, *Ein Winterabend* ('A Winter Evening'). *Die Sprache im Gedicht*, in comparison, cites, or sites, no fewer than forty-three of Trakl's poems in the course of a wide-ranging search for the well-spring of their peculiar language. Outside of these two texts Heidegger makes only glancing references to Trakl's work and to the impact it had on his own thinking.

The 1953 essay consists of three numbered sections of uneven length, prefaced by a short untitled introduction or prologue. These basic partitions are not interrelated according to any conventional pedagogical principle, and do not unfold the stages of a developing argument. It is, for instance, very difficult to discriminate between the essay's three main sections in terms of theses or themes, since each successive section recollects the discussion of the last and subtly displaces it. To depict this complex progression it is perhaps necessary to borrow the 'metaphor' Heidegger himself calls upon, that of a *wave*, which describes motion coiling into an enigmatic pulsion and cyclical repetition. Yet the peaks and troughs that alternate within Heidegger's text do not follow the regular trace of an oscillograph; they cut a jagged and confusing path. As they rise a distinct 'theme' emerges, momentarily isolated from a maelstrom of interweaving currents. Due to the intensity of Trakl's language, and to the momentum historically invested within it, each theme shatters into blinding foam when swept to its apex, and sinks again into swirling depths. In this essay I shall only attempt to explore limited stretches along a single of these interwoven currents: pursuing elements of reflection and dispersion in Heidegger's reading of Trakl's poem *Geistliche Dämmerung*.

Heidegger's readings of poetry are perhaps most distinctively characterized by the refusal to participate affirmatively in the discourse of European aesthetics, and the associated project of rigorously bracketing subject–object epistemological categories. He argues that when the categories of aesthetics are carried into the domain of linguistics or other varieties of language study they take the form of a distinction between a normal and a meta-language. The minimal notion of meta-language is a technical terminology which is distinctive to the critical or interpretative text. This terminology traces an ancestry for itself that is divergent in principle from that of the texts to which it is 'applied'. The kinship of 'thinker' and 'poet' is annihilated. At variance to this sedimenting of metaphysics, Heidegger pursues a tendency towards the uttermost erasure of terminological distinctiveness. The language of poetry is not to be translated, but simply guided into a relationship with itself. And this guidance is not to be that of the thinker *qua* subject, but that of an impersonal thinking which is no longer disguised in the cloak of philosophy. Philosophy would no longer be the guardian of this relation, since the epoch of philosophy is simultaneous with that of meta-language. Or, put differently, meta-language is pre-eminently the language of meta-physics.

The final essay in *Unterwegs zur Sprache*, entitled *Der Weg zur Sprache*, begins by citing a sentence from Novalis's 1798 text *Monolog*: 'Precisely what is most peculiar about language, that it only concerns itself with itself, nobody knows' (*US*, p. 241; N, p. 5). It is from this thought – of language accounting for itself in itself – that Heidegger begins his meditation on poetry. The vocabulary for the meditation is to stem from the reading itself. Indeed, thought is to be carefully dissolved into poetry, but only in such a way that poetry is strengthened in its thinking. Heidegger trusts that the key to what is said in the reserve of Western languages, while itself reserved, is yet able to be elicited. He suggests:

Thus released into its own freedom, language can concern itself solely with itself. This sounds like the discourse upon an egoistic solipsism. But language does not insist on itself in the sense of a self-centred all-forgetting self-mirroring. As saying, the weft of language is the propriative showing, which precisely deflects its gaze from itself, in order to free what is shown into its appropriate appearing. (*US*, p. 262).

Language is to be understood in a way that could be misread as a theory of narcissism, since it relates itself to itself, and this could be taken to be analogous to the self-regard of a subject enraptured by its own reflection. The discourse on language must therefore fend off a misinterpretation that threatens to appropriate it, or at least deflect it, into a psychoanalysis of the sign. At this crucial moment the circle of language seems to symptomize a type of auto-eroticism, displacing itself into a geometric figure of desire. In insisting that his approach to language is not to be confused with a dissolution of the subject into unconscious energetics – and in the prologue to *Die Sprache im Gedicht* the reference to psychoanalysis is explicit – Heidegger marks a crucial historical crossroads in the interpretation of Nietzsche's doctrine of the cosmic circle, the eternal recurrence of the same. Heidegger seeks rigorously to distinguish his own reading of eternal recurrence – as the last attempt to conceive the temporality of beings, as recapitulation of the history of being, as the circle of language, and even as Trakl's 'icy wave of eternity' – from what has been interpreted within the Freudian research programme as the 'death drive', as the economy of desire, and as the return of the inorganic. Return, which is perhaps the crucial thought of modernity, must now be *read elsewhere*. The dissolution of humanism is stripped even of the terminology which veils collapse in the mask of theoretical mastery. It must be hazarded to poetry.

*Geistliche Dämmerung*[1] is the only poem cited by Heidegger in its entirety in the essay, and this is of some considerable significance. Dissolving the unity and specificity of the separate poems plays a vital role in Heidegger's project of uncovering a site (*Ort*) that relates to the Trakl corpus indifferently and as a whole. Up to the point at which *Geistliche Dämmerung* is introduced Heidegger conserves the status of this site as the sole 'ontologically' significant totality by splintering, rearranging, and repeating fragments of the individual poems. The resilient integrity of this particular poem in Heidegger's text might therefore indicate a special difficulty, one that obstructs the process of assimilation and resists the hegemony of the site. If this is so it is possible that an issue is at stake in the reading of this poem which resists absorption into any readily *communicable* truth of Trakl's poetry, an issue that perhaps remains in some sense exterior to a 'thinking dialogue' with the poet, but one that also retains a peculiar insistence. As Heidegger's reading unfolds it comes to chart a closure of communication of precisely this kind.

There is no unambiguous point at which the discussion of *Geistliche Dämmerung* begins. It is approached through a discussion of the final lines of *Sommersneige* ('Summer Solstice') in which the steps of a stranger ring through the silver night, and a blue beast is brought to the memory of its path, the melody of its spiriting year. To this is conjoined the hyacinthine countenance of twilight from the poem *Unterwegs* ('Underway'). Heidegger introduces the poem in order to address what is named in its title, without any hint that the perplexing figure of the sister is to haunt it both here and in its later citation (*US*, pp. 67–81), displacing all other preoccupations. It reads:

> *Stille begegnet am Saum des Waldes*
> *Ein dunkles Wild;*
> *Am Hügel endet leise der Abendwind,*
>
> *Verstummt die Klage der Amsel,*
> *Und die sanften Flöten des Herbstes*
> *Schweigen im Rohr.*

*Auf schwarzer Wolke*
*Befährst du trunken von Mohn*
*Den nächtigen Weiher,*

*Den Sternenhimmel.*
*Immer tönt der Schwester mondene Stimme*
*Durch die geistliche Nacht.*

(At the forest's rim silence meets / A dark beast; / Quietly, on the hill, dies the evening wind, // The plaint of the blackbird ceases, / And the gentle flutes of autumn / Fall silent in the reed.// On a black cloud you sail, / Drunk on poppies, / The nocturnal pool, // The starry sky. / The lunar voice of the sister sounds unceasing / Through the spiriting night.) (*US*, p. 48; *T*, p. 66)

The translation of 'beast' for *Wild* is of course unsatisfactory. In German the word *Wild* denotes a feral animal, especially one hunted as game, and sometimes it specifies such animals as deer. In addition it connotes wildness and wilderness, since the adjective 'wild' exists in German as well as English. Furthermore, it is probably etymologically related to the similar word *Wald* (forest). This network of associations seems impossible even to approach in translation. Such difficulties are particularly frustrating inasmuch as this translation must bear almost the entire weight of Trakl's exploration of animality, and the further stresses of Heidegger's response to it.

For Heidegger the 'dark beast' is *clearly* the 'blue beast' who negotiates the diffference between animality and the opening of the horizon of being – *der Mensch*. The wildness of the beast is not swallowed by the forest; instead it gives to the forest a margin. But this margin is not a fixed demarcation, and is not illuminated by the light of day. The shadowy animal, trembling with uncertainty in the evening wind, is man:

The blue beast is an animal whose animality presumably rests, not in animalness, but rather in that thoughtful gaze, after which the poet calls. This animality is yet distant, and scarcely to be registered, so that the animality of the animal noted here oscillates in the indeterminate. It is not yet brought into its weft [*Wesen*]. This animal, the one that thinks, *animal rationale*, humanity, is, according to Nietzsche's words, not yet firmly established [*fest gestellt*]. (*US*, p. 45).

Heidegger takes the weave of the distance separating humanity from the beasts of the wilderness to rest in a type of thinking that is irreducible to adaptive biological calculation. Such thinking is rooted

in the temporalization of the ontological difference, and has been traditionally unified – if only confusedly so – about the thought of transcendence. Transcendental thinking has the peculiar characteristic of
relating itself to the thematic of thought itself, a tendency which has
been systematized within epistemological philosophy. Within the
western tradition this type of cognition has been designated 'reflection'. The human is that animal caught in the play of its reflection.
The line of approach that Heidegger follows, in what is to be his first
and sole decisive encounter with the poem, begins with its final
stanza:

The starry sky is portrayed [*dargestellt*, staged, placed there, the *stellen* is
always decisive for Heidegger] in the poetic image of the nocturnal pool. So
our habitual representation [*vor-stellen*] thinks it. But the night sky is in the
truth of its weft this pool. Over against this, what we otherwise call the night
remains only an image, namely, the faded and vacuous after-image
[*Nachbild*, perhaps also 'copy'] of its weft. (*US*, p. 48)

The insistence that the night sky is in truth a pool is not irreducible either to Heidegger's phenomenological stubbornness, or to a
defence of the primordiality of metaphor. It is far more intimately
connected with the problematic of spatiality in post-Kantian thinking, and beyond this with the Greek thought of the heavens as χαος.
These concerns are bound up with Heidegger's pursuit of that reflection which yields an image of human transcendence, and therefore
marks a firmly established separation of Dasein from the psychology
of animals. This pursuit is perhaps the aspect of Heidegger's work
which is closest to the concerns of the ontotheological tradition, the
point where his thinking is most 'human, all-to-human'. But there is,
nevertheless, something both crucial and 'technically' precise at issue
in this play of mirrors. The passage continues:

The pool and the mirror-pool often recur in the poet's poetry. The water,
sometimes blue, sometimes black, shows humanity its own countenance, its
returning gaze. But in the nocturnal pool of the starry sky appears the twilight blue of the spiriting night. Its gleam is cool. (*US*, p. 48)

The starry sky has an integral relation to reflection, but one which
is of daunting complexity. Heidegger first turns to the pool itself,
besides which humanity lies, lost in narcissistic reverie. Here
humanity gazes upon itself, although we are not told whether, like
Narcissus, this gaze is inflamed with desire.

Heidegger finds the compulsive character of Trakl's imagery to be indicative of a repression, but one which does not seem to be – at least superficially – primarily sexual. He takes the reflectivity of Trackl's mirrors to exceed all representation and ontical objectivity (*Vorhandenheit*). In the darkened pool the gaze does not return in a familiar form; it reveals instead an abyssal twilit blue, which colours both the dawn and dusk of the spiriting night. The image of no thing returns. Reflection is shattered against the impersonal, against the impassive shade of a pure opening or cleft in beings. Humanity is thus reflected as the default of an (ontical) image; as a lack of ground or *Abgrund* which is the transcendental condition of any possible ontology. The heavens are an abyss: χαος. As we follow Heidegger's discussion of *Geistliche Dämmerung* further, this classical comprehension of chaos enters into a problematic negotiation with the contemporary sense of the word as disorder. It is this negotiation which re-opens the path to Trackl's most crucial explorations.

As the reading of *Geistliche Dämmerung* proceeds Heidegger's discussion suddenly changes key, without indicating that there is any thematic unity between the mirror and the mysterious figure who is now introduced, the sister:

> The cool light stems from the shining of the lunar woman [*Möndin*] (Selanna). Ringing her luminosity, as ancient Greek verse says, the stars fade and even cool. Everything becomes 'lunar'. The stranger [*der Fremde*, the German masculine] stepping through the night is called 'the lunar one'. The 'lunar voice' of the sister, which always sounds through the spiriting night, is then heard by the brother in his boat when he attempts to follow the stranger in a nocturnal journey across the pool, which is still 'black' and scarcely illuminated by the stranger's goldenness. (*US*, pp. 48–9)

The sister is allied to the moon, and thus to the luminosity of the night. Her power to render a world visible holds sway in the epoch of world-calumniating darkness initiated by the flight of the Hellenic gods, whose end is heralded by the stranger's goldenness, which is the flickering light of a new dawn. It is the sister who guides the path of the wanderer throughout the nihilistic metamorphoses, during which the securities of ontotheology lose their authority and disappear into their twilight, and before the arising of that new thinking which betrays itself only in scarcely perceptible hints. The sister is associated with transition, and with the indeterminacy of an unthreaded time. Even the corrupted seals that stamped the distinctive mark of scholasticism and theological apologetic are broken, and no new type has taken their place. The haunting voice of the sister is heard as the brother drifts away from the ancient genus of theological metaphysics and towards the genus of the stranger. Yet the sister's voice cannot be identified with the type of the past or with that of the future, it cannot be subsumed within a genre.

The passage is not so easily reduced to even this tentative metaphysico-historical familiarity, however, since Heidegger does not only mention the sister, but also Selanna; the strangers (*der Fremde, der Fremdling* – the gender of *das Fremde* from *US*, p. 41 – has now strangely metamorphosed); and the sister's brother. What is the meaning of this perplexing cast? What relation does Selanna, the lunar woman, have to the sister who speaks in lunar tones? Of Selanna, David Farrell Krell writes: 'Heidegger recollects the way the ancient Greek lyricists speak of the moon and stars; in the context of abscission, of the confluent twofold, and *seléné*, who as Semele is the mother of Dionysos . . .' (IM, p. 171). In the classical myth Semele is tricked by Hera into demanding that her lover (Zeus) reveal himself to her in his full presence, and when he does so she is killed by his radiance. An event that might suggest some relation to the 'stranger's goldenness'. But even following this apparently un-ambiguous path quickly leads us into a kind of mythological *aporia*, since, as Robert Graves notes in *The White Goddess*:

The Vine-Dionysus once had no father, either. His nativity appears to have been that of an earlier Dionysus, the Toadstool-god; for the Greeks believed that mushrooms and toadstools were engendered by lightning – not sprung from seed like all other plants. When the tyrants of Athens, Corinth and Sicyon legalized Dionysus worship in their cities, they limited the orgies, it seems, by substituting wine for toadstools; thus the myth of the Toadstool-Dionysus became attached to the Vine-Dionysus, who now figured as a son of Semele the Theban and Zeus, Lord of lightning. Yet Semele was the sister of Agave, who tore off her son Pentheus' head in a Dionysiac frenzy. (*WG*, p. 159)

The attribution of a (patrilinear) genealogy to Dionysus is complicit with a project of repression. An intoxication that came from nowhere, from a bolt of lightning, is asked to show its birth-certificate. Wine, which Plato will later accommodate even to dialectic, displaces the fungus of the Dionysian cults (*Amanita Muscaria*). The sacred mushroom of the cults is held to be responsible for those socially unassimilable deliria which are a threat to the πολις.

But what is the relation between this ancient policing of social pathology and Heidegger's interpretation of Trakl? How can a bridge be built between such ontic-empirical history, and the onto-transcendental question concerning the site of poetry? The spanning of such a gulf has been hindered by the medicalization of the history of derangement, and its reduction to the historical and psychiatric study of madness. But this regional investigation is nothing other than the contemporary instance of that discourse of the πολις which first instituted a genealogy of Dionysus. Such a construction patently fails to mark the inherently delirious character of western history, and, therefore, of scientificity itself. This is not only a matter of ontotheology being rooted in a specific amnesia. A delirium integral to the western graphic order implies, more radically, that any possible history must arise out of the forgetting (or secondary repression) of a constitutive arche-amnesia (the ellipsis integral to inscription). Klossowski has even been led to suggest that western science is aphasic, because it is initiated in the default of a foundational discourse (*NC*, p. 16). This default is not merely a passively accepted pathology, it is an inscribed, prescribed, or actively administered pharmaco-pathology. The response of the West to the writing of itself has been that of a poisoning. This is why the fact that Selanna substitutes for a delirium without origin – which is equally a delirium of origins – seems to resonate with what Derrida entitles an *aggression pharmakographique*.

In Trakl's *Geistliche Dämmerung* the path of the pharmakon, the intoxicated voyage across the nocturnal pool, seems to evade *Geschlecht* (the general resource of typography). Instead it crosses the starry sky, through which the lunar voice of the sister resounds. A problematic of the moon is introduced, demanding some minimal gesture of interpretation. Perhaps to speak of the 'lunar' in this fashion is simply to speak of the way things appear in the night.[2] In the poem *In der Heimat*, for instance, the sister is seen asleep bathed in moonlight:

> *Der Schwester Schlaf ist schwer. Der Nachtwind wühlt*
> *In ihrem Haar, das mondner Glanz umspült.*
> (The sister's sleep is heavy. The nightwind burrows
> In her hair, bathed in the gleam of the moon.) (T, p. 35)

This apparent reduction or simplification of the problem only displaces our difficulties however. The Traklean night (*Nacht*) is, as we

have seen, the time of derangement (*Umnachtung*), consonant perhaps with the 'mania' that stems, like moon (and 'mind'), from the
Indo-European road (*\*men(e)s-*). That the moon is associated with
woman is indicated by the etymological relations between 'moon',
'month', and 'menses', but it is also the companion of lunatics and
werewolves; figures with whom the reader of Trakl is certainly familiar.

It is, fittingly, in the culminating lines of *Traum und Umnachtung*
that this imagery crosses a climactic threshold:

*Steinige Oede fand er am Abend, Geleite eines Toten in das dunkle Haus des Vaters.
Purpurne Wolke umwölkte sein Haupt, daß er schweigend über sein eigenes Blut
und Bildnis herfiel, ein mondenes Antlitz; steinern ins Leere hinsank, da in
zerbrochenen Spiegel, ein sterbender Jüngling, die Schwester erschien; die Nacht das
verfluchte Geschlecht verschlang.*
(He found a petrified desolation in the evening, the company of one deceased
as he entered the dark house of the father. Purple clouds enwreathed his
head, so that he fell upon his own blood and image, a lunar countenance; and
fainted petrified into emptiness when, in a shattered mirror a dead youngster
appeared, the sister: night enveloped the accursed genus.) (T, p. 84)

With a passage of such beauty and labyrinthine depths any
response is likely at worst merely to irritate, and at best to increase
our perplexity. I will only try to ask one simple question. Is there a
connection to be made between the shattering of the mirror and a
movement of astronomical imagery; between an explosion of desire
that exceeds all introversion or reflection on the one hand, and a nocturnal or lunar *process* on the other? If such a connection were to be
made it would surely pass by way of the sister, who is herself a
threshold between the reflective order of the father's house and the
illimitative difference of the night sky. It is the 'night pool' with its
subtly differentiated luminosities – a series of intensities which defy
resolution within any dialectic of presence and absence – that flood
onto the mirror with the sister; shattering every power of representation. At the point of a certain nocturnal delirium (or lunacy) the relation of the sister to the family is metamorphosed. She no longer
obeys the law of the boundary by mediating the family with itself,
sublimating its narcissism, or establishing its insertion into the order
of signification by disappearing (leaving the father's house according
to the exchange patterns of patrilineal exogamy, and thus as a meta-
bolic or reproductive moment within a kinship structure). Instead
she breaches the family, by opening it onto an alterity which has not
been appropriated in advance to any deep structure or encompassing

system. A night that was an indeterminable alterity such as this would be a fully positive differentiation from the day.[3]

Perhaps the single most important Trakl text on this theme, in addition to the culmination of *Traum und Umnachtung*, is a poem called *Geburt* ('Birth') (T, p. 64) where lunar imagery functions similarly as a haemorrhaging of familial interiority. The poem pivots upon a line at the end of the third stanza in which a sublimated incestuality works a stifling movement of interiorization: *Seufzend erblickt sein Bild der gefallene Engel* ('Sighing the fallen angel glimpsed his image'). It might seem as if the birth of the sister is to be absorbed in a retreat into the claustrophobic heart of the *Geschlecht*. But although the fourth stanza begins with an awakening in a musty room (*dumpfer Stube*) the one who thus awakes is 'a pale one' (*ein Bleiches*); 'lunar'. The eyes of the mother (or the midwife) (*steinernen Greisin*) are described as 'two moons', a reference taking us back out into the night (whose 'black wing touches the boy's temple'), and back to a crucial image from the second stanza; that of the decayed moon:[4]

*Stille der Mutter; unter schwarzen Tannen*
*Oeffnen sich die schlafenden Hände,*
*Wenn verfallen der kalte Mond erscheint.*
(Silence of the mother; under black pines / The sleeping hands open out / When the cold and ruined moon appears.) (T, p. 64)

It would be possible to interpret this ruin of the moon as a dialectical restoration of the inside, its order and its securities, as if what had defied the inside was now falling away into self-annihilation. It might thus be asserted: 'This nocturnal path, departing from everything we have always believed in, it has all collapsed into chaos now. Wasn't it obvious it was going to go terribly wrong? You should have listened to your priest/parents/teachers/the police.' Yet this is not the only reading open to us.

The ruin of the moon might seem to block the nocturnal movement that passes from a claustrophobic interior into endless space, and that conjugates the dynasty with an unlimited alterity. But this would not be the case if the moon itself was, at least partially, a restrictive element across the path of departure, rather than being the sole gateway into the heavens. The ruin of the moon would then be a protraction of the nocturnal trajectory; a dissolution of the lunar that proceeds not as a negation of the night, but as a falling away of what is still too similar to the sun. This second possibility is supported by the terms of Heidegger's reading. He is very precise, in his interpretation of the delirious journey across the nocturnal pool, about what he takes the meaning of the moon to be: a constriction of stellar luminescence rather than the ultimate elimination of sunlight; a fading and cooling of stars:

The cool light stems from the shining of the lunar woman (Selanna). Ringing her radiance, as ancient Greek verse says, the stars fade and even cool. (*US*, pp. 48–9)

This interpretation might seem to lack all philosophical rigour, and perhaps even to forsake any possible 'theoretical' reference. In fact it contributes to a problematic of enormous importance, although one that has been fragmented and largely obliterated by the constitution of astronomy and astro-physics as positive sciences in modern times. This problem is that of real (and astronomically evident) differences that are *in principle* irreducible to mathematical formalism, and which are furthermore – as Deleuze has demonstrated in the closing sections of *Différence et Répétition* (Paris, Press Universitaire de France, 1968) – a potential basis for a quite other and more comprehensive approach to mathematization (or theoretical quantification) without any recourse to ultimate identity or equalities. The obscuration of such differences within the constitution of astro-science has been a deferral rather than a resolution of the problem of radically informal differences, leaving this matter as an explosive threat to the foundations of modern cosmology. Perhaps the last confident, unitary, and explicit treatment of the question is to be found in Hegel's 'Encyclopaedia', in the *Zusatz* to the transition from Finite Mechanics to Absolute Mechanics:

One can admire the stars because of their tranquillity: but they are not of equal dignity to the concrete individual. The filling of space breaks out [*ausschlägt*] into endless kinds of matter; but that [i.e. the casting of the stars] is only the first outbreak [*Ausschlagen*] that can delight the eye. This outbreak of light [*Licht-Ausschlag*] is no more worthy of wonder than that of a rash in man, or than a swarm of flies. (HE, p. 118)

Philosophy is to turn its gaze away from the stars, learning from Thales perhaps, who fell into a hole whilst absorbed in astronomical contemplation. In a subtle but vigorous neo-Ptolemaism, Hegel subordinates the stellar moment to the concrete and ordered bodies of the solar system, and these bodies are in turn subordinated to the development of terrestrial life. This is due to the dialectical dignity of particularized actuality in comparison with abstract principle, so that astro-physical laws are sublated into their successively more concrete expositions in geology, biology, anthropology, and cultural history. Yet there is something more primordially and uncontrollably disturbing in the vast and senseless dispersion of the stars, something which is even hideous, like a disease of the skin.

What offends Hegel about the stars is the irrational facticity of their distribution; a scattering which obeys no discernible law. He expresses his disdain for this distribution, and his anxiety before it, in a word that is also both a powerful description and an acknowledgement: *Ausschlag*, which can mean swing or deflection, but in this context means 'outbreak' in the sense of a rash. The verb *ausschlagen* is even more multi-faceted, and can mean (among other possibilities) to knock or beat out, to waive, to burgeon or blossom, or to sweat. But Hegel is not speaking of the blossoming of the stars here, or at least, he does not want to do so. We must be careful not to lose track of the 'object' Hegel is isolating here: it is a differentiation that is at once senseless and sensible, an outbreak of irrationality in the redoubt of reason similar to that which Kant acknowledges in the *Schematismuslehre*. It is the differential principle of stars, flies, flocks of birds, and dust; of astronomical, geological, ornithological,[5] and epidermal eruptions. Trakl names it with deft precision *Staub der Sterne* ('the dust of the stars'). In his reading of Trakl Heidegger also acknowledges this unity of *aus* and *Schlag* as a disruption 'of' sentience, but only if the 'of' is read according to the subversive syntax of Heideggerian thought; as an 'of' that no longer presumes a prior and undisrupted subject. For Heidegger sentience is not exploded or threatened from without by the *Ausschlag*, it is always already under the sway of the outbreak that will be derivatively apprehended as its subversion:

Trakl sees 'sentience' [*Geist*] in terms of that weave [*Wesen*] that is named in the primordial signification of the word *Geist*; since *gheis* means: incensed, dislocated, being outside oneself [*aufgebracht, entsetzt, außer sich sein*]. (*US*, p. 60)

Hegelian sentience could be described as *entsetzt* by cosmological eruption, but the sense of this outrage changes with Heidegger's radicalized approach, in which *Entsetztheit* cannot be thought as a delimiting response to the anarchic explosion of cosmic debris but only as its inertial protraction. Heidegger thus provides us with a hermeneutical key according to which every sentient reaction to the *Ausschlag* can be read as a symptom or repetition of the outbreak 'itself'. It is no longer even that sentience is infected by irrationality; it is rather that sentience has dissolved into the very movement of infection, becoming a virulent element of contagious matter.

Since the light of the stars is not a transcendental ground of phenomenality, but rather a differential effect stemming from the isolation or uneven distribution of intensities, Hegel takes its claim to philosophical dignity as an offence. He determines starlight as a pathological luminescence, without order or intelligibility. The fading of stars is, therefore, among other things, a name for a necessary stage in Hegel's system. The senseless distribution of stellar material is repressed in the interest of the particularized (sub-)planetary body, which in turn furthers geocentrism and the infinitizing of light. This movement crushes difference under a logicized notion of significance. In contrast, Trakl brings the thought of the sign together with that of stellar dispersion, writing: *O, ihr Zeichen und Sterne* ('O, you signs and stars') (T, p. 63). And – partially echoing Rimbaud's words – *Un chant mystérieux tombe des astres d'or* (' – a mysterious song falls from stars of gold') – he mentions *die Silberstimmen der Sterne* ('the silver voice of the stars') (T, p. 53) and *Das letzte Gold verfallener Sterne* ('The last gold of ruined stars') (T, p. 50). The German word *Stern* derives from the Indo-European root *ster-* meaning to extend or spread out. It is from this root that the English word 'strew' – as well as 'star' – descends. The stars are traces of a primordial strewing; an explosive dispersion, which in its formlessness, defies mathematization or the reduction to order. It is the shock wave of this metaphorics which sweeps through Trakl's specifications of the sign, and it is perhaps for this reason that Trakl writes of ruination (*Verfallen*) in this context. Any order which is to be extracted from the strewing of difference will be dependent on this 'spreading out' (Latin *sternere*), it will not be metaphysical – dependent upon a transcendental difference – but '*stra*tophysical'; a movement between planes, or grades, of dispersion. Where metaphysics has always fixed disorder in a dichotomous relation to an absolute principle of coherent form or ultimate lawfulness, a stratophysics would locate regional order within a differentiation in the rate of dissipation. It thus constitutes an abyssal relativism, although not one that is rooted in subjective perspectives, but rather in the open-ended stratifications of impersonal and unconscious physical forces. Astrophysics is marked by its etymology as stratophysics – a materialist study of planes of distributed intensities – and therefore can be seen to abandon its most extreme potentialities when it subordinates itself to mathematical physics.

The question of strata can insinuate itself into every word of Trakl's text, because it is at the 'core' of any rigorous graphematics. Each stratum is a dimension of dispersion, flattened like a spiral galaxy. This flatness is just as crucial to the study of intensities as the trajectories traced within it, since the stratification or stacking of organizational levels is the basic form of any possible energetic surplus, the irreducible or final principle of 'real form': redundancy. Each stratum has its specific 'neg-entropy' or positive range of compositions, 'selecting' only a relatively narrow series of combinations from the stock of elements generated by its substrate. A stratum thus inherits an aggregate 'degree of difference' or grammar, distinguishing it from a certain potentiality of 'randomness' (unproblematic reducibility into its substrate), and constituting a potential for teleological illusion (unproblematic reduction of its substrate). This stratification of intensive positivities, which is most clearly indexed by the successive unities of letter, word, sentence, etc. that are precipitated out of a common 'graphic plasma' or semiotic substance within alphabetical regimes, is the only rigorous basis for an architectonics of the sign. Only because of such a graphic redundancy – for example, that stored in the difference between letter and word – *between the words an alphabet makes possible and those which are realized* – can energy be unevenly distributed within a stratum, and intensities generated.[6] Trakl acknowledges this excitatory axis, which punctures and intensifies each plane of distribution, in the use of words related to the German verb *sinken* (to sink). Thus he writes:

*Von Lüften trunken sinken balde ein die Lider*
*Und öffnen leise sich zu fremden Sternenzeichen.*
(Drunken with breezes the lids soon subside / And open themselves to strange star-signs.) (T, p. 18)

And:

*Zeichen und Sterne*
*Versinken leise im Abendweiher.*
(Signs and stars / Sink quietly in the evening-pool.) (T, p. 51)

The explosion of stellar and semiotic materials generates a combination of intra-stratal and trans-stratal processes, the former of which have been historically determined as 'causal' or 'legislated' and the latter as 'intellectual', 'teleological', or 'legislative'. This is a ramification (speculative I admit) of Trakl's vocabulary of *Stufen* ('steps') of terraced differentiation (a theme I hope to explore more thoroughly elsewhere). Stratification is the complex physiological process, the only one, in which the distinction between matter and meaning cannot be sustained.[7]

The tools Heidegger relies upon in his approach to the issues of exile into the night and astronomical dispersion stem from the 'ecstative analyses' of his Marburg meditations. The term he focuses upon as a possible entry point for such a discussion is 'flame'. He first gathers Trakl's stellar thematic into that of flame with the suggestion: 'The night flames as the lightening mirror of the starry sky' (*US*, p. 66). He then proceeds: *Das Flammende ist das Außer-sich, das lichtet und erglänzen läßt, das indessen auch weiterfressen und alles in das Weiße der Asche verzehren kann.* ('That which flames is the outside itself, that which lightens and lets gleam, and that which in doing so can expand voraciously so that everything is consumed to become white ash.' [The expression *Außer-sich* is such a clear index for Heidegger's notion of ecstasis that Hertz employs 'ek-stasis' as its translation in his rendering of this sentence]) (*US*, p. 60). The flame of the stars is explosive – or outside of itself – but this *Ausschlag* can be a gentle illumination *or* an uncontrolled devastation (an *Aufruhr*, 'revolt', 'turmoil' [*US*, p. 60]). It is about this 'or', with which I am attempting to indicate Heidegger's hope that the *Weiterfressung* can be deflected or suspended in contingency, that the ambiguous path of his reading turns.

Ten pages earlier Heidegger poses this sense of an alternative between castings (*Schläge*) most acutely, and in so doing returns us to the question of infection. Examining Trakl's expression *das verfluchte Geschlecht* ('the accursed genus') (T, p. 84) he points to a Greek word that can be translated equally as either *Schlag* or *Fluch*; πληγη ('curse'). πληγη is also translated by the Latin *plangere*, from which we derive the English 'plague', and the German *Plage* (found in the sixth line of Trakl's poem *Föhn* [T, p. 67] and in the fifteenth line of *Allerseelen* ['All Soul's Day'] [T, p. 211]). Heidegger's text (which I cannot confidently hazard to my translation alone) reads:

*Womit ist dieses Geschlecht geschlagen, d.h. verflucht? Fluch heißt griechisch* πληγη, *unser Wort 'Schlag'. Der Fluch des verwesenden Geschlechtes besteht darin, daß dieses alte Geschlecht in die Zwietracht der Geschlechter auseinandergeschlagen ist. Aus ihr trachtet jedes der Geschlechter in den losgelassenen Aufruhr der je vereinzelten und bloßen Wildheit des Wildes. Nicht die Zwiefache als solches, sondern die Zwietracht ist der Fluch. Sie trägt aus dem Aufruhr der blinden Wildheit das Geschlecht in die Entzweiung und verschlägt es so in die losgelassene Vereinzelung. Also entzweit und zerschlagen vermag das 'verfallene Geschlecht' von sich aus nicht mehr in den rechten Schlag zu finden.* (With what is this gen-us cast, i.e. cursed. Cursed names the Greek πληγη, our word 'casting'. The curse of the decomposed gen-us consists in this, that this ancient gen-us is cast apart into the discord of gen-ders. Each of the genera strives for unleashed revolt in an always individuated and naked wildness of the beast. It is not the twofold that is the curse, but rather the discordance of the two. Out of the revolt of the blind wildness it carries the gen-us, cast away into torn duality and unleashed individuation. Thus divided and cast down the 'ruined gen-us' is no longer able to find the 'right cast'.) (*US*, p. 50)

It would be possible to read this passage as if it were a development entirely internal to Heidegger's 'philosophy', and as if the reading of Trakl in which it is embedded were a mere eccentricity or modulation in the vocabulary of an unswerving intellectual pursuit. Such a reading would recall that according to Heidegger, ontotheology is the curse that leads beings to strive towards absolute mastery of the earth, erasing every trace of their dependence upon being. That difference of each being with respect to being is displaced by the differences among beings, and being is converted into a mere disputed territory to be subdivided among conflicting beings. It would also recall that within this history everything thought of as 'real' has been distributed among exclusive concepts, through which beings represent themselves to themselves in their competitive distinctiveness, so that the differences, discriminations, and determinations of beings cease to speak of being. It would conclude that what is metaphysical (in the sense that Heidegger understands as the ontotheological) in dualities of genre is not that they are binary, but that this binarity monopolizes the interpretation of the being's difference from being. What is lost in ontical interpretation is the being of genre itself, the composition of ontical difference from out of the non-ontic. In other words, to think *Geschlecht* abstractly, but in a certain sense beyond ontotheology, it would be necessary only to insist (in a decisive Heideggerian trope) that ontical differentiation is not itself anything ontical.

Yet Heidegger is not simply interpreting a word that circulates freely within the German language. He is attempting to read this word as he encounters it within the tortuous and vespertine labyrinth of Trakl's poetry. We must return to Heidegger's question, and attempt to ask it along with him: what is this cast, this curse or epidemic? We are assisted in this by Trakl's words, which lend us a faltering answer to place alongside Heidegger's discussion; the cast that has cursed us, surely that is what Trakl names *Aussatz*; leprosy, infection, and (thus) exclusion. The spaces of difference across which the *Zwietracht* stretches and displaces itself (following the semantic instabililty of *Geschlecht*) are never to be found described by Trakl in terms that could be reduced to formal disjunctions or negative articulations. Instead he writes of *Mauern voll Aussatz* ('walls full of leprosy') (T, p. 41) echoing Rimbaud who, during his *Saison en Enfer* finds himself *assis, lépreux, sur les pots cassés et les orties, au pied d'un mur rongé par le soleil* ('sitting, leprous, upon broken pots and nettles, at the foot of a wall gnawed by the sun') (R, pp. 302–3). It seems at first surprising that Heidegger makes no mention of the frequent references to leprosy throughout Trakl's poetry,[8] since *Aussatz* points to an *Aus-setzung* (the Old High German source *Uzsazeo* means 'one who has been *ausgesetzt* or "cast out" of society'), a coinage which profoundly accords with the ecstative orientation of Heidegger's reading. Heidegger even has a space specifically allocated to disease in his reading. Not that he is particularly concerned with the German equivalent of this word: *Krankheit* (although he quotes Trakl's line *Wie scheint doch alles Werdende so krank!* ('How sick everything that is becoming seems!') (T, p. 29; *US*, p. 64). The disease which finds a place in Heidegger's text is the same as that which obsesses Trakl; it is the searing of stars, or the primordial and contagious eruption of the pathological. But Heidegger's supplement to Trakl's text is disappointingly regressive on this issue, and my brief concluding question touches on an example of the repugnant obstinacy and piety of the 1953 essay in asking: why does Heidegger refuse to follow Trakl and name ecstative eruption *Aussatz*?

In concluding the question of the curse that abuts onto Trakl's thema of *Geschlecht*, Heidegger distinguishes between two cast(e)s and two dualities. There is a cursing cast or stamp that is associated with a reckless and destructive individualization and that generates antagonistic or conflictual binarity (*Zwietracht*), and there is a gentle *sanft* binarity (*Zwiefalt*) that escapes the contagion of the curse. As is so typical of Heidegger, *Zwiefalt* simultaneously marks an aspiration towards the (Schellingian) post-philosopher's stone of a-logical intervallic difference and the theologian's dream of an immaculate or uncontaminated conception. Drawing upon a thought of pain *Schmerz* as a threshold and relation Heidegger seeks to ameliorate the pathological scorching of the stars: 'gentleness is, following the word *das Sanfte*, the peaceful gatherer. It metamorphoses discord, in that it turns what is injuring and searing in wildness to soothed pain' (*US*, p. 45). This attempt to establish pure and dichotomous distinctions that both explicate and escape the history of oppositional thought necessitates a discrimination between (two) *types* of duality. (It is precisely because Derrida will refuse to underwrite such a discrimination that he turns instead to a re-inscription of continuities that are able to encompass and partially assimilate the 'ruptural' aspect of his own work, resigned to a 'structurally necessary inadequacy' in the prosecution of deconstruction. Both Heidegger and Derrida seem to concur, however, in taking the sense of dichotomy to be irredeemably polar and reciprocally ultimate rather that stratal and unilaterally or impulsively protractile.)

The historical predicament that Heidegger and (in a different way) Derrida trace out here, and which finds its symptom in this problematic 'antinomy' of escape and re-capture, hope and despair, with all the unstable compromises and evanescent moments of indecision or indifference it generates, is too complex to delineate in this paper. I will only venture to suggest that by holding *Zwietracht* and *Zwiefalt* apart at this point, and refusing to abandon the hope that formal or ultimate dichotomy might be redeemed by a future thinking, Heidegger is engaged in what we could legitimately describe as a 'gentle critique' of the history of metaphysics, a grotesque recapitulation of Kant's compromise with ontotheological tradition (and tradition always belongs to the church). Heidegger's attempt is to limit the *Aufruhr* which constitutes the intensive undertow of Traklean textuality. His is the sterile hope of an aging philosopher with Platonic instincts, the delusion that the climactic dissipation of Western civilization can be evaded, and that the accumulation of fossilized labour-power can found an eternally reformable social order. He was not completely unaware of the profound struggle between the weary regimentation of the patriarchal bourgeoisie, and a fluctuating pool of insurrectionary energy tracing its genealogy to the ur-catastrophe of organic matter. But he felt nauseous at the thought of losing control, and perhaps he still believed in God. *Zwiefalt* would surely be a distantiation from this noise and restless ferment, an end to contagion, a final peace? It is according to this deeply rooted 'logic' of purification and transcendence, the most insidious trope of a decomposing theology, that the irruption of ecstative difference refuses the name *Aussatz*, and Heidegger – exhausted and uncomfortably feverish – lays down his copy of Trakl's poems, and closes his eyes.

## Abbreviations

Ba    Otto Basil, *Trakl*, Reinbek bei Hamburg, Rowohlt, 1965.

GT    Herbert Lindenberger, *Georg Trakl*, New York, Twayne Publishers, 1971.

HE    G.W.F. Hegel, *System der Philosophie. Zweiter Teil. Die Naturphilosophie*, from Sämtliche Werke, Band 9, Stuttgart, Fr. Frommanns Verlag, 1929.

IM    D.F. Krell, *Intimations of Mortality*, University Park, Penn. State University Press, 1986.

N    Novalis, *Dichtungen*, Reinbek bei Hamburg, Rowohlt, 1963.

NC    Pierre Klossowski, *Nietzsche et le cercle vicieux*, Paris, Mercure de France, 1978.

OC    Charles Baudelaire, *Oeuvres complètes*, Paris, Gallimard, 1975.

R    Arthur Rimbaud, *Collected Poems* (Parallel text), Harmondsworth, Penguin, 1986.

T    Georg Trakl, *Das dicherische Werk*, München, Deutscher Taschenbuch Verlag, 1972.

US    Martin Heidegger, *Unterwegs zur Sprache*, Pfullingen Neske, 1982. Translated by Hertz and Stambaugh as *On the Way to Language*, London, Harper & Row, 1982.

WG    Robert Graves, *The White Goddess*, London, Faber & Faber, 1961.

## Notes

1 The German *Dämmerung* is as ambiguous as the English 'twilight', and can mean the half-light of dawn as well as that of dusk. As Baudelaire is almost certainly Trakl's first major poetical influence (Ba, pp. 42–9) it is tempting to read the title *Geistliche Dämmerung* as a translation of *L'Aube spirituelle* ('Spiritual dawn'), the forty-seventh poem of *Spleen et Idéale* (*OC*, vol. 1, p. 46). Heidegger, however, is determined to maintain the ambiguity of *Dämmerung* in his interpretation (*US*, pp. 42–3), and the

importance of *Abend* ('evening') in Trakl's poetry lends weight to this 'decision'.

2 Trakl ends the poem *Am Moor* ('At the Moor') with the line *Erscheinung der Nacht: Kröten tauchen aus silbernen Wassern* ('Appearance of the night: toads dive out of silver waters') (T, p. 54) suggesting that there is indeed an issue of nocturnal luminacy in Trakl's poetry; a becoming visible in the night, which is also an appearance of the night itself. The night is not merely a formal condition or scene for certain apparitions, it is also what is 'expressed' in the silver light of the moon and stars. The night itself finds a voice in 'the lunar voice of the sister', that is also a *Silberstimme* ('silver voice'), a word that is used in the poem *Hohenburg* (T, p. 51), and twice in the poem *Sebastian im Traum* (T, p. 53).

3 The sister is also associated with the moon towards the end of the prose poem *Offenbarung und Untergang*, first in the line *hob sich auf mondenen Flügeln über die grünenden Wipfel, kristallene Klippen das weiße Antlitz der Schwester* ('lifted by lunar wings above the greening treetops, crystal cliffs of the sister's white countenance') that ends the penultimate paragraph. The final paragraph begins *Mit silbernen Sohlen stieg ich die dornigen Stufen hinab* ('With silver soles I climbed down the thorny steps') and speaks of *ein mondenes Gebilde, das langsam aus meinem Schatten trat* ('a lunar shape, that slowly stepped from out of my shadow') (T, p. 97). By stepping out of her brother's shadow the sister escapes the determinations of image, reflection, or copy that could be returned to the same; to a self-mediated narcissism playing with representations as its own (or proper) alterity.

4 The ruined moon is also mentioned in *Sebastian im Traum* in the line *Da in jenem März der Mond verfiel.* ('Then, in that march, the moon was ruined.') (Ruin, from the Latin *ruere* 'to fall', cannot be used intransitively to capture the precise usage of *verfallen* in this case.) (T, p. 53). The ruin of the moon is here taken as a datable event, emphasizing its referential entanglement in the processes of genre. Trakl's deployment of astronomical metaphor is not a retreat from history into timeless or archetypal symbolism, it is, on the contrary, a historicizing of the heavens; the opening of a genealogy through conjugation with astronomical forces. For Heidegger's most explicit comments on Trakl and history see *Die Sprache im Gedicht* in particular (*US*, p. 80).

5 The association of bird-flight and the emergence of signs is one of the richest threads of Trakl's poetry. In *In einem verlassenen Zimmer* ('In an Abandoned Room') occurs the line *Schwalben irre Zeichen ziehn* ('Swallows trace demented signs') (T, p. 16); the final stanza of *Traum des Bösen* ('Dream of Evil') begins *Des Vogelflugs wirre Zeichen lesen / Aussätzigen* ('Lepers read the confused signs of bird-flight') (T, p. 19); the second stanza of *An den Knaben Elis* ('To the Youth Elis') ends with the words *dunkle Deutung des Vogelflugs* ('the dark significance of bird-flight') (T, pp. 17, 49) and *Der Herbst des Einsamen* contains the line *Der Vogelflug tönt von alten Sagen* ('The flight of birds resounds with ancient sagas') (T, p. 62).

Wherever there is erratic dispersal and movement in undemarcated space Trakl anticipates the arising of sense, and a question of reading.

6 Claude Shannon's theory of information understands redundancy as the dimension of a message that does not function at the level of communication, but rather functions as a resource for the discrimination of the incommunicative ('noise') from communication in general, thus providing a layer of insulation against the degradation of the message. This formulation seems to me to lack two crucial elements: 1) It fails to provide any suggestion as to how the message participates in the constitution of redundancies (thus taking redundancy as a transcendental condition of communication). This first default leads to the preservation of the metaphysical distinction between semiotic and material processes (messages and techniques), which is otherwise profoundly shaken by the thought of redundancy; the thought, that is, of an isolation or 'de-naturalization' of the semiotic stratum proceeding by means of intensities or surpluses that invoke no element of negativity, but only gradations. 2) It fails to acknowledge the political dimension of redundancy as a means of trapping disruptive signals. It is this 'trapping' within an intermediate zone between strata that first enables the categories of madness, perversion, deformity, disobedience, and indiscipline to be constituted, thus providing the basis for the associated but counterposed disciplinary programmes of pedagogy, psychiatry, punition, etc. To fail to acknowledge such questions is to take the notion of noise as a purely passive and non-sentient interruption rather than as a strategically oriented 'jamming' of the message, and thus to ignore the conflictual aspects of both grammars and anti-grammatical subterfuges as they contend within the fluctuating space of redundancy or control. This default is typical of a technocratic scientificity which takes the question of power as having been always already resolved prior to the question of technique.

7 For a discussion of strata which is, I think, based upon different principles, see the beginning of Deleuze and Guattari's *La géologie de la morale (pour qui elle se prend, la terre?)* in *Mille Plateaux*, pp. 53–60.

8 For instance, in *Kleines Konzert* ('Little Concert') *Aussätzigen winkt die Flut Genesung* ('The torrent beckons lepers to convalescence') (T, p. 25); in *Drei Blicke in einen Opal* ('Three Glimpses in an Opal') *Die Knaben träumen wirr in dürren Weidensträhnen / Und ihre Stirnen sind von Aussatz kahl und rauh.* ('Youths dream confusedly among the pasture's dry bales / And their brows are naked and raw with leprosy') (T, p. 39) (see also T, p. 40); towards the end of *Helian* (in a line I have already cited) *Helians Seele sich im rosigen Spiegel beschaut / Und Schnee und Aussatz von seiner Stirne sinken* ('Helians soul gazes on itself in the rosy mirror / And snow and leprosy sink from his brow') (T, p. 43); and in *Verwandlund des Bösen* ('Metamorphosis of Evil') there is a *Minute stummer Zerstörung; auflauscht die Stirne des Aussätzigen unter dem kahlen Baum* ('moment of mute devastation; the brow of the leper hearkens under the naked tree') (T, p. 56).

# · 4 ·

# Derrida, Mallarmé, and Anatole

## JOHN LLEWELYN

*Parmi le long regard de la Seine entr'ouverte*
Paul Valéry, *Valvins*

In memoriam Carl Barbier,
Mallarmé scholar and friend

A parenthetical codicil appended to his article on Mallarmé in a *Tableau de la littérature française* lists various other questions of which Derrida says he 'should no doubt have spoken'.[1] Among them is the question of Anatole.

Anatole, Mallarmé's only son, died in the autumn of 1879 at the age of eight. To have spoken of him would therefore have been to begin to speak of Mallarmé's griefs and of the work of mourning which Derrida says his article also no doubt ought to have treated. Mourning is a topic of which Derrida does treat elsewhere, most explicitly in 'Fors' and in *Glas*, which refers to his own father's recent death. To mourn – *se douloir*, as the obsolete French form put it – is to live with the pain (*douleur*) of a death. Mourning (*deuil*) is therefore a topic of which I no doubt should have spoken when, after listening to a paper in which I had referred to *Glas* and 'Fors',[2] Ruben Berezdivin asked how I supposed that Derrida could regard pain as anything other than something negative. The time lost in giving my lame excuse for not giving a direct answer would have been better spent hearing Derrida speak for himself. When asked after the formal period for discussion what he himself would have said, his reply, if I recall aright, was that pain itself involves a regarding, an evaluation, and is not a sheer datum. Hence it is not negative if by that is meant something other and over against me. Derrida might agree with Nietzsche that 'one does not *react* to pain. . . . Pain itself is a reaction', the natural reaction being the value judgment 'harmful' and aversion, moving away.[3] And to the extent that a reaction is an action, pain is as much action as passion. That is one reason for thinking that pain is not something merely received or reacted against. But the reaction which consists in judging something harmful does not entail the reaction which consists in shunning that thing. Different things are harmful in different ways, and what is harmful in one respect may nevertheless be sought after. We are not conceptually bound to say No to it. We can say Yes. This is a second sense in which pain, meaning by that a pain, what is painful, need not be valued negatively. This brings us up against the question of whether this valuing can be a feeling, and how such a feeling is to be construed and deconstrued, particularly the feeling of a felt loss. That question would call for consideration of the question as to how a 'pleasure' can be felt as a pain.[4] Nothing will be said about these questions here. What can be said however is that whatever Derrida's response might be to the remarks cited from Nietzsche and to the questions these remarks raise, we can be sure that his fine ear picks up the difference Nietzsche makes between two sorts of Yes. Although Zarathustra's Yes, cited by Derrida in 'Ja, ou le faux-bond' and toward the end of *Glas*, is 'tremendous and unlimited', it is an affirmation that is laced with negation. For it says No to the Yes which merely endorses whatever is, including whatever is painful, as does the big-eared donkey, the camel, and the Christian,[5] and it says No to the determinate double negation of dialectic. With Nietzsche classical being becomes becoming, becoming becomes revalued being, revalued being is affirmation, and affirmation is creative revaluation, not the affirmation which takes being as its object and burden.[6] It would be ingenuous to say that Derrida simply endorses this view, but I have a hunch that it is the kind of thing he would say he would like to like. Witness the aforementioned references to the 'das ungeheure unbegrenzte Ja'[7] of Zarathustra and the paragraphs at the end of 'La Différance' where Derrida writes of 'différance' that it must be '*affirmed*, in the sense in which Nietzsche puts affirmation into play, in a certain laughter and a certain step of the dance',[8] 'un certain pas de la danse'. A Terpsichorean No? Not, for sure, a dialectical negation. It is precisely from that and its dialectically affirmative partner that Derrida and Nietzsche want to dance laughingly away. Not from negativity as such, such as might or might not characterize the pain of grief, and is not to be laughed away. But from a philosophical thesis of *determinacy* resulting from negation and the negation of negation. Not toward some indeterminacy, back, say, to an indeterminate Being or Nothingness. But toward an undecidability for which Being and Nothingness are misnomers. Which has no proper name. And not because it is a noumenon or is unmentionably numinous. But because it is the *affirmation jouée*, the played, worked, operated, gambled affirmation that is the condition of the possibility of determinacy, indeterminacy, naming – and misnomers. And 'undecidability' is a misnomer at least in the sense that it has the disadvantage of suggesting something neutral or repressively negative. Perhaps 'indecidability', although or because it is not standard English, would be nearer what Derrida's *indécidabilité* would mark. But then we should lose the implication that Derridian undecidability is an *ana*-logical take-off of the neutral third value of Gödelian *Unentscheidbarkeit*, an effect similar to that which Derrida gains by pouring new wine into the old bottle of 'condition of possibility' to summon the bouquet of what is *before* the law, *Vor dem Gesetz*.

How can Derrida's reiteration of Nietzsche's Yes be squared with the way he reads Mallarmé? Despite the recourse both Nietzsche and Mallarmé have to the throwing of dice, despite the priority they both give to art, despite the proclamation they both make that God is dead, and despite the fact that they both address their words only to the few who have ears fine enough to hear, surely Mallarmé's outlook is the epitome of that of the man of resentment, morbidity, and melancholia rather than, like Nietzsche's, that of the lover of strength, health, and life? Does not a brief perusal of the Contents pages of Mallarmé's *Oeuvres complètes* suffice to show that he is in love with death? Among the poems of his earliest years are two entitled *Sa fosse est creusée!* . . . and *Sa fosse est fermée* . . . . The third part of *Hérodiade* is a poem on the death of John the Baptist. *Remémoration d'amis belges* speaks of the 'pierre veuve' and the 'canal défunt' of a town commonly known as Bruges-la-Morte. The prose poem *Réminiscence* begins 'Orphan, I wandered in black'.[9] It is as though a drowning takes place in *Un coup de dés*. The section of *Igitur* printed last in the Pléiade edition carries the title 'Il se couche au tombeau'. There is a poem in memory of Gautier called *Toast funèbre* and a series of elegies called *Hommages et Tombeaux*. One of the *Contes indiens*, the one entitled *Le mort vivant*, begins under 'un nuage de tristesse' which brings darkness at noon: 'Le deuil régnait, And there is a *Deuil* on Maupassant. Furthermore, in a letter dated 3 May 1868 Mallarmé mentions that he is rereading *Melancholia*. Of this collection of poems which his friend Henri Cazalis published that year Mallarmé says that it is 'une de mes lectures favorites en mon état'.[10] In other words, throughout Mallarmé's life and works there sounds what Baudelaire calls, in the introduction to his translation of Poe's 'The Philosophy of Composition', an essay in which Mallarmé found much to admire, 'un glas de mélancolie'. *Le glas* (*le glas*, *le glas*) is heard as one turns page after page. Mourning and melancholy. *Trauer und Melancholie*. If there is a theme that pervades Mallarmé's works, can it be anything but death? And if there is a theme that pervades the works of Nietzsche, what else can that be but life? What pervades the works of both Nietzsche and Mallarmé on Derrida's reading of them is life-death. Not however as theme, but as trace. Wake. Wake!

Consider first some of the comments Derrida makes about Nietzsche in *L'oreille de l'autre*. On the 'date' of his forty-fifth anniversary, Nietzsche writes, at what it is reasonable to count as the mid-point of one's life, under the eye of *Midi là-haut*,

On this perfect day, when everything is ripening and not only the grape turns brown, the eye of the sun just fell upon my life: I looked back, I looked forward, and never saw so many and such good things at once. It was not for nothing that I buried my forty-fourth year today; I had the *right* to bury it; whatever was life in it has been saved, is immortal. The first book of the *Revaluation of All Values*, the *Songs of Zarathustra*, the *Twilight of the Idols*, my attempt to philosophize with a hammer – all presents of this year, indeed of its last quarter! *How could I fail to be grateful to my whole life?* – And so I tell my life to myself.[11]

'Und so erzähle ich mir mein Leben.' What is meant by 'mir'? Kaufmann translates it 'to myself'. Derrida gives 'je me raconte', which allows both for 'to myself' and for the 'for myself', 'pour moi', that Derrida also gives. Nietzsche affirms his life. He apposes his signature, his *firma*, his mark. Nietzsche's autobiography, Derrida says, is *auto*biography not, or not just, in the sense that it is his life that it tells, but in the sense that he is telling it to himself, its first, though not its only, addressee. The I, *ich* (a chiasmic *chi*, pronounced by French speakers as *qui*, who) who recites the life is not its first addressee, prior to the recitation of that life. It is the eternal return that reaffirms, repeats 'Hear hear'. But where is the ear of this repetition? What is the position of the apposition? Where is its here? Where does it take place? It does not take place, not at any definable here and now. As Mallarmé writes, nothing takes place except the place which is not a location that is simply *fort* or *da*, but is instead an unhomely *loc. cit.*, like that of the above-cited exergue of *Ecce Homo*, between the title and Nietzsche's text, after his preface but before his story, before history, neither inside nor outside the life and the work, yet both.

*Entre*, between, in the way that the writer Friedrich Nietzsche and the writings to which he appended his name are between the father who died before him and the mother who died after him. Not only is the person who signs himself F. N. their heir, the heir of two sexes, their two laws (the civil law that Creon obeys and the law of the family followed by Antigone), but the heir of life and death. Because he signs for them, not just for their sakes but on their behalf, they have a say in what he says. The deed he performs in signing and what he subscribes to depend, as that Anglish Nietzschean John Austin would say, on their uptake.[12] They are co-signatories of recorded deliveries, both senders and receivers. They are correspondents with political responsibility, for if Nietzsche's *enseignement*, i.e. his mark and his message, are opened up in this way, the question as to his and our heirs becomes a question of general interest where it is no easy task to determine who's who and who bequeaths what to whom. This is not only Nietzsche's problem. It is a problem for us his interpreters, whoever we are, for the interpreters of Mallarmé, for Mallarmé and his mother and father. And for his only son, Anatole.

The testamentary structure that Derrida uncovers in Nietzsche's writing is discernible also in Mallarmé's. Mallarmé himself says that nowadays to write a book is 'faire son testament', to make one's will.[13] Or, rather, the will of more than one, since the signature is, as Villiers de l'Isle Adam's title has it, an intersign. Mallarmé says too that a book is a tomb.[14] Among the notes for his Tombeau d'Anatole we find the following: 'mère identité/de vie mort/père reprend/ rythme pris ici/du bercement de/mère/suspens — vie/mort —/ poésies — pensée'.[15] The mother rocking the child dictates the rhythm of the poetry in which the father gives posthumous life to the son who carries the father's name to the grave. But as well as this hymen between mother and father and life and death, there is a hymen of the father, who is already the legatee of his deceased mother and father, and the son, who is also the father of the man in that he gives his life for his father to help him write the work: 'il fallait — /héritant de cette/merveilleuse intelli-/gence filiale, la/ faisant revivre/— construire/avec sa (nette)/lucidité — cette/oeuvre — trop vaste pour moi/', a work so vast that the father has had to sacrifice his own life to and for it.[16] Having made this sacrifice he need have no qualms that he is exploiting the death of his son, particularly if he is *encrypted* in a tomb-tome engraved in language that is not language of the tribe and the market-place (forum), not language that is *profane*. In the 'claustration' of this book father and son give their lives for each other: 'je me sens couché en la tombe à côté de toi'.[17] They also give their lives to each other. For in the book, in the poem, death is thought. Anatole's physical extinction is an undeniable event, but as such it belongs to the world of contingencies in which, since the crisis of 1866, Mallarmé sees nothing but nothing. If however one thinks that one is dying, death is no longer sheer waste. But in realizing it one makes it all the more real, all the more painful. This is a dilemma which Mallarmé's mourning of his son attempts to resolve. In *Igitur* he writes: 'Je pense que je meurs — donc je meurs'. In the notes toward a Tombeau d'Anatole, from this swift syllogism, as Richard calls it,[18] thereby distancing it from the Cartesian non-syllogistic *cogito*, Mallarmé hopes to derive on behalf of his son a denial of the consequent from a denial of the antecedent. Formally, this is as invalid as the 'therefore' of the hypothetical in *Igitur* is hasty. But perhaps it is out of place to apply formal principles here. It is not the mortality of Caius that Mallarmé has in his mind or heart. As we have already said, Mallarmé does not deny his son's physical extinction. His hope is that he can die for his physically dead son, really die the death that requires realization. At first suffering pangs of guilt at the thought of concealing from his son that he is dying, of depriving him of his death in order to save him from the pain of its realization, the father comes to hope that he and his son may attain to the best of both worlds through a mourning in which the son's unconsciousness of his dying is compensated for through the father's consciousness of his dying, his son's and his own: 'je veux tout souffrir/pour toi/qui ignores — /rien ne sera/soustrait (qu'à/toi) du deuil inouï'.[19] Death is deceived if it thinks it can inflict on Anatole the thought that he is dying: 'mort — ridicule ennemie/ — qui ne peux à l'enfant/infliger la notion que tu es!'[20] But is not Stéphane Mallarmé deceiving himself if he thinks he is not deceiving his son? Let him who would cast the first stone remember that the son is an eight-year-old child, that the father's conscience may nevertheless remain unclear over whether he is deceiving his son or not, and that there also remains another thought that gives him anguish: the thought that the disease from which the son is dying may be congenital. So there remains something for which the 'tombeau idéal' would be a compensation and an atonement in a quite precise sense if indeed Anatole is its co-author – and co-reader, in that one writes also for and to the dead, including the bearer of one's name and, since every name is testamentary, the name he bears. The name of Mallarmé. The name of Derrida.[21]

So the ideal tomb-tome that snatches the dead from death would seem to be the complete writing cure. A *pharmakon*. Could a more 'successful', 'normal' mourning be imagined? But could it be more than imagined? Could it, when we understand what we are asking this *Denkmal* to do, even be imagined? Could the ideal Tombeau ever be real?

The Tombeau d'Anatole was never constructed. It is no more than a handful of fragments, a handful of dust. Like the *Livre* projected in the little pile of notes while the shadows gathered to wipe away his thoughts of death (to spit into the eye of the 'ridicule ennemie' is to spit into the wind), Mallarmé requested it to be burned, for 'there is no literary inheritance there, my poor children'.[22]

So is Anatole still waiting to be buried, still not sublimed, 'résorbé,[23] into eternity, still waiting for his father to transmute him into himself? Yes and no. In the so-called autobiography sent to Verlaine, Mallarmé says that the present time is an interregnum, a time of obsoletion in which the poet can do no more than work 'avec mystère' preparing for what will come 'later or never'.[24] This reference to the present time echoes the 'nowadays' of the previously cited observation that 'Aujourd'hui écrire un livre, c'est faire son testament'. The implication seems to be that the *Livre* with a capital 'L' or the *Oeuvre* with a large fully-rounded 'O' is not impossible in principle, however much the literary efforts of Mallarmé and his contemporaries are destined to fail because they live at a time of catastrophe,[25] a bordertime of *Crise de vers*, crisis of towardness, between the desire and its consummation, the performance and its memory: 'between desire and fulfilment, perpetration and remembrance: here anticipating, there recalling, in the future, in the past, *under the false appearance of a present*'.[26] But it is only at the present time that the present is a false appearance? Is it only the late nineteenth century that is a tunnel leading from Hugo up into the light that streams through the glass canopy of 'the almighty station of the virginal central palace, that crowns', the station dedicated to Saint Lazarus? Or are the only stations we can expect to reach always underground stations, like the Gare des Invalides? Mallarmé's 'indication', as I read it, is that the 'integrity of the Book' does not presume a Present. The glass crown of the Gare St Lazare is multifaceted, like the diamonds in the poem that crown the writer's scrupulous labour. The totality of the Book is a totality of glittering fragments, a 'représentation fragmentaire'.[27] The Book explodes 'diamantairement', 'in our time and for ever'. If we mean by the Book what Mallarmé had been preparing in the manuscript he asked to be committed to the flames, we learn from the fragments toward it published by Scherer that the 'integrity' of the Book was to combine an extraordinary level of organization with an extraordinary degree of flexibility. Nothing and everything was to be left to chance. Its volumes were to be designed so that they fitted together to form a monumental block like a deconstructible Rubik cube. The three hundred and twenty pages of each of the twenty volumes would be folded in such a way that no paper-knife would be needed to make the text visible, and since the pages would not be sewn or glued, there would be a wide range of orders in which they could be read. With the result that 'the volume, although giving the impression of being fixed, becomes by this play, mobile – from death it becomes life'.[28] Some of the preliminary papers calculate meticulously the mathematics and dynamics of the Book, the contrapuntal and harmonic permutations open to its operator. The Book, for which everything in the world exists,[29] would be a word-processing machine for translating chance into necessity.[30] And this is why it is destined to remain unrealized. The Book is bound to *faire faux-bond*, as Derrida says, not simply because Mallarmé lacked energy, ingenuity, or time, but because the twenty years he told Aubanel he would need to complete the work would still not be enough, for the reason he himself gives in *Un coup de dés*. If a throw of the dice will never abolish chance and writing is a throw of the dice, Mallarmé has good reason to expect that his project of the Book will be considered an 'acte de démence'. When he describes this project as his 'tapisserie de Pénélope' he is forgetting that she did eventually complete Laertes' shroud.[31] Mallarmé's task, like Igitur's, is a *folie* and, like the task of the old man in *Un coup de dés*, an absurdity. When finally the old man raises his arm, with the dice in his still-clenched fist, his gesture is no more than the mime of a throw from someone who (not waving, but drowning) is over-whelmed by the paralysing thought that he who wins loses and he who loses wins. Since 'Toute Pensée émet un Coup de Dés', even that desperate, demented last deed in which the arm effects a circuit between the sea of chance and the fixed constellations of the sky, writes a momentous, *augenblicklich*, remark to the effect that writing is aboriginally absurd.

The absurdity of writing is, if not the message or the theme, per-haps a motif of Mallarmé's project toward the *Grand Oeuvre*. The *Grand Oeuvre* is in principle incompletable and therefore in a sense not even begun. Yet in another sense it has extant provisional parts: the programmatic notes published by Scherer and maybe *Un coup de dés* and other 'exercizes' included in the Pléiade *Oeuvres complètes*; maybe also the sketches for a Tombeau d'Anatole. In this sense the unrealized Book, fated to be forever *unterwegs*, already exists, as *débris de. . . .* Mallarmé recognizes this when he says to Verlaine:

I shall perhaps succeed, not in finishing this work in its entirety (I do not know who one would have to be to be capable of that!), but in producing a completed fragment, in making the *glorious authenticity* of a portion of it scin-tillate, only hinting at all the rest for which a lifetime would not be enough. To prove by the parts that have been executed that this book exists, and that I have known what I shall not have been able to accomplish.[32]

Thirteen years earlier he had written, of a word he himself uses again and again: 'I predict it: the word *authentic*, which was, for many years, the sacramental term of antiquarians, will soon no longer have any meaning.'[33] As for the glory, this is the glory of a Lie. In the tun-nel of the 'night of Tournon' he had learned the lesson of Plato's cave. All matter is illusion. All is lies. Except for Poetry – and, he later adds, friendship and love. Poetry itself is a lie, but a glorious lie. Man may be a reed, but he is a thinking reed whose most sublime achievement is that of having invented God and the soul and works of art in which the poet sings 'en désespéré'[34] his 'explication orphique de la terre':[35]

I have every admiration for the great Magus who searches inconsolably and obstinately for a mystery that he knows does not exist, and which he will pursue for ever precisely on account of his lucid despair, since *that would have been* the truth![36]

When he speaks of the poet's orphic explication of the earth Mallarmé knows that Eurydice is led forth no further than the exit from her grave. As Anatole remains at the mouth of his. Neither above ground nor below, *subjectile*, 'entre le dessus et le dessous, le visible et l'invisible, le devant et le derrière, l'en-deçà et l'au-delà. Entre gésir et jeter'. On the subtle threshold between transitive *iacere* and intransitive *iacere* – (c)I-gît-(t)ur.[37]

'Introjection/incorporation: everything is played out on the threshold which divides and opposes the two terms.'[38] Ashes to ashes, dust to dust. But Derrida elicits from Mallarmé and from elsewhere an explication why the project for an orphic explication of the earth was bound to fall short, *faire faux-bond*, and hence why no book could be a spiritual instrument in which the soul of the departed could be safely entombed, if by safe entombment is meant what some psycho-analysts mean by introjection. Mallarmé himself says that we have *invented* the soul, and this invention plays no little part in the defini-tion of introjection that Maria Torok develops from Ferenczi. Introjection, as this is held to take place in 'normal' mourning, is con-ceived as the inclusion in oneself of the lost object and the drives it occasions,[39] the lost loved one and one's love, the love and friendship that Mallarmé excepts from his principle that all is lies. Introjection is a last supper, a cannibalistic ingestion of the loved one's spirit. How, as Hegel would have asked, can introjection succeed if what it aims to include is the loved one's free spirit? This question is all the more pertinent in view of the fact that Mallarmé, as so many of his commentators insist, had learned something about Hegel from Villiers de l'Isle Adam and others,[40] if not directly from the writings of Hegel. What we may provisionally call the Hegelian moment in Mallarmé's thinking is evinced in his assertion that Literature sup-presses 'le Monsieur qui reste en l'écrivant'.[41] At Igitur's midnight, which is a 'milieu, pur' between night and day, at the zero hour at which the old man of *Un coup de dés* is expected to throw the dice, in the decisive *clin d'oeil* when the flashing blade brings to John the Bap-tist deepest darkness and at the same time brightest light, at the dead of Mallarmé's own long 'night of Tournon' whose 'nuit' suggests the brightness of the day whose 'jour' suggests the sombreness of night,[42] at such critical epochs *cogito* is phenomenologically reduced to *cogitatur*. At the 'instant spécial' there is, as Heidegger says in 'What is Metaphysics?', no I or you, only one, the authentic counterpart of the inauthentic *das Man* ('Daher ist im Grunde nicht "dir" und "mir" unheimlich, sondern "einum" ist es so'). As Mallarmé himself says, 'my thought thought itself', 'I am now impersonal, and no longer the Stéphane you knew, – but an aptitude that the spiritual universe has to see itself and develop itself through what was once me',[43] to develop itself in the Book, 'the Text speaking there for itself and without the author's voice'.[44] Not that the text speaks with the 'voiceless voice' of what Levinas calls the *il y a* or of what Blanchot calls 'nothingness as being, the idling (*désoeuvrement*) of being'.[45] The voice is a middle voice, neither simply active nor simply passive, that is incomprehensible (*inouïe*) within the categories of nothingness and being. It does not even *belong* to a person,[46] and the personage through which the voice speaks has no selfconsciousness. The depersonalization (*śunyāvadā*)[47] here in question is a kind of death. Mallarmé writes: 'I am dead', 'I am perfectly dead'. This is not the kind of death of which Igitur says 'I think that I am dying – therefore I am dying', since for want of a mirror the selfconsciousness of the I has died. The 'personage whose thinking is not conscious of him'[48] has died into the poem or the book which is now not only the tomb of the ancestors of Igitur, the Tombeaux of Poe, Baudelaire, Verlaine, and Anatole, but of him who is no longer Stéphane. 'L'objet perdu-moi'.[49] All that survives is the objective-subjective, subjectile, 'operator' of the spiritual instrument – as with the performer of *sean-nós* in the southwestern corner of Ireland who faces away from the mirroring looks of the listeners as she or he sings – so that *il s'agit*. It is a question of, *es geht um*, my death, the 'idiomatic mode of "I am dead" that manoeuvres me or with which I ruse',[50] a ruse that is not an act of will and war performed by a Mr So-and-so; rather a calculus that operates itself.[51] *Wo ich war . . . il s'agit (Ça gît, Sa gît)*.[52]

But *il s'agit* thanks to the voice (*glas*) and the black on white, the black and the blank. And the black is not just the simple opposite of the white, any more than writing is the opposite of speech. Speaking/writing: everything is played out on the threshold which divides and opposes the two terms. Somewhat as writing is to speaking and hypomnesis and anamnesis,[53] so incorporation is to introjection and melancholia to 'normal' mourning. That, at any rate, is how I take Derrida's hint that so-called normal introjective mourning may be no more than a dream:

The question could of course be asked as to whether or not 'normal' mourning preserves the object *as other* (a living dead person) inside me. This question – of the general appropriation and safekeeping of the other *as other* – can always be raised as the deciding factor, but does it not at the same time blur the very line it draws between introjection and incorporation, through an essential and irreducible ambiguity?[54]

The line is blurred, as hinted in Abraham and Torok's heading 'Deuil *ou* mélancolie, Introjecter-incorporer'.[55]

What is incorporation? To incorporate is to mimic introjection. While introjection speaks, incorporation is, to use the words of the title of a series of letters and articles by Poe that Mallarmé perhaps knew, Secret Writing. Incorporation is cryptography. It encrypts the lost object whose loss it pretends not to acknowledge, by hiding it in a tomb that is simultaneously inside and outside the self that has the gaol of introjection for its goal. In *Cryptonymie: le verbier de l'homme aux loups* Nicolas Abraham and Maria Torok apply to the case of Wolfman this distinction made in earlier papers between two kinds of appropriation.[56] There is no question of pursuing that application here, or indeed Derrida's analysis of it in 'Fors'. The most we can do is approach some of the implications it might have for a reading of Mallarmé.

'Fors' is subtitled 'Les mots anglés de Nicolas Abraham et Maria Torok'. It treats of words that fish for complements and is subtended sideways on from Mallarmé's *Les mots anglais*. It is related to it *diamantairement*.[57] Neither is introjected in the other. Mallarmé and Derrida both say that introjection is no less a deception than incorporation appears to be. Indeed, incorporation, regarded as *maladie du deuil*, invalid, invalide, grief, is the place to look for the key to the structure of 'normal' grief and of what is called introjection. Somewhat as Sartrean *mauvaise foi* is the place to look for the key to the structure of what he calls good faith. Somewhat as what is ordinarily understood by writing conceals the key to the structure of speech. The operation of this structure or, better, substructure or, still better, destructure, is forcefully caricatured by Mallarmé as he is read, say, in 'La double séance' and the essay on Mallarmé mentioned in the opening sentence of the present essay. Mallarmé is continually taking calculated risks with his readers. For instance, of *Igitur* he writes: 'Ce Conte s'adresse à l'intelligence du lecteur qui met les choses en scène, elle-même.' This is borne out by the title, namely *Igitur ou la Folie d'Elbehnon*, that has preceded and by the synoptic note that soon follows. 'Igitur' can be 'therefore', *ergo* the 'donc' of 'je pense donc je suis' and the 'donc' of 'je pense que je meurs – donc je meurs', of the 'il faut' of the proof of the patronymic title that Igitur's ancestors foolishly expect him to provide. 'Igitur' can also be the first word of

*Genesis* 2: 'Igitur perfecti sunt coeli et terra et omnis ornatus eorum.' One commentator questions this reading on the grounds that 'there seems to be little if any relationship between this summing up of Creation and Mallarmé's prose-poem'.[58] But there is a close relationship surely if Igitur is being asked to vindicate his race and declare that 'it was good'. The same commentator is reluctant to accept the suggestion that Elbehnon is El behnon, the son of the Elohim,[59] because Semitic grammar would call for the 'el' to come second. I suspect that Mallarmé would have said 'Let it call', and welcomed Richard's suggestion 'El be none' or, come to that, Butler's anglish Erewhon and Dylan Thomas's Anglo-Welsh Llareggub. Only one word ago he has hazarded an anagram, *folie*, of *fiole*, the glass phial containing the *pharmakon* that would give Igitur his quietus. Anyway, it is often as much for its sound as for its sense that Mallarmé uses a name. Rather, he purports to show that they cannot be separated at least in the language 'remedied' by the poet,[60] and in the English Language as he found it and described it in *Les mots anglais*. If we are allowed an anglish extrapolation from English to French, we can say that in 'L'infini sort du hasard' of what the Pléiade edition has as the Argument section of Igitur, the *s* of 'sort' represents 'le jet indéfini'[61] and – perhaps its 'principle sense' – *incitation*.[62] This extrapolation is warranted by Mallarmé's adherence to the notion that sound and sense are intimately connected at the origin of language, and by his statement in *Diptyque*, where he is not thinking of one language in particular, that the letter *s* is 'la lettre analytique, dissolvante et disséminante, par excellence'.[63] What Mallarmé is dissolving here is the opposition of speaking and writing, oral value and purely hieroglyphic value, *grimoire*, by appealing to an occult space of forces and forcings (*forçage*?)[64] that are not simply forced meanings, not purely semantic values, nor purely syntactic or grammatical ones.(*grimoire* has the same root as 'grammar'), but 'une secrète direction confusément indiquée par l'orthographie et qui concourt mystérieusement au signe pur général qui doit marquer le vers', where, I dare say, 'vers' is not only verse or a line of poetry, but also the divagating approach of the serpent in the garden and the worm in the ground. 'L'infini sort du hasard' is indecidably-undecidably 'The infinite emerges from the throw of the dice' and/or 'The infinite destiny of chance'. A monstrous offspring of a hymeneal interlude between semantics and syntax, where 'infini' is not simply an adjective or simply a noun, where 'sort' is not simply a noun or a verb, and where the fragment 'or' may be an adjective suggesting the colour of innumerable Mallarméan sunsets and/or the noun that names the metal of political economy[65] and/or the orchestra's sonorous brass and/or the temporal adverb 'now' at this fatal hour of 'Le vierge, le vivace et le bel aujourd'hui' and/or the conjunction[66] that suggests the 'or' of the to-be-or-not-to-be of vie/mort, for instance the life and/or death of Anatole.

For Igitur, whether the dice (*assahar*) are cast or not, *kif-kif*, 'il y a et il n'y a pas le hasard'. As the poem with its rhymes that toll a hymen of sound and sense 'reduit le hasard à l'infini', so the poetic afterlife of Anatole is infinite if by that is meant the unfinished 'bad' infinity of 'le jet indéfini', but not infinite if by that is meant a 'good' infinity safe from risk. Because his entombment is not introjection, but 'deep' incorporation, the archi-incorporation, both *vicieuse* and *sacrée*, the *introjecter-incorporer* that is the abyssal 'condition of the possibility' of the opposition introjection/incorporation, of the bad *Erinnerung* which is incorporation and the good *Erinnerung* which is introjection, but makes these possible only as scenic, *forcené* effect, *crayonné au théâtre*. The elegy would be an appropriation of the death of the loved one that gives him or her new life. In the poem the one who is lost would be resurrected 'Tel qu'en Lui-même l'éternité le change'. But this new life turns out not to be the Platonic or Hegelian eternal truth of Anatole or Poe. The poem is a fabrication which is, as in Mallarmé's reading of the story of Penelope's weaving of the shroud, never complete. Its thread, the thread between life and death cut by Iris – the iris being the flower that Mallarmé *says*, the flower that is, as Derrida says, 'l'absente de tous bouquets',[67] the flower whose varicolours make up the colourlessness of which light – is rewoven with a shuttle that eternally returns. And although, after being worked by day and unworked by night, Penelope's shroud appeared to reach completion, this completion was never more than appearance. If the *hymne* to Anatole had been finished, it would still have been unfinished, a hymen of the undone and the done. If we imagine that Anatole could have been laid to rest in his poetic grave, we are forgetting that the black letters are inscribed 'parmi le blanc du papier',[68] whose white is not whiteness, but the blank *entre* between perversely dark *jour* and perversely bright *nuit*, a perverse deception for whose remuneration through verse one may harbour a hope, a *souhait* that may turn out to be no less a deception, *mon songe*, than that for the stone *dite philosophale*.[69] Nevermore.

No more than Mallarmé's literary progeny, is Anatole *hermetically* encrypted. He remains 'captif solitaire du seuil',[70] at the pale of the blank between Mallarmé's whites, the *blanc de blancs*: of, as Derrida conjugates them, the snow, the cold, death, marble, and so on; the swan, the wing, the fan, and so on; virginity, purity, hymen, etc.; the page, the veil, the sail, gauze, milk, semen, the milky way, the star . . . ; and the white of Pierrot's face. But also the entres between 'entre' (mentioned) and entre ('used') and *antre* and *autre*, the unreadable cryptic space between meaning and the mark, sense and sound, life and death, the *milieu, pur, de fiction*, that calls to be recited indefectibly forevermore, *à jamais* '. . . le perpétuel suspens d'une larme qui ne peut jamais toute se former ni choir . . .' (. . . the perpetual suspense of a tear that can never be entirely formed nor fall . . .').[71]

## Notes

1 Jacques Derrida, 'Mallarmé', in *Tableau de la littérature française: De Madame de Staël à Rimbaud*, Paris, Gallimard, 1974, pp. 368–79.

2 Derrida, 'Fors: les mots anglés de Nicolas Abraham et Maria Torok', Introduction to Nicolas Abraham and Maria Torok, *Cryptonymie: le verbier de l'homme aux loups*, Paris, Aubier-Flammarion, 1976, pp. 7–73; trans. Barbara Johnson, *The Georgia Review*, 1977 vol. 31, pp. 64–116. *Glas*, Paris, Galilée, 1974; Paris, Denoël/Gonthier, 1981. John Llewelyn, 'A Point of Almost Absolute Proximity to Hegel', in *Deconstruction and Philosophy: the Texts of Jacques Derrida*, edited by John Sallis, Chicago, University of Chicago Press, 1987, pp. 87–98.

3 Friedrich Nietzsche, *The Will to Power*, trans. Walter Kaufmann and R.J. Hollingdale, London, Weidenfeld & Nicolson, 1967, pp. 371–2.

4 'Fors', p. 44; p. 93. On these questions of pleasure and/or pain, life and/or death, see Derrida, *La carte postale*, Paris, Aubier-Flammarion, 1980, a crucial text I lack the nerve to speculate on here.

5 Derrida, *L'oreille de l'autre*, Montreal, VLB Editeur, 1982, p. 70.

6 Gilles Deleuze, *Nietzsche et la philosophie*, Paris, Presses Universitaires de France, 1962, p. 213.

7 Derrida, 'Ja, ou le faux-bond', *Diagraphe*, 1977, vol. 11, p. 100; *Glas*, p. 291; p. 365.

8 Derrida, *Marges de la philosophie*, Paris, Minuit, 1972, p. 29; *Margins of Philosophy*, trans. Alan Bass, Chicago, University of Chicago Press, 1982; Brighton, Harvester Press, 1982, p. 27. See 'Ja, ou le faux-bond' p. 111: 'Il faut qu'au-delà de l'infatigable contradiction du *double bind*, une différence affirmative, innocente, intacte, gaie, en vienne *bien* à fausser compagnie, échappe d'un saut et vienne signer en riant ce qu'elle laisse faire et défiler en double bande. Lui faisant d'un coup faux-bond, ne s'expliquant soudain plus avec la double bande. C'est ce que j'aime, ce faux-bond, celui-ci (à ne pas confondre avec les rendez-vous manqués, ni

avec aucune logique du rendez-vous), tout ce que j'aime, c'est l'instant du *"ungeheure unbegrenzte Ja"*, du "oui prodigieux et sans limite" qui vient à la fin de *Glas* (système de la D.B.), du "oui qui nous est commun" et depuis lequel "nous nous taisons, nous nous sourions notre savoir", dit Zarathoustra.'

9 Translations are my own unless stated otherwise.

10 Henri Cazalis (Jean Lahor), *Melancholia*, Paris, Alphonse Lemerre, 1868. The poem entitled *La voie lactée* contains a line which in this edition runs: 'Ils vont par l'infini faire des cieux nouveaux'. Mallarmé has 'Ils vont par l'Infini faire des lieux nouveaux'. See Stéphane Mallarmé, *Correspondance 1862–1871*, Paris, Gallimard, 1959, p. 273. Of this line Mallarmé writes to Eugène Lefébure that it is 'Un bien beau vers, et qui fut toute ma vie depuis que je suis mort'. With reference to the question asked by Ruben Berezdivin mentioned above, it may be noted now that one of Mallarmé's favourite words is *ennui* and that the first entry for that word given by Littré (1863) begins: 'Tourment de l'âme causé par la mort de personnes aimées . . .'

11 Nietzsche, *Ecce Homo*, in *On the Genealogy of Morals* and *Ecce Homo*, trans. Walter Kaufmann and R.J. Hollingdale, New York, Knopf and Random House, 1969, p. 221.

12 Derrida, 'signature événement contexte', in *Marges*, p. 383; p. 322.

13 Robert Greer Cohn, *L'oeuvre de Mallarmé: Un Coup de dés*, Paris, Librairie des Lettres, 1951, p. 422, citing *L'amitié de Stéphane Mallarmé et de Georges Rodenbach*, Geneva, Pierre Cailler, 1949, p. 120.

14 Stéphane Mallarmé, *Oeuvres complètes*, Paris, Gallimard, 1945, p. 379: in the section 'Le Livre, Instrument Spirituel' of *Quant au Livre*.

15 Mallarmé, *Pour un Tombeau d'Anatole*, Paris, Le Seuil, 1961, leaflet 128.

16 ibid., leaflet 14.

17 ibid., leaflets 15 and 79.

18 ibid., p. 65.

19 ibid., leaflet 130.

20 ibid., leaflet 77.

21 Derrida, *L'oreille de l'autre*, p. 74.

22 Henri Mondor, *Vie de Mallarmé*, Paris, Gallimard, 1941, p. 801.

23 Mallarmé, *Pour un Tombeau d'Anatole*, leaflet 117.

24 Mallarmé, *Oeuvres complètes*, p. 664.

25 Derrida, 'Fors', p. 56; p. 102.

26 Mallarmé, *Mimique*, *Oeuvres complètes*, p. 310. Derrida, 'La double séance', in *La dissémination*, Paris, Le Seuil, 1972, p. 201; *La dissémination*, trans. Barbara Johnson, Chicago, University of Chicago Press, 1981; London, Athlone Press, 1981, p. 175.

27 Jacques Scherer, *Le 'Livre' de Mallarmé*, Paris, Gallimard, 1957, leaflet 93(A). Derrida, *La dissémination*, p. 255; p. 226. 'Each session of play being a game, a fragmentary show, but sufficient at that unto itself . . .'

28 Scherer, op. cit., leaflet 191 (A).

29 *Oeuvres complètes*, p. 378.

30 Jean Hyppolite, 'Le coup de dés de Mallarmé et le message', *Les études philosophiques*, 1958, vol. 13, pp. 463–8.

31 As I forgot until reminded by Geoff Bennington. I thank him and all the other signatories of this paper who participated in the workshop on Philosophers, Writers, and Poets held in July 1985 at the University of Warwick, where a version of it was first read, and Stephen Houlgate for spotting unintended malapropisms.

32 *Oeuvres complètes*, p. 663. Emphasis added.

33 ibid., p. 684. Mallarmé's emphasis.

34 *Correspondance 1862–1871*, p. 208. Letter to Cazalis of the end of April 1866.

35 *Oeuvres complètes*, p. 663.

36 Letter of February 1889 to Odilon Redon cited at Cohn, op. cit., p. 124, and Henri Mondor, *Vie de Mallarmé*, pp. 452–3. Cf. Mallarmé's 'ce devait être très beau' in his 'Recommandation quant à mes papiers' cited by Mondor at p. 801, and the following comment of Jean-Pierre Richard, *L'univers imaginaire de Mallarmé*, Paris, Le Seuil, 1961, p. 437: 'Tout l'oeuvre de Mallarmé doit ainsi se lire en même temps à l'indicatif et au conditionnel: il faut voir en elle comment cela *est* beau, mais aussi, pour reprendre la si juste parole testamentaire de Mallarmé, comment "*cela devait être très beau*".' A double reading.

37 Derrida, 'Forcener le subjectile', *le Matin*, 26 July 1985, p. 25, fragments of the preface of a collection of drawings and paintings by Artaud to be published by Gallimard in 1986. I am grateful to Nelly Demé for forwarding the cutting to me. Derrida, *La dissémination*, p. 308; p. 276. Mallarmé, *Oeuvres complètes*, p. 901: 'Les mots, dans le dictionnaire, gisent . . .'

38 Derrida, 'Fors', p. 15; p. 70.

39 Nicolas Abraham (and Maria Torok), *L'écorce et le noyau*, Paris, Aubier-Flammarion, 1978. p. 236 of Maria Torok, 'Maladie du deuil et fantasme du cadavre exquis'; pp. 259–73, Abraham and Torok, 'Deuil *ou* mélancolie, Introjecter-incorporer'.

40 Among these other sources, according to L.-J. Austin, may have been Edmond Scherer, 'Hegel et l'hégélianisme', *Revue des deux mondes*, 15 February 1861 vol. 31, pp. 812–56, 'Mallarmé et le rêve du "Livre" ', *Mercure de France*, 1073, 1 January 1953 pp. 81–108, cited by Gardner Davies, *Vers une explication rationnele du Coup de dés*, Paris, Corti, 1953, p. 33.

41 *Oeuvres complètes*, p. 657. 'La Littérature, d'accord avec la faim, consiste à supprimer le Monsieur qui reste en l'écrivant, celui-ci que vient-il faire, au vue des siens, quotidiennement?' Cited by Philippe Sollers, 'Littérature et totalité', in *Logiques*, Paris, Le Seuil, 1968, p. 116.

42 *Oeuvres complètes*, p. 364.

43 *Correspondance 1862–1871*, p. 242. Letter to Cazalis of 14 May 1867. Cf. p. 249, letter to Lefébure of 17 May 1867: '. . . me sentir un diamant qui réfléchit, mais qui n'est pas lui-même . . .'

44 *Oeuvres complètes*, p. 663.

45 Maurice Blanchot, *L'espace littéraire*, Paris, Gallimard, 1955, p. 136.

46 *Pace* Leo Bersani, *The Death of Stéphane Mallarmé*, Cambridge, Cambridge University Press, 1982, p. 63.

47 Julia Kristeva, 'Poésie et négativité', in *Semeiotike*, Paris, Le Seuil, 1969, p. 212. Robert Magliola, *Derrida on the Mend*, West Lafayette, Purdue University Press, 1984, p. 89 and other pages listed in the index under *Sūnyāta*.

48 *Oeuvres complètes*, p. 439. In the letter referred to in note 41 Mallarmé writes: 'j'ai encore besoin, tant ont été grandes les avanies de mon triomphe, de me regarder dans cette glace pour penser et que si elle n'était pas devant la table où je t'écris cette lettre, je redeviendrais le Néant'.

49 Abraham (and Torok), ' "L'objet perdu-moi". Notations sur l'identification endocryptique', in Nicolas Abraham (and Maria Torok), *L'écorce et le noyau*, pp. 295-317.

50 Derrida, 'Entre crochets', *Digraphe*, 1976, vol. 8, p. 108.

51 ibid., p. 105; p. 107.

52 Derrida, 'Fors', p. 23; p. 76.

53 Derrida, 'La pharmacie de Platon', in *La dissémination*.

54 Derrida, 'Fors' p. 17; p. 71.

55 Abraham (and Torok), *L'écorce et le noyau*, p. 259.

56 See note 39.

57 *Oeuvres complètes*, p. 373. Derrida, 'Fors', p. 63; p. 108.

58 A.R. Chisholm, *Mallarmé's Grand Oeuvre*, Manchester, Manchester University Press, 1962, p. 130.

59 *Oeuvres complètes*, p. 1580.

60 ibid., p. 364. Cf. *Correspondance 1862-1871*, p. 154, Letter to Lefébure of February 1865: 'Le peu d'inspiration que j'ai eu, je le dois à ce nom, et je crois que si mon héroïne s'était appelée Salomé, j'eusse inventé ce mot sombre, et rouge comme une grenade ouverte, Hérodiade.'

61 ibid., p. 953.

62 ibid., p. 948.

63 ibid., p. 855.

64 Derrida, 'Entre crochets', p. 105.

65 *Oeuvres complètes*, pp. 399-400. Derrida, *La dissémination*, pp. 198, 318; pp. 172, 286.

66 Derrida, 'Mallarmé', p. 371.

67 *Oeuvres complètes*, p. 857. On p. 56 (*Prose pour des Esseintes*) *iridées* rhymes with *Idées*.

68 Scherer, *Le 'Livre' de Mallarmé*, leaflet 2.

69 See note 62.

70 *Oeuvres complètes*, p. 69: *Sonnet (Pour votre chère morte, son ami)*. Derrida, *La dissémination*, p. 243; p. 214: 'the threshold never crossed'.

71 *Oeuvres complètes*, p. 296, cited at Derrida, *La dissémination*, p. 206; p. 180.

# · 5 ·

# On the Subject of the Subject: Derrida on Sollers in La dissémination

## MARIAN HOBSON

### Texts in/on Texts

Everyone has noticed that Derrida writes about texts, at very close distance and sometimes with no holds barred: but the idea that Derrida writes *on* a text has made possible many accounts of deconstruction which find themselves able to leave out almost entirely the text he is referring to. Gerald Bruns writes for instance: 'The presupposition of monologue or text as something to be analysed makes deconstruction possible, and in the same stroke it makes dialogue (and therefore hermeneutics) seem prehistoric.'[1] Bruns, like many others, has picked out the policing, predatory nature of some of Derrida's analyses, the way he locates and raises to the surface a wreck in the argument, rather than giving assistance to those arguments in difficulty. But Bruns, like many others, has quite brushed aside the fact that other of Derrida's texts move in a quite different way – they elaborate the text they are writing about, they carve it up, they plethorize it, they swell bits of it up, they blister it locally. *Glas* is like this, and so is the article 'La dissémination'. It would be better to speak of Derrida *in* Sollers.

Or 'Derrida' in 'Sollers'? Should the scare quotes recognize that the appropriation of a text to a proper name, the tying of it to an origin, to an authorizing instance or subjectivity, has been questioned precisely in Derrida's work on Sollers? (Ezra Pound, for example, makes an appearance there as 'Pound'.) That this 'authorization' has been made uneasy by the circumstances of the article's publication? The journal *Critique* published 'La dissémination' in two parts, in February and March 1969, as a review of Philippe Sollers' novel *Nombres*, published in the spring of 1968. Derrida had published several times in Sollers' journal *Tel Quel*, most recently the article 'La Pharmacie de Platon', and was giving papers at the *Tel Quel* seminar ('La double séance', given on 26 February and 5 March 1969 was published in *Tel Quel* in 1970). These articles, with 'La dissémination' and 'Hors Livre', a preface about prefaces, were put together to form the volume *La dissémination*, published in 1972 in the publishing house Le Seuil's *Tel Quel* collection.[2] The *Tel Quel* group was famous for its quarrels and its political radicalism; Sollers and Kristeva had just turned Maoist (Sollers quotes Mao in *Nombres* and was translating some of Mao's poems). Derrida does not restrict himself to *Nombres* – he quotes other Sollers novels (*Le Parc* and *Drame*) and the collection of writings on theory and literature, *Logiques*, which also appeared in 1968. He may refer to the long article on *Nombres* entitled 'L'Engendrement de la formule' published by Sollers' wife, Julia Kristeva, slightly later the same spring in *Tel Quel*; her article certainly refers to his.[3] Minimally then, there is mutual support in the post-May 1968 period; Sollers, for instance, wrote an article on Derrida for the *Times Literary Supplement* of 25 September 1969, attacking Jean-Pierre Faye, who is said to have insinuated that Derrida had taken up a Nazi ideology.[4] By the Cérisy colloquium of 1972, however, they had moved apart.

'In' as a relation between these texts becomes something like a cellular telephone network; this is complicated by the fact that each text is in turn exploring the receiving and transmitting relation between texts. The net of immediate interests shared by Derrida and the *Tel Quel* group is wide: they published, for instance in spring 1967, Genet's 'Ce qui est resté d'un Rembrandt déchiré en petits carrés bien réguliers et foutu aux chiottes', which is one of the host texts in *Glas*, and which is printed, in a version of the printing of *Glas*, in two columns, the left text in roman, the right-hand text in italics. In the same number as Kristeva's article, they published part of Starobinski's work on Saussure's manuscripts, which like 'La dissémination' takes the form of italicized quotations and commentary in roman print. Moreover, Starobinski is dealing, as is Kristeva, with the question of the formula: in his case, the hypograms, anagrammatic citings of a key word, often a proper name, which Saussure thought might control the phonetic development of a Latin poem – one of the titles to a section of Derrida's article is written as a hypogram, 'EcriT, EcrAn, EcrIN' [WriTing, EncAsIng, ScreeNing], where the upper-case letters spell *tain*, the word for the reflective backing on a mirror. Starobinski's manner of thinking the problem posed by Saussure's theories has clearly been affected by *Tel Quel* and by Derrida's own work.[5] He will end the article by asking whether the hypogram, as subset of a discourse is the infrastructure of the set, or its antecedent – precisely the question Kristeva's article will address, when she relates what she calls the 'formula' to the 'genotext' and the 'phenotext, that is, to reworkings of Chomsky's distinction between deep and surface structures. She also relates it to Sanskrit linguistic theory for she was about to get published an article by the Estonian, Linnart Mall, on Indian Buddhist theories of language. She quotes Benveniste's work on the phoneme *Tr* which links 'trait' and 'trace' and +*r* in Derrida's text '+R' (1975).

More generally, *Tel Quel*'s leanings include: an espousing of Mallarmé,[6] of surrealism, or rather a surrealist pantheon,[7] an interest in automatic writing; a slightly single-minded materialism; ultra-left politics;[8] aggressivity to the intellectual establishment, and an insistence on the superiority of writers over critics, especially university ones. This is the ambient milieu of *La dissémination*. Behind this milieu, detached from it and opposed to it, is perhaps the figure of Sartre.

This multiple intersecting occurs not just in relation to others, but also in relation to his own work. Derrida in or on Derrida? The book *La dissémination* groups papers connected with *Tel Quel* together (whereas *Marges* published a bit later the same year is a collection of work of heterogeneous origin). All are divided into two parts; all are concerned with presence as presentation or representation and illusion. In a process of continuous expansion, they take texts of Plato (*Phaedrus, Republic, Gorgias*), Mallarmé (*Mimique*), Sollers (*Nombres*), and work outwards from one text along certain paths which then intersect with those coming off another. 'La Pharmacie de Platon' unravels the complexities of Plato's attitude to writing: seen as secondary, an activity related both to the creation of false appearances, to *mimetike fantastike*, and to the vain preservation of dead or merely external knowledge, and thus to sophist dialectic; yet also a preserver of the inner voice, written into the soul itself. Derrida shows within the platonic text the operation or decision, which will be confirmed by Plato's spiritual descendants, whereby a composition of opposites is separated out and the signifier classed lower than the signified, whereby the true is taken to be manifested presence which is stable and certain, not manifesting appearance, which is always referring back to what appears. And his method of work on Plato, to show 'different functions of a same word in different places, relations which are virtually but not necessarily citational' (*D*, 111; 98) is a microversion of what is going on in his own book. Both work on 'mimesis' and method are expanded in 'La double séance', where Mallarmé's *Mimique*, like the mime who is its hero, is not imitating anything final, but is caught in and is playing on exactly the unstabilizable chain of further reference that Plato disliked in pictures. There is no one thing which precedes the imitation and interrupts the chain, says Derrida of this text, nor does it climax in a performance which might create, by a kind of performative utterance, the imitation that it is. Instead, in a version of the Platonic cave (with a pun on 'antre', cave and its near homophone 'entre' between) we have writing with a trap door, a double bottom, a 'double fond', where we never accede to the *ontos on*, the really real. 'Polysemia'[9] – construction of a set of thematic subjects – stabilizes a text into themes, and cannot therefore take into account the constant displacement of the 'fond', the bottom. For an appearance points to what it is an appearance of, which in turn points beyond itself, creating only a chain of endless simulacra, only a process of 'dissemination'.

Derrida's 'La dissémination' was preceded on its first publication, as he reminds the reader with a note in *La dissémination*, by the statement:

The 'present' essay is but a tissue of 'quotations'. Some are in quotation marks. Generally faithful, those taken from *Nombres* [*Numbers*] by Philippe Sollers are written, unless otherwise indicated, both in quotation marks and in italics (Editor's note). (*D*, 319; 287)

However, Sollers' novel itself could also properly be called a 'tissue of quotations' – unattributed though marked off by inverted commas (perhaps not always – who can tell?) Derrida and Kristeva put forward: Pascal, Nicholas of Cusa, Mao, Marx, Bourbaki, Wittgenstein, Dante. From heterogeneous sources, the quotations are inserted without modulation, so that they remain heterogeneous to their surroundings in the novel. They often provide a sudden switch which moves the narration from the writing of experience to the experience of writing:

/'From the river comes the picture, from the lake comes the book'/: at the end of these words was something spinning and cold, but I could not go as far as to turn back onto myself. (*N*, 58, section 2.42)

There is a powerful exploration of a divorced relation to the body and to writing, and imposed on this or in this, an exploration of writing as a machine, as an unspontaneous, an almost involuntary and alienated activity; these maintain a constant uncertainty as to whether it is the novel or the body that is being written about.

However I found again my mutilated body and it was as if the flesh had been ploughed and the sexual organ sown together and raised like an ear of corn, closed and hardened [. . .] It was me, I was sure, I had waited for my sleep [. . .] I began to work at the linkings, at the novel to which its figures were coming back, on a luminous and empty background where they were disintegrating in the end. (*N*, 43, section 1.29)

Yet this dismembered body and mutilated text is no body of Osiris to be brought together into unity by Isis after long searching. The parts germinate of themselves, in intense localized heterogeneous and sometimes social activity.

In fact, the same work was at work everywhere, stirring and drowning groups in their progression, changing the relationship of forces, of production, making transformations appear, permutations, and it was in this way that the fight spread, with its jumps of inversions, of generation . . . Everywhere distributed, everywhere active, everywhere brought back to life and never finished, what I call here 'the fight' could be extracted at all levels, that is a handful of earth, the particle vibrating and disappearing, the cells, the kernels, the words, the patient rise of the masses really uncapturable at that depth. (*N*, 72, section 3.55)

Snatches coalesce into a kind of love story (section 58) or patches of erotic description or description of execution; east is contrasted with west, where signs have no purchase on what is outside, where hallucination is neutralized; whereas in the east there is people, not crowd, and the 'invisible force of remainderless mutation', where text or appearance are both cause and consequence – ' "the product of the appearance that it itself must produce" ' (*N*,37, section 3.23). Writing is a constant passage between, on the one hand, the experience of dismemberment and of germination in destruction, and on the other, the construction of the novel through violent mutilation (*N*, 62, section 3.47).

'Dissemination' is used by Sollers of this complex movement of self-loss and self-reassertion, of ejaculation from and attracting to, of chaos and writing, where words and seed move from generalization (Sollers quotes without quote marks his own epigraph from Lucretius, 'Seminaque innumero numero summaque profunda'), from mention (symbolized by quotation marks) to use, to application to you, to meaning for the apparently individual case, who can be the recipient of the novel or of the dedication (*N*, 101, section 4.80). The novel (so called on its title pages) constricts these snatches by its formal apparatus: it is divided into one hundred sections which rotate in groups of four. Each section bears two numbers, its place in the group of four and then in the total; they are not paragraphs, in that they don't begin with a capital letter, though frequently they begin with dots; they always end with a dash. The fourth sections are always closed off by brackets, and this excepted nature is confirmed by the tense – it is invariably in the present tense, whereas the other sections tend to use the imperfect or both perfect and present participles without main verb. This is further confirmed by the system of pronouns – they are usually in the apostrophic form 'vous', 'you', whereas the other sections use 'she', 'he', 'I', and their plurals. The material organization goes beyond punctuation, for a good many sections end with a Chinese character; there are diagrams, all of which except one are developments of a square; it is dedicated in cyrillic characters to Julia (Kristeva), and the vowels from her name – which are also those of Sollers' family name – are played with as a formula (*N*, section 55, quoting section 3).[10]

The novel has worn well. The constant superimposition of body on text and text in body, the complex numerical and syntactic patterning, provide and divide effects. Its jacket announces a dialogue between west and east, and a passage from alienated writing to 'une écriture traçante', writing as trace – a term probably adapted from Derrida. In the companion volume of essays, *Logiques*, published the same year, Sollers sketches a view of the novel's position in intellectual history, as being part of a move from writing alienated in capitalism and trapped in representation, to writing as production: 'Infinite, grid, double, materialism, dialectics, space' (*Logiques*, 13), which 'functions as an apparatus' (*Logiques*, jacket). Texts as apparatus, appearance as being produced by what it produces, heterogeneity as seminal (seed and term, 'germe' and 'terme' constantly echo in both texts ) – all this is at work in 'La dissémination' as well as in *Nombres*. The disparate nature of Sollers' quotations (Derrida adds to them, but he also alters unmarked quotations)[11] is inserted into his own text by Derrida with the quotations themselves, and perhaps thus exacerbated, re-marked in the Derridean sense; and he elaborates on the heterogeneous modes of their reference, the different tacks of their insertion (*D*, 372; 334). As does the epigraph he has picked out from Sollers' *Logiques*, Derrida calls this process the *graft*: texts are not assimilated into the host text but made to remain as foreign bodies and to continue to radiate towards the text they came from (*D*, 395; 355). And this commentary is of course self-commentary: for although his article is published as a review on *Nombres*, he scarifies the novel, he takes cuttings from it and enlarges them, grafting them on to the concerns of 'La Pharmacie de Platon' and 'La double séance'. Buzz words common to Sollers, Kristeva, and Derrida ('dissemination', 'double bottom', 'column') are elaborated on, forcibly collocated with more idiosyncratic kernel phrases ('surjet' [overcast], 'futur antérieur' [future in the past], 'greffe' [graft]) or syntactic forms – use of the future in the past, or of the propositional form 'this is that' – some of which will have notable and extensive futures in his writing, whereas others will be left high and dry.

'Citation', as Derrida points out, is the nominal form of the frequentative of 'to move': it fits the complex calling up and overlaying of references that he operates. 'Quotation', derived from numerical methods of reference might seem to fit Sollers' text, with its cyclic number system. Both might appear to be explicit, even accelerated versions of Kristevan 'intertextuality'. Kristeva models 'intertextuality' on Husserl's 'intersubjectivity': I shall speak later of this 'evincing' (Kristeva, 378) of the subject by the text. Of intertextuality she writes:

Every text constructs itself as a mosaic of citations, every text is absorption and transformation of another text. (146)
The text is thus a *productivity*, which means: 1. its relation to the language in which it is situated is redistributive (destructivo-constructive), and as a consequence it is approachable through logical rather than through linguistic categories; 2. it is a permutation of texts, an intertextuality: in the space of one text several statements, taken from other texts, cross and neutralise each other. (113)

She describes, with what could be called peremptory intuition, intertextuality as a function, a mapping ('application logique', 146).

Ultimately then, it must associate, must map elements of one text on or into another. There is then a necessary hierarchy between the elements of analysis and the operation – in fact she speaks of 'level'. Whereas, with Derrida, we have 'citational effects' (334). The plurals, the lack of hierarchy, allow only for dissemination – there can be no stable typology.

## Parody and Presence

Conscious and persistent quotation looks uncommonly like parody – parody has frequently used the technique of an anachronistic insertion of a piece of text into a context to which it is alien. This is not necessarily hostile: a seal of importance on the parodied text may be bestowed thereby. The repetition can act as an acknowledgement of the parodied text's force of example at the same time as the strange context makes possible disinvestment.[12] But to quote extensively in contexts which are left heterogeneous, from a text which itself quotes constantly, duplicates the gesture. Can this be a parody of a parody? Derrida's 'La dissémination' does mimic a certain elliptic irony, a certain kind of difficulty and abruptness found in Sollers (in particular much of it imitates the direct address found in the fourth sections of the novel, speaking or pretending to speak to 'vous', you). Beyond this, some of the complication has a precautionary nature, putting forward in a perhaps slightly placatory mode an embarrassment at working over in a review a text to which its author has attributed literary status.[13] The mimicry allows both the acknowledgement and the disinvestment spoken of earlier, but it also acquires a sharp philosophical point, since it effaces any simple distinction between itself and Sollers' text, for its irony dissolves both texts into a 'generalized simulacrum'. *Nombres*, says Derrida, is already a commentary on what it presents, so that his review is a review of a commentary and there is no primary text which might be present to review, but only presentation and appearance of presentation. His text mimes the presentation of *Nombres*, their re-presentation and their account, inventory, review (*D*, 326; 294). It mimes the relation 'on' and turns it into 'in'.

But how exactly? A *topos* of criticism at the time – though not of Kristeva, Sollers, or Derrida – was the *mise-en-abîme*, where an object or incident in the work reflected the whole, and whereby, if he noticed it, the reader would become aware that what he was reading was an organized piece of writing. Jean Ricardou will develop this into an opposition between a novel's 'dimension référentielle' and its 'dimension litterale',[14] (crudely put, the 'story' and 'the text' and its techniques for reminding the reader that it is there); and Kristeva herself had in 1967 earlier created a related but subtler opposition between 'verisimilitude' and the 'productivity called text' in an article of that name. What is interesting is that both Sollers and Derrida move well beyond the binary relation implied in these accounts of what came to be called textuality. This is done first by multiplying the mirror (Sollers: 'mirror', *N*, 20, section 2.6; 'black mirror', *N*, 39, section 1.25; 'the mixture from before the mirror', *N*, 47, section 3.31; 'this crossing of the mirror', *N*, 65, section 1.49; 'La dissémination': 'these mirror effects through which the texts quotes, quotes itself', *D*, 361). But we don't see what is mirrored. These are reflecting surfaces only: they do not order and focus, they are not put in an order of imbrication, unlike in so many earlier novels, Diderot's *Jacques le fataliste* for instance.

But if novel and account of its writing, commentary, and commented text are not in a binary relation, indeed if they cannot be divorced, does this mean that the texts perform themselves, that they do as well as say; or do they 'produce' themselves to use a term of Kristeva's? It is striking that Derrida disowns the word for its relation to unproblematized presence (*D*, 328). And in 'La double séance', a passage from Mallarmé used in 'La dissémination' to introduce the notion of generalized simulacrum is the occasion for Derrida to deny that the performative mode, where the utterance acts as it speaks, is adequate to account for the Mallarmean text, or for any text, since it retains notions of presence in the performance itself, and thus stabilizes the relation between appearances and what appears (*D*, 232–4; 205–7). Some of the way Derrida writes can be understood as implicitly disenabling two common critical tools for analysing fiction: the *mise en abîme*, where the text is said to reproduce itself within itself; the performative, where language becomes act – which in later texts he will explicitly make less certain in their distinction between object and image or speech and act. For the very possibility of a one-to-one reflexion necessary for the *mise en abîme* will be questioned; and the mimicry of what in Sollers' novel is already a heavy apostrophic gesture – the use of the 'vous' [you] form in the fourth sections – sets in doubt the value of 'performance'. In

'La dissémination', modes of presence are parodied: the relations 'on' and 'in' are scrambled, they are not distinguishable.

## Forged References and False Starts

The effect of unlocalized quotation in Sollers is to 'derealize' the referent, to move it from designation of something thought of as existing outside the novel to entrapment in a system of references. 'What is being effected is [. . .] a generalized putting-in-quotation-marks of literature, of the so-called literary text: a simulacrum through which literature puts itself simultaneously at stake and on stage' (D, 323; 291). But such is paradoxically also the effect of what seems to be the reverse procedure: common nouns display tendencies to become proper names, they try to move from type to token, from use to mention, and to being 'rigid designators'. Sollers has both hidden and revealed himself by embedding his own names in the text. Yet, as Derrida points out, this covert self-citing doesn't function as an à clé reference: the puns on his pen name (Sollers/soleil [sun]) are not references but screens to hide (D, 328–9 quoting Nombres, 1.25) and Derrida himself puns on Sollers' family name, Joyaux, through a quotation from Mallarmé. So we do not issue out onto the authorial instance but are spun further into the tissue of quotation. Even the proper name is not singular, not the indivisible individual, not the place of last resort.

This uncertainty about indication and quotation, designating and using is repeated à propos of the event that novel and commentary might be taken to be. The 'generalized simulacrum' is said to oscillate 'here' between the texts (note how 'entretexte' puns on 'intertexte', the Kristevan term for the tissue of relations between individual texts and 'antretexte', text as Platonic cave and representation of illusion); between the so-called primary text and its so-called commentary. This process he will call 'the double bottom' and it refers in particular to the way Derrida gets his text going. He starts with a section headed 'Déclenchement', the 'Trigger', and then its dictionary definition: 'automatic start of a mechanism'. This mechanism, the textual apparatus, is a kind of theatre (see diagram 1), one of whose surfaces gives rise to the effect of presence, to the effect of events happening, to the effect of experience. But before developing this, Derrida starts by raising the question of the singular event (the incident-room version of the proper name – both are referents, supposed nuggets of reality to which we point or which we speak). Is Sollers' novel a singular event, indeed is his own writing?

This time at last. 'This time at last' does not mean that what had always obscurely until now been sought has finally, in a single blow – a stroke of the pen or a throw of dice – been accomplished. (*D*, 323; 291)

The singular event that is Sollers' novel is not singular, but a 'generalized putting-in-quotation-marks of literature' because it is double from the word go. Likewise, Derrida's text has got itself going by reduplicating, by containing its own beginning, by quoting itself – 'Cette fois enfin' appears first a page earlier and in italics. 'Because it begins by repeating itself, such an event at first takes the form of a story' (*D*, 324; 292). This is what Derrida maintains happens in texts by Blanchot[15] and in a poem by Ponge.[16] No more than the proper name is the event first or single; what precedes turns out to be a reproduction of what it precedes. Is this looping back of the text created in 'la dissémination' by mere typography, the italics? Not that that, I think, would worry Derrida. (The whole paradoxical nature of what one might call the 'ouverture' in Derrida deserves further study.[17]) But more is at stake than what could be called a missed quotation from Mallarmé: 'what had always obscurely until now been sought' (*D*, 323; 291). There is no eschatology, literature seeks but will not find, and where one thinks to find original text there is altered quotation. So no more than the proper name is the event first and single; what precedes turns out to be a product of what it precedes. Sollers writes.

The real text is conceived as a product of a duality which it produces (*Logiques*, 12) and in a quoted passage in *Nombres*:

'each one of the appearances that can be seen realising itself is the product of the appearance which it must itself produce'. (*N*, 37, section 3.23)

The notion of production is being bent round into a kind of circle. Likewise, Derrida's repetition of 'this time at last' suggests that by this doubling back what starts is not the beginning but the consequence. But there is more. The doubling back operated by Derrida means that his text reflects itself without containing itself (the *mise-en abîme* is disenabled). It is both open and closed – closed through the reflexion of itself which might seem to complete, as a mirror image may complete an object; open because the reflexion is not complete, nor indeed one way.

Moreover, as Sollers superimposed text and self, or text and body, Derrida links the text's skewed self-reflexion to the self-reflexion of consciousness:

> The world comprehends the mirror which captures it and vice versa. [This is a parodistic reworking of Pascal's 'Par l'espace, l'univers me comprend et m'engloutit comme un point: par la pensée je le comprends'.[18]] In the whole of what it captures, and because it can capture the whole, each part of the mirror is larger than the whole; but then it is smaller than itself. (*D*, 351; 316)

Derrida in 'La dissémination' (as he does in other parts of his writings) is crossing four kinds of reflexion: as a model for self-consciousness, in subjects or in texts; reflexion in a mirror; reflexivity as a one to one relationship; and the reflexive as a grammatical relation. In each of these there is a kind of short-circuiting – the reflexion is not perfect but skewed.

1 Sollers' novel and Derrida's article revise what is put forward as the habitual model for consciousness and self-consciousness which become unlimpid and troublesome.

2 The model of a different kind of mirror is suggested, one whose mercury misreflects – it is a revision of the 'speculative' mirror of Hegelianism (*D*, 39; 33).

3 Reflexivity is a one-to-one relation; but certain sets of entities can be put into a one-to-one relation with parts of themselves – this is true of the natural numbers, for instance, which have the same cardinal number as their sub-set, the even numbers (this is sometimes known as the paradox of Galileo). This paradox of the container contained is hinted at several times (cf. Sollers, *Logiques*, 12).

4 There is in Derrida's article a constant use of reflexive verbs, a constant play with their curious power, perhaps peculiar to the French language, to hover between passive and active meanings so that one of the crucial distinctions possible to make about a human subject is queered.

'La dissémination' with its false start starts up an interweaving of these reflexions; it lifts itself into orbit, boots itself, bootstraps itself, in computer terminology, it doubles back so that the distinction between Sollers' text, Sollers' text's commentary on Sollers' text and

Derrida's text's commentary on Sollers' text, and Derrida's commentary on its own commentary, etc. is not possible, or rather not meaningful. This is not sympathetic osmosis, but, as we shall see, a destabilizing of certainty about what is said about what – subject and object are not to be cleanly separated, predication becomes problematic, nor can any kind of order of priority be established; moreover, an uncertainty about the individual, the singular, is written into the text and brought about in the text.

## The Subject of Illusion

Derrida's piece begins with its own reproduction. Sollers' novel, said to be a textual machine, places the reader in the position of a spectator who is up on the stage. The novel contains diagrams, most though not all of which are variants of a square open on one side. The first seems to be an account of perception, of the creation of a thinking subject, and finally an account of the projection of events apparently in three dimensions on to the two dimensions of the page; the second diagram in 4.24 speaks of a theatre where is 'the old text which speaks of truth and error, of life and death', where the five squares of the diagram are the earth whose middle empty place is chance; and the third diagram, in 4.48, double the second, is described as the 'portico of history' – Sollers parodies at this point St Jean Perse's *Anabase* where it speaks of a kind of parousia; and the fourth diagram is called 'the sequence in white of the present', the 'separation and confusion of life in common' (4.52), that is, the indistinctness of separate identity, of singular and non-singular. Here the 'love story' and the themes of subject and object, and of politics, seem to merge. Yet having said this of the novel, Derrida's warning should be noted. 'Polythematics', that is the eliciting of a plurality of themes, is merely an imposition on a text of deferred presence. Created by the copula 'is', by identifying – 'this *is* that' (*D*, 389; 350) it essentializes the text, it immobilizes it by a process of creeping predication. Likewise, reading 'est' as 'East', it is not the end or aim of the West (no teleology, no eschatology) 'forever producing itself, it never comes to be. Like the horizon' (*D*, 393; 353).

Kristeva, though she will later write an important article on predication, 'Objet ou complément', reprinted in *Polylogues*, 1977,

# from Sollers' *Nombres*

4.8

4.24

4.48

4.52

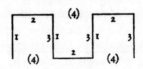

c'est-à-dire, d'une surface à son opposé

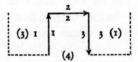

c'est-à-dire, d'un ensemble à l'autre, d'un blanc au
blanc redoublé,

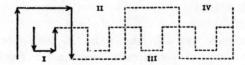

picks out in her article on the novel the dismemberment of the individual subject. Of the first diagram, Sollers had written:

This fourth surface is in a way made in the air, it allows the words to get heard, the bodies to get themselves looked at, one forgets it easily as a result, and there probably is the illusion or the mistake. Indeed, what one takes too easily for the opening of a stage is still a deforming wallsheet, an invisible and impalpable opaque veil which for the other three sides takes on the function of a mirror or a reflector and towards the outside (that is to say towards the possible spectator, that is as a consequence always pushed back, multiplex). (*N*, 22, section 4.8)

From this, he says, comes the impression of depth, of representation, of reflexion. Kristeva calls the first diagram a theatre, an axial topology, a machine in which 'je' (I) is dethroned:

The textual topology is theatrical: it posits a stage where the 'I' plays itself, multiplies itself, becomes an actor and calls into the act the spectator comprehended and played out as one of the parts of the scenography which are not privileged. Pierced by the axis and as if reflected by it and in it, the entity 'I' is no longer a unity doubled into 'body' and 'language'/'sense' and a corporeal meaning or a signifying body, unified and out of kilter in relation to themselves in one and the same movement. (351)[19]

Likewise, Derrida shows how in *Nombres* the thinking subject is the illusionary subject of an unrecognized theatre. (The reminiscence of Brechtian criticisms of bourgeois theatre is strong.) The set of fourth sequences, the opening of the diagram on the fourth side resemble the structure of that old-fashioned theatre, and they too are dead because the consciousness that stands as spectator and consumer of the represented present or meaning – 'you' – believes itself to move in the freedom of pure appearing, while it is only an effect, the drifting, reverberation, transported, cast-off effect, forever turned back or thrown away (*D*, 341–2; 307–8). And the consequence is that

He who says 'I' in the present tense, in the so-called positive event constituted by his discourse, would be capable of only an illusion of mastery. (*D*, 330; 298)

The transcendental subject, the 'I' who contains the world, like the bearer of the text who is external to the text, are no more, for as the latter has become part of the text, it is a 'pure place of passage' so the subject is only a 'differentiated structure of organisation' (*D*, 332; 299).

Now, as Manfred Frank has pointed out,[20] Lacan had discussed consciousness and its derivation from a mirror effect in a seminar published in 1978 but dating from 1954–5, and in *Ecrits* (1966). And in differentiating his position from the behaviourists who, like him, try to make consciousness an epiphenomenon but who, unlike him, cannot take account of intersubjective relations, Lacan says:

Consciousness, that gets produced [se produit] each time there is given a surface such that it can produce what is called *an image*.[21]

Slightly earlier in the same passage he had linked the emergence of consciousness to the existence of our eyes or ears. Derrida similarly links consciousness to a surface: it is a 'conditioned product, a surface effect [or an effect of surface]' (*D*, 332; 299). However, unlike Lacan, he disenables the metaphor of the mirror, making it transparent and deforming. Our apprehension of things out there is due to a 'frons scaenae', a proscenium opening which seems to be the opening on to the immediate where we are unconscious of the medium through which we see; but this apprehension is only the appearance of appearance.

So that quite unlike Kristeva's position, it is not merely the subject, but all phenomena, all events, all history, which are multiple and the products of a network of differential relations. Furthermore, again unlike Kristeva, Derrida sees Sollers' novel as explaining how the illusion of subject in particular, and presence in general, comes about. As a machine for denouncing illusion, Derrida compares the novel to the Platonic cave. However, whereas in the cave the shadows reflected the external realm of light, in the novel, mirrors are not in the world, but the *ontos on*, the really real is now contained within the mirror (*D*, 360; 324); instead of a binary opposition reality/appearance there is merely differentiated appearance.[22] This is an attack on the 'subject' and on 'presence', cast in the role of illusions. But if there is no real against which they can be set, it may be that the attack is rather on their use as the privileged pole of a distinction. For through the reference to Plato, and as we will see, to Kant, these illusions are latched into a complex philosophical tradition. Though they are not given the paradoxical roles of other concepts (like *hymen* or *parergon*) they do have conferred on them a more complex philosophical status than that of dead ends or dead entities.

The presentation of an object, of an event; the constitution of an object as being opposite one – these are created by the textual machine (*D*, 330; 297). Just as the novel, in its bits and pieces way, nevertheless coalesces into a representation which its own machine undoes, so by analogy, the constitution of an object as being there, in front of me, here and now, is merely an effect of presence, 'après coup', 'nachtraglich'.[23] But 'effet de' with its conjoint implication of the unreal and the posterior, begins to receive definition, for this error is said to be non-empirical, it is a variety of 'transcendental illusion' (*D*, 329; 297).

'Transcendental illusion' in Kant's *Critique of Pure Reason* 'does not cease even after it has been detected and its invalidity clearly revealed by transcendental criticism'. We have to think like that, in order to be able to think at all; such reasoning is not illicit, a 'logical paralogism', but a condition of possibility for intellectual activity, a 'transcendental paralogism'. Such reasonings are 'sophistications not of men but of pure reason itself. Even the wisest of men cannot free himself from them.' Kant suggests that whereas the sophists' dialectic produces an illusion which can be dispelled, the transcendental dialectic, the dialectic of pure reason, 'even after its deceptions have been exposed will not cease to play tricks with reason'.[24] And the first example Kant gives is the illegitimate conclusion from the transcendental concept of the subject 'a bare consciousness which accompanies all concepts' to the absolute unity of the subject itself. Derrida seems to bring together what Kant divided; the transcendental 'vehicle' for concepts is an illusion, and not merely, as with Kant, its psychological twin, the unified subject. But it is an illusion that is not always avoidable.

This odd status is repeated in the model for consciousness, reflexion. For consciousness, it is implied, has been analysed as reflexive, as turning itself back on itself, as if it were obtaining a perfect 'mirror image' of itself. It is this capacity to watch itself that has made possible the notion that the thinking subject comprehends in some sense the world, that the self thus transcends the world. Derrida emphasizes that this containing self is in fact contained, always sited (Derrida, and Kristeva, quote Mallarmé's 'nothing will have taken place but the place' 330; 297) so that the reflexion is always decalated, is never simultaneous with the object. Moreover, the mirror is not the containing mirror, but the mirror of Sollers' fourth surface, for where we think there is direct givenness onto appearance there is the 'closed opening' (349; 314), in the subject as in the text. It is a mirror whose mercury is transparent, or rather deforming. The 'I', then, is a secondary creation:

I opened my eyes, I watched coming towards me what would in the end force me to say 'I' (N, 28, section 1.13)

and immediate appearance is apparent immediacy, 'a surface effect' (D, 332; 299).[25]

## The Appearance of Presentation

The novel is a textual apparatus which writes the 'I': 'and I is only the differentiated structure of the organisation' (D, 332; 229). The 'I' may be a post-ego, the result of a ricochet effect off everything else; but it is always part of what it claims to focus and gather. It is 'not some singular and irreplaceable existence, some subject or "life", but only, moving between life and death, reality and fiction etc. a mere function or fantom' (D, 361; 325). The illusion is the result of the relation of the non-representable to the representation (D, 330; 297).[26] The 'singular mirror' (D, 331; 298) reflects no reality, but only produces 'effects of reality'. Like the creating of an 'I' as a transcendental illusion, the novel fashions its reader by creating the rhetorical effects which in a sense *are* the novel, 'the product of the appearance that it itself must produce' (N, 37, section 3.23). One of the ways of considering 'La dissémination' is as an examination of how these effects come about.

Novels can address 'you', make you present at fictional events; and if they reveal how they do so then the level of events becomes the appearance and the presenting of the fictional workings becomes the present – the present is not undercut, merely pushed one stage further back. But *Nombres* is different. So that if the host text is already parodically moving between presentation of appearance and appearance of presentation, and if the review text repeats and generalizes that movement, then

The mirror in which these *Numbers* are read, in its capacity for seeing you, will of course be broken, but it will reflect that breaking in a fiction that remains intact and uninterrupted. (D, 327; 295)

Fiction and commentary, illusion and breaking of illusion are not alternating, discrete moments. They resemble Derrida's definition of 'being in the process of', which like Newton's light takes the form both of wave and corpuscle:

A movement that is at once uninterrupted and broken, a continuity of rifts that would nevertheless not flatten out along the surface of a homogeneous, obvious present. (*D*, 345; 310)

In the novel *Nombres*, there is representation, effect of presence, appearance of presentation. The novel appears to present, it seems. One of the ways it does this is by the address in the fourth sequences 'vous' [you], which has two senses – Derrida calls it 'le discours d'assistance', the attending discourse. It seems to 'put the reader in the picture', to make him present; but it also, while edging her into reading it, gets there before him or her, makes him or her super-numerary. It writes what it claims to be (*D*, 362; 326):

In this duality triggered off by writing, it pretends to account – and to give a reason – for what you are seeing, feigning to tell you the presence of your present, whereas this pretense is itself part of a writing process. (*D*, 362; 326).

Derrida by writing in the same 'you' form, presents in turn a simulacrum. 'Effects of presence' and 'affects as presence' are not distinct.

The novel takes apart another effect of presence, the present tense. Sollers had said, in a section which begins with a diagram called the 'portico of the story [of history]':

The problem being the following: how to transform point by point a space into another space, the imperfect into the present, and how to include oneself in this death. (*N*, 64, section 4.48)

(The fourth sequences are always written in the present tense.) So this remark could be interpreted as asking how to make a story present; or how to make history reach to the present.[27] It seems to use what it denounces as illusion of presence and originariness. Sollers, Derrida points out, in the previous novel, *Drame*, had used verbs in the present tense both with inverted commas and also without. There is on the same page in *Drame* a simple present, and 'the present that enounces or denounces its relation to the other tenses in a "scientific" discourse' (*D*, 343; 309). *Drame* called the tense the 'plupresent'.

The plupresent in sequence four thus envelops both the person 'lived' by you, in the 'illusion' of one who lives, reads, speaks in the present, your eyes riveted to the classical scenario and its violent reinscription in the theatrical arithmetrical machine: *Numbers* read see and speak, you. (*D*, 345; 311)

So the novel affects the reader as present, at the same time as it shows up presence as an illusion. How can it do this? By a tense that mirrors the plural and differential nature of what we call the present. For the 'plupresent' operates in the novel by a 'future in the past'. Writing that is representing the irrepresentable is what makes the 'taking place' appear to happen; but writing works by an infinite process of references forward and back (*D*, 345; 311). The systematic use of quotation is not a mosaic, not a laying down of elements not further analysable – they must keep their heterogeneity, they must not dissolve seamlessly. They must not form a 'last analysis' but a constant exchange. Likewise in the case of time – the present is not 'here' and 'now' but the effect of an infinite process of overlaying, operated by past projections and future retentions.

In a way then that develops the traditional analysis of rhetorical effects, the reader can be passively affected: 'The tale is thereby addressed to the reader's body, which is put by things on stage, itself' (*D*, 322; 290; Barbara Johnson has pointed out that this is a misquotation from Mallarmé, who used the word 'intelligence'). But since the effect of presence is the effect of writing, and the effect of 'I' is the effect of a constant reference, text and consciousness become more than analogies, they become intertwined. Subject and object, active and passive relation are thus disturbed; the subject turns into object because, far from surveying the object from a privileged vantage point, the subject is always framed by the text, always object, and has no place from which he can be excepted. But this strong materialist debunk of the subject (Derrida speaks of his being 'taken apart' [démonté]) is not simple. The reader 'receives' the novel's effects: but that 'reception' is the illusion of spontaneous action.[28] This is marked in Derrida's as in Sollers' text by the play on the 'vous' [you] form – it implies both activity on the part of 'vous', reader or author, and the removal of the margin for reaction in the part of reader/author by the near imperative form. In Derrida's text it is the book which becomes active:

*Numbers* read, see and speak, you, in the process of reading *you*, seeing *you*, speaking (to) *you*, 'in the process' meaning at the moment that, non-presently, you are being read, seen, spoken etc. (*D*, 345; 311)

This reversal of the relation between book and reader smudges our usual attribution of action and animation to the human subject. In the case just quoted, the passage receives its tension precisely from its contravening of our expectations. Elsewhere, it is the very opposition between active and passive which is undermined, for Derrida uses the French reflexive a great deal and exploits its indeterminacy between 'voices': witness the very first lines:

Telle autre énumération, tout carrément écrite, se garderait pourtant indéchiffrable. (*D*, 321)
Some such other enumeration, altogether squarely written, would nevertheless remain undecipherable. (*D*, 289)

Les *Nombres* s'énumèrent, s'écrivent et se lisent. Eux-mêmes, d'eux-mêmes. Par quoi ils se remarquent aussitôt. (*D*, 322)
These *Numbers* enumerate themselves, write themselves, read themselves. By themselves. Hence they get themselves remarked right away. (*D*, 290)

The subject may have been dethroned, he may be the object of language:

My own presence to myself has been preceded by language. Older than consciousness, older than the spectator, prior to any attendance, a sentence awaits 'you': looks at you, observes you, watches over you, and regards you from every side. There is always a sentence that has already been sealed somewhere waiting for you where you think you are opening up some virgin territory (*D*, 378-9; 340)

but language itself is active.

There may be here a complex and shadowy dialogue with Sartre (as there may be in *Glas* later). When Derrida writes:

At the very moment he [he who says 'I'] thinks he is directing the operations, his place - the opening toward the present assumed by whoever believes himself capable of saying 'I', I think, I am, I see, I feel, I say (you, for example, here and now) - is constantly and in spite of him being decided by a throw of dice whose law will subsequently be developed inexorably by chance (*D*, 330-1; 298)

the reference to Mallarmé's *Coup de dés* is patent; but so also is the contradiction of Sartre's article on Mallarmé. For Sartre, Mallarmé knows that poetry is a kind of act where chance is denied through poetry's necessity. And this is developed in *The Idiot of the Family*, again implicitly in relation to Mallarmé:

The dice throw will never abolish chance because it contains chance in its practical essence; yet however the player performs an act, he throws the dice in a certain way, he reacts in one way or another to the numbers that come up and tries, in the following moment to use his good or bad luck.[29]

Sartre's writer, Flaubert or Mallarmé, can if he chooses (and he can choose) create necessity out of chance by action. Choice, action, creation are impossible, however, if the external causes acting on a man cannot be internalized by an act of will. And this is what a passage quoted by Derrida (from a twentieth-century author, perhaps Merleau-Ponty? but it repeats eighteenth-century materialist arguments about human agency) will assert:

A difference: the cause is radically that. It is not a positive difference, nor is it one included within the subject. It is what the subject is essentially lacking. (*D*, 337; 304)

Sartre argues in *The Idiot of the Family* as he had argued in his book on Mallarmé that though language forms us, it is also an act; language exists in that it is spoken; man is not merely spoken, in that he is born into a linguistic network as into a web of causes, but he also speaks. Only a month after the publication of 'La dissémination', in an article in *Temps Modernes*, which caused a scandal by printing a tape-recording of a psychoanalyst's session with a patient, Sartre wrote:

Who is this A who is speaking? A blind process or the going-beyond of this process through an act? I don't doubt that the least one of his words nor that all his behaviour can be interpreted analytically: on condition of bringing him back to his status of analytical object. What will disappear with the subject is the inimitable and singular quality of the scene; its synthetic organisation; in other words, action as action.[30]

This is a protest that language cannot just be seen as at work in the subject. And behind this is clearly a defence of the subject as such:

Man is never an individual; it would be better to call him a *universal singular* [universel singulier]: totalised and thus universalised by his epoch, he retotalises it in reproducing himself in it as a singularity. Universal by the singular universality of human history, singular through the universalising singularity of his projects. (*The Idiot of the Family*, vol. 1, 7–8)

The very possibility of Sartrean totalizing is criticized in the passage on cause just quoted from 'La dissémination' – what is lacking from each particular thing is infinite and cannot therefore be totalized, nor included in the subject. Derrida, in what reads like a reply to Sartre's 'universal singular' - a reply couched in the tense of the future in the past - speaks of a 'singular plural [singulier pluriel], which no single origin will ever have preceded' (*D*, 337; 304). Derrida's phrase, more than Sartre's, makes one hesitate in deciding which of the two adjectival forms must be treated as the noun, a hovering not unlike the effect of his use of the reflexive. The world is not a totalization of singulars, however universal they may be, there are no elementary particles, no indivisible individuals, no final atomic constituting part, because each term is also a germ (*D*, 338; 304). Dissemination is not multiplicity coming after a primary unity which has split up, but on the contrary, it is a working towards a unity which cannot come about except through a plural. It is this primary unity which is traditionally the condition of possibility of transcendental subjectivity; it is also an impossible unity, and thus a condition of the impossibility of transcendental subjectivity; every circumscription of the singular, and of the so-called 'individual' opens it out to numbers, to plurality, to plethora. Only the plural, says Derrida, can have identity, since the unique, the singular in time, is that which cannot be repeated in its identity (*D*, 405; 365). The unique is the *apeiron* (what is not known); consciousness is a two-place relation: '[there is] no simple originary unit prior to this division through which life comes to see itself' (*D*, 338; 304).

If Derrida is denouncing the illusion of the individual, he is also showing how it comes about, as part of the presentation of appearance, or in Sollers' novel the appearance of presentation. The column, which in Sollers' text appears as the penis, the column of text, a column of air pressure, sometimes a gap, and which in Kristeva's text is the fourth side of the theatre (361), in Derrida's becomes the placeholder for presence:

The column is nothing, has no meaning in itself. A hollow phallus, cut off from itself, decapitated (i), it guarantees the innumerable passage of dissemination and the playful displacement of the margins. It is never itself, only a writing that endlessly substitutes it for itself, doubling it as of its very first surrection. (*D*, 381; 343)

It is what makes possible the copula, the assertion 'is', the calm mastery of consciousness in the operations of predication, indication, perception; what makes possible the Western phantasms of mastery (*D*, 391; 351-2). Yet its phallic significance is only a 'semic effect' for it is replaceable infinitely. The odd status of 'concepts' in Derrida's work is clear from the column: taken over from a text worked on, subject to 'dérive', (derivation/slippage), in *Parergon*[31] it will be stretched to relate Kant's concept of the 'colossal' to the supplement; in *Glas* it will refer to Hegel's account of religion as well as to the twin columns in which that text is printed. Neither 'theme' nor 'metaphor', not a reducible content, nor a substitute for some other defined content. Yet in both 'La dissémination' and in *Glas* it joins up with Derrida's analysis of fetishism.

Sollers' text, with its mirror effects and self-quotation, makes the preservation of a statement, its fetishization, its investment with 'scientific' value impossible (*D*, 351; 315). Derrida's evocation of the fetish occurs just after a quotation from Sollers where the latter reworks Marx's definition of value:

Sollers: By means, therefore of the value-relation expressed in our equation, the bodily form of commodity B becomes the value-form of commodity A, or the body of commodity B acts as a mirror to the value of commodity A (3.67; 351; 315).

Marx: A use value represents the exchange value for another use value.
Lacan: A signifier is what represents the subject for another signifier.[32]

The reification of a value in an object is fetishism (one version of the column in *Glas*). Derrida maintains that Sollers' textual theatre unpicks any fetishism. Now Sartre, in the third volume of *The Idiot of the Family* in what is clearly an attack on structuralist and post-structuralist theories of language will speak of the 'thingism [chosisme] of the signifier'. And this analysis is a development of the criticism of structuralism expressed in the revue *L'Arc* in 1968 and earlier in the parts of *The Idiot* published in 1966 in his journal *Temps modernes*, where, moreover, there is implicit but clear reference to Lacan. Such theories, Sartre maintains, turn language into a thing, cutting off the living relation of author and reader. Although they claim to be interested in exchange (the linguistic version of difference) the system of linguistic exchange has been reified, and language becomes a fetish. (Kristeva in her article on Sollers' novel picks up the phrase *a contrario* and speaks of a 'signifying volume which is not turnable into a thing [volume signifiant non-chosifiable]' (285).)

Has the signifier, has the structure of language been turned into a bogus intellectual entity? The spectre of fetishism, having appeared at the disseminating banquet, is waved away in 'La dissémination' but not in *Glas*. The aggressive acronym in *Glas*, SA, stands for 'savoir absolu', absolute knowledge, Hegel's absolute knowledge, the point at which what is known and what is real are one (I can't go into the complexities of that 'stands for' here). But SA was commonly used at the time in the pair Sé/Sa, signified/signifier and must also refer to the signifier (certainly by *Glas*'s time become of contentious value in intellectual exchange). The account in *Glas* of fetishism, of how fictitious and stabilized values are created, is complex and difficult. But *La dissémination* contains signs of increasing engagement with the problems of fetishization and some of these signs read like unflagged disagreements with Kristeva. The article 'La double séance' warns against ontologizing Mallarmé whether towards mimesis or towards 'actuality, reality or even materiality' (*D*, 266; 235). And in the preface to the book there is a warning to the *Tel Quel* group that Kristeva's reliance on the value of materiality (which is what enables her to continue allegiance to materialism) is in fact a kind of idealism, in which matter, or history, or the real have become a transcendental signifier (*D*, 51; 43). Derrida repudiates 'production' (*supra*, p. 119). And it is striking that whereas Kristeva à propos of Sollers will speak of 'engendering' Derrida will speak of 'dissemination'.

The odd sense in which number theory speaks of 'generating' or 'engendering' numbers is picked up by the novel which plays a numbers game designed to appear machinelike. Derrida says that the 4 which Sollers places in the present tense is not the triad of Oedipus, the Trinity, nor of Hegelian dialectic (*D*, 392; 352) 'which have always governed metaphysic', but the opensided quatrilateral and he develops this numerology in the preface written for *La dissémination*. Whereas Sollers starts each section with the double number, it is by numbers as words that Derrida builds in the number four throughout his text – 'cadre' [frame], 'écart' [gap], 'carré' [square], 'carrément' [frankly], 'carrure' [build] are only a few. 'Carrefour' brings French and English together. He quotes Heidegger who 'crosses' out Being [Sein] and who speaks of the 'fourfold' [das Geviert] and the 'fouring' [die Vierung] where earth and sky, mortals and immortals are united. Heidegger's texts – and Derrida appears to use *Zur Seinsfrage* [*The Question of Being*], *Bauen Wohnen Denken* [*Building, Living, Thinking*], and *Das Ding* [*The Thing*], the latter in a composite quotation – are all concerned with subjectivity, and with the development of the relation of subject and object, and of an instrumental attitude to the world. And he relates this four to the Sollers diagram, with the blank middle box; the blank is what allows us to say 'is', to predicate. But the diagram, like Heidegger's four, frames the subject; it is what limits, what stops the infinite of the Kantian ideas, what folds us always into a place. Kristeva will take issue with this, one might almost say, will reverse it – the fourth surface is the surface where the formula is realized, 'It is in relation to the fourth surface – "you", phenomenon, formula – that the infinite germination can articulate itself' (363). *Nombres*, she says, is an

arrival at the edge of a new epoch which, crossing Christianity and refusing 'surreal' mystifications as well, foresees its own outside and firmly calculates its own formula. (363)

If she rejects the Saussurean sign in terms which recall Derrida's *De la grammatologie*, and the Hegelian 'pyramid', the 'triadic matrix' in a numerology which points forward to *La dissémination*'s preface, the Heideggerian four is refused as well. The crossing through is, she says, a 'crucified *ontos*', is merely the last defence of what is crossed through, it 'denies what *is* to relegate the infinite in the non-Being of a constant becoming of Being, and points to a transcendental space where a compact, homogeneous undifferentiated uncountable Being reigns' (364). So that, consonant with her use of structures derived from Saumjan's form of transformational grammar, she describes the genotext as not present in the sense of there, but still actualizable, and thus not disseminated, but still available as History (308). Kristeva's panlogism seems to rest on History, on matter, in a way impossible for Derrida.

It is in this light that Derrida's way of writing can be seen – a disenabling of any 'thingism of the signifier', a making impossible of the treatment of textuality as a system with precise causative power, as an absolute system, and I would add, making difficult any talk about deconstruction as if it were homogeneous. The terms he uses, very different one from another in tone, provenance, and shelf-life, cannot be knitted into a system where all the concepts are the same dimension.[33] Now Kristeva, too, has a plethora of theoretic entities: 'signifying differential', 'signifying complex', 'textual unit'. . . . But she works between 'genotext' and 'phenotext'; they are encased in a diagram (287), the plethora is not assumed and explored; it is an heuristic link between textual and political revolution.

The text shows indeed: '4.76. how it is now a question of a revolution operating no longer with substances or units [unities] but with whole continents and texts . . .' In this continent of a new reality which it [the text] opens, it necessarily summons the revolutionary practices of today. (370)

Derrida in *La Voix et le phénomène* had used a similar pathos to speak of a future. Here he does not. Instead there is an insistence on the extreme plurality of Sollers' novel: 'an ordered series of displacements, slips, transformations and recurrences' (*D*, 333; 300). The textual unit in Derrida is not simple nor stable: not the section, not the phrase, not the word, not the metaphor, but moving between these, making a web of multiple reference – approaching the technique he will use in *Limited Inc., a, b, c,* where John Searle's article, to which Derrida replies, comes close to being quoted in its entirety, but bit by bit and in jumbled order. And out of this web is spun that difficulty in Derrida's text which is at once the most intractable and the most revealing: the extent to which any commentary on his text is preempted by his text itself; a commentary resolutely 'on' gets sucked in and changes status.

In 'La dissémination', the margin of difference with Kristeva and Sollers is there but not made patent. In these texts – Kristeva's, Sollers' Derrida's – which talk about texts, there are words, topics, attitudes which transmit on the same frequency, but it is as if each writer moves between these frequencies in different orders and at different rates. The resulting texture of the three as of the one Derrida text, is very varied. The heterogeneity of Derrida's approach, the cuts and quotes, the arbitrary localizations in terms of what bit or whom he chooses to anchor his text to, all these shock or sit one up. Powerfully.

## Notes

1 Gerald L. Bruns, 'Structuralism, Deconstruction, and Hermeneutics', *Diacritics*, spring 1984, p. 15.
2 Derrida, *La dissémination*, Paris, Le Seuil, 1972; *Dissemination*, translated, with an Introduction and Additional Notes, by Barbara Johnson, London, The Athlone Press, 1981. References will henceforth be given in the text, to the French first, to the English second (e.g.: *D*, 111; 98).
3 Julia Kristeva, 'L'Engendrement de la formule', in *Semiotike: Recherches pour une sémanalyse*, Paris, Le Seuil, 1969. Philippe Sollers, *Nombres*, Paris, Le Seuil, 1968. References to these will hereafter be in the text, in my translation (e.g.: *N*, 58, section 2.42). I will also refer to Sollers, *Logiques*, Paris, Le Seuil, 1968, in my translation.

4 'Un Pas sur la lune', *Tel Quel*, 39, autumn 1969, pp. 3–12.

5 'Thus the conclusion is reached that every discourse is a *set* which allows the cutting out of a *subset*: this latter can be interpreted: a) as the latent content or the infrastructure of the set; b) as the antecedent of the set. This leads to the question whether, in turn each discourse, which has provisionally the status of a set cannot be regarded as the subset of a "totality" not yet recognized. Every texts surrounds and is surrounded. Every text is a product which is productive', Jean Starobinski, 'Le Texte dans le texte', *Tel Quel*, 37, 1969, p. 33.

6 Julia Kristeva, *La Révolution du langage poétique*, Paris, Le Seuil, 1974.

7 Or post-surrealist – Bataille, Artaud, with Lautréamont and Roussel as precursors.

8 It is striking that *La dissémination, Positions* (Paris, Minuit, 1972), and *Glas* (Paris, Galilée, 1974) seem to contain the only references to Marx in Derrida's work.

9 The concept of *polysemia* was developed by Jean Richard in his work on Mallarmé.

10 There are curious and deliberately private references using this acronymic form in a recent Derrida text, *Feu la cendre*, a text printed with its Italian translation by Stefano Agosti, Sansoni Editore, Florence, 1984.

11 Barbara Johnson in the introduction to her translation has pointed out that these are sometimes misquotations with a very precise point.

12 Margaret A. Rose, *Parody, Metafiction – An Analysis of Parody as a Critical Mirror to the Writing and Reception of Fiction* (London, Croom Helm, 1971), was first, to my knowledge, to see the importance of parody in Derrida and Foucault.

13 Sollers allowed it to be called 'roman', 'novel', on the endpapers. In *Logiques* he emphasizes the superiority of 'textual writing'. Writing, he says, can only be studied by the practice of writing, by which ultimately, and in spite of his championship of Bataille and Artaud, he means what used to be called 'creative' writing; a kind of rank-pulling that Derrida does not go in for.

14 Jean Ricardou, *Le nouveau Roman*, Paris, Le Seuil, 1973, p. 63.

15 For instance, Derrida, 'LIVING ON: Border lines', in *Deconstruction and Criticism*, London, Routledge & Kegan Paul, 1979, pp. 75–176.

16                     Fable

> Par le mot 'par' commence donc ce texte
> Dont la première ligne dit la vérité,
> Mais ce tain sous l'un et l'autre
> Peut-il être toléré?
> Cher lecteur, déjà tu juges
> Là de nos difficultés . . .
> (Après sept ans de malheur
> Elle brisa le miroir).

Francis Ponge, *Le Parti pris des choses*, Gallimard, Paris, 1967, p. 126, discussed by Derrida in a seminar given at the University of Geneva in 1978.

17  See for example the beginning of 'La Loi du Genre', *Glyphe*, 7, Johns Hopkins University Press, Baltimore, 1980, pp. 176-232.

18  Pascal, *Pensées*, ed. Lafuma, Le Seuil, Paris, 1962, p. 67.

19  This is the doxa of the death of the subject expressed vigorously, if crudely, by Kristeva elsewhere, in sketching her own location: 'After the destruction of the "subject" by marxism, and its structural reading [Althusser], after the freudian and post-freudian revelation of the complicity between representation, consciousness, knowledge [Lacan], after the Heideggerian showing of the rationalist limits of the logos, semiology seems to be constituting itself today as that place from which our culture thinks itself with the maximum of distance.' (Julia Kristeva, 'Distance et Anti-Représentation', *Tel Quel*, 36, winter 1968, p. 49.)

20  Manfred Frank, *Was ist Neostrukturalimus?* Suhrkamp, Frankfurt, 1983.

21  Jacques Lacan, *Le Séminaire livre* II, Paris, Le Seuil, 1978, p. 65.

22  Diderot in the article 'Fragonard' published in *Salon de 1765*, uses the Platonic cave as a kind of cinema of illusion – the prisoners are turned to the back wall and are watching a deluding show put on for them by kings and priests who are stationed behind them with a magic lantern.

23  The importance of art as a model for ideas about the subject echoes the use made of 'fiction' by Hume for instance in his *Treatise of Human Nature*; see Marian Hobson, *The Object of Art*, Cambridge University Press, Cambridge, 1982, p. 31.

24  Immanuel Kant's *'Critique of Pure Reason'*, translated by Norman Kemp Smith, 1929 [1970], p. 299; p. 327.

25  It had already been shown in *La Voix et le phénomène* à propos of Husserl that the relation to the self is always mediate, always a product of a spacing, a detour.

26  This is a difficult passage in the text; the work of C.M. Johnson, *Writing and System* (thesis in the University of Cambridge) elucidates it.

27  'Textual writing, excluded by definition from the "present" (whose function is to fail to recognize it) precisely constitutes the deferred history [or the story] – and the ideological stripping of this present' (*Logiques*, p. 14).

28  Heidegger had reworked Kantian intuition, moving it towards receptivity, in *Kant and the Problem of Metaphysics* (1929). Trans. J.S. Churchill, Bloomington, Indiana, 1962.

29  Jean Paul Sartre, *L'Idiot de la famille*, Paris, Gallimard, 3 vols. 1971-2; vol. 1, p. 59; cf. preface to *Stéphane Mallarmé: Poésies*, Gallimard, 1977 [1952].

30  'L'Homme au magnétophone', *Temps Modernes*, avril 1969, p. 1818.

31  'Parergon', in Derrida, *La Vérité en peinture*, Paris, Flammarion, 1978, pp. 19-168.

32  Manfred Frank, op. cit., points out these deliberate echoes.

33  Cf. Marian Hobson, 'History Traces', in *Post-Structuralism and the Question of History*, edited by Derek Attridge, Geoff Bennington, and Robert Young, Cambridge, Cambridge University Press, 1987, pp. 101-15.

# · 6 ·

# Sartre and the Language of Poetry

## CHRISTINA HOWELLS

Sartre: We must carry out an analytic cleansing operation which will free words of their contingent, accidental meanings. (*Sit. II*, p. 305)

Nothing is more harmful than the literary exercise called, I believe, poetic prose, which consists in using words for the obscure harmonics resounding around them, made of connotations in conflict with their clear meaning. (*Sit. II*, p. 305)

Mallarmé: To evoke, in a deliberate shadow, the object kept silent, by allusive words, never direct, reducing themselves to silence.[1]

Sartre: The writer's commitment aims to communicate the incommunicable (lived being-in-the-world) by using the *disinformation* obtained in everyday language – the materiality of language which seems to have an independent life. (*Sit. VIII*, p. 454)

What is this *nothing*, the silent unknowing which the literary object must communicate to the reader? (*Sit. VIII*, p. 437)


Between 1947 and 1972 Sartre's conception of the role of literature, the nature of commitment, the function of poetry, and the power of language changes radically. And it is, throughout, Mallarmé who provides him with the test-case, and the most radical example of how poetry works.

The views on literature expressed in *Situations, II* of 1947 constitute a kind of familiar, 'classical' Sartre; committed literature aims to change the world: 'I hold Flaubert and Goncourt responsible for the repression which followed the Commune because they didn't write a line to prevent it' (*Sit. II*, p. 13). Prose can be, and therefore, according to a circular polemical logic, must be committed. Poetry, like the fine arts, cannot and must not try to teach. Twenty years later Sartre's position is equally clear: poetry performs an ethical function (*Sit. IX*, p. 62). Flaubert and Mallarmé are committed writers (*Sit. IX*, 14). Sartre seems to have recanted; the apparent *volte-face* in fact reflects a refining of his aesthetic ideas which depends ultimately on an evolution in his conception of the nature of language.

In 1947 Sartre lumbered himself with a somewhat conventional distinction between prose and poetry, which he spent the rest of his life trying to attenuate. Prose is committed because it communicates ideas, and all ideas can be communicated. Poetry, on the other hand, uses words as objects rather than means, that is to say, as images. Prose works through the *signification* of words, poetry through the *sens*. No true synthesis is possible because as attitudes to language the two genres are mutually antagonistic.

Prose is related to perception, poetry to imagination. The poet invites us to imagine language; he effects 'a strange alteration in the role of the sign' (*I*, p. 40) whereby 'the physiognomy of the word comes to represent that of the object' (*I*, p. 91). But the word can't be sign and image simultaneously (*I*, p. 112), and it is the poet's *in*ability to use language to signify which leads him to make use of its materiality.

Since he doesn't know how to use the word as a sign of an aspect of the world, the poet sees in the word the *image* of one of these aspects. (*Sit. II*, p. 65)

The radical separation of perception and imagination, word as sign and word as image, has multifarious consequences. In the first place, it makes of poetic prose an uncomfortable hybrid, and by the same token prose is stripped of its suggestive qualities just as poetry is removed from the domain of communication and *a fortiori* commitment. Sartre is not suggesting that the two language uses do not affect and contaminate one another, but he does not accept a notion of gradual transition between prose and poetry. Two crucial footnotes indicate that it is possible to see the poet as committed in a different way; precisely because of his failure to communicate conceptually he stands outside the language, and therefore the ideology of a bourgeois society. This is an example of *qui perd gagne* – loser wins. In so far as the poet fails to communicate, he suggests incommunicability itself. Contemporary poetry – by which Sartre means post-Romantic, Baudelaire, and more particularly Mallarmé – is committed to failure. And the poet's individual failure bears witness to the failure of humanity in general. This line of thought is not developed in *What is Literature?*, but is a major concern in Sartre's work on Flaubert, *The Idiot of the Family*. Failure is envisaged as the one means of escape from totalization. Failure is radically inassimilable to the historical process.

Of course Sartre's recognition of the poet's 'failure' to communicate in no way implies a belief in the 'ineffable'. He rejects entirely the notion that thought precedes language and is distorted by its verbal expression. His own view is that the two realms are dialectically inter-dependent: thought comes into being through language; language clarifies and defines thought. He never went back on this position, but after 1947, he became increasingly aware of the fact of alienation as it affects self-expression. Already in *L'Etre et le néant*, Sartre acknowledged that language, as part of *l'être-pour-autrui*, is open to misunderstanding by others (*EN*, p. 441) but, he maintained, it nonetheless coincides, at its source, with thought. By 1960, in the *Critique de la raison dialectique*, the emphasis has shifted; Sartre is concerned to show how language too is part of the *practico-inert* whereby man's free activity, his *praxis*, becomes rigid and objectified, part of the external situation of both himself and other men. He no longer envisages the individual listener as the chief source of the alienation of the speaker; the very structures and semantics of language are now held responsible. Sartre has not rejected his earlier assertion of the interdependence of thought and language, but he now maintains that we are fundamentally incapable of thinking certain thoughts, which we might, in a sense, be groping towards, because language, as it is given to us, cannot provide adequate expression for them.[2] Our thought is not distorted *après coup*, by its verbal expression, it is vitiated from the outset by the limitations of the language in which it is attempting to realize itself.

*Orphée noir* (1948) and *Saint Genet* (1952) appear as early explorations of the alienating power of language. The language of the white man or the bourgeois alienates the thought of the negro or the thief. Genet's alienation is an extreme example of the basic loneliness and singularity of each individual human experience. Man's inner moods and feelings are fundamentally incommunicable; the only communication which can take place is conceptual, for the very universalizing power of language which permits communication destroys the individuality of the experience expressed. Language can convey 'le savoir' but not what Sartre later calls 'le non-savoir' or 'le vécu'.

In *Glas* (1974) Derrida seems wilfully to misrepresent Sartre's analysis of Genet, implying a reductivism and psychologism at odds with the text of *Saint Genet* itself. If Sartre talks of a *key* to Genet's writing it is precisely his *difference* from what was made of him. And rather than *translate* Genet's images, Sartre uses them to illustrate the inadequacy of any poetry susceptible of a prosaic translation. Genet revels in the alienating power of language, the impression of being spoken rather than speaking, the 'prestigious' power of certain words, overdetermined, one might say, in their connotations, or alternatively communicating *nothing*. One of Sartre's examples is Genet's 'moissonneur de souffles coupés' – reaper of mown breath (breath that has, literally, been *cut*). 'Allusive words, reducing to silence' as Mallarmé's ideal proclaims – capturing something, but only to destroy it; the line, Sartre argues, means nothing, or rather means Nothing.

It is perhaps in *Saint Genet* that Sartre's attitude to communication is most pessimistic; the rationalism of *L'Etre et le néant* has been whittled away, and the notion of another kind of communication through style, which comes to the fore in *L'Idiot de la famille*, has not yet been developed. But, paradoxically, this pessimistic awareness of language as *practico-inert* seems to have liberated Sartre's criticism. Having recognized the extent of language's power to alienate, he became increasingly sensitive to the ways in which the writer succeeds in overcoming this alienation. As a result, his conception of the nature of literary communication underwent a radical transformation.

In a series of interviews and lectures given in the main in 1965–6, which complement the views of the *Critique*, Sartre turns repeatedly to the theme of language as at once 'too poor' and 'too rich' (*Sit. VIII*, p. 434), too conceptual and rigid to express the real adequately, but also overlaid by secondary connotations which may interfere with the intended meaning. Communication is distorted in two very different ways. Sartre's eventual optimism is based on his realization that the second form of distortion can be used to compensate for the first. In fact these secondary connotations are not limited to a purely semantic level; they permeate language in all its dimensions. For example, what Sartre calls the *particularités* of any language, its specific morphological and syntactic structures (gender, word-order, etc.) do not, in everyday speech, draw attention to themselves, but they may at times hinder comprehension and so become, in Sartre's terms, *désinformatrices*. A deliberate instance of *désinformation* is Genet's attempt to disorientate the reader through gender: 'les brûlantes amours de la sentinelle et du mannequin' (*Sit. VIII*, p. 434): 'the burning loves of the soldier and the model'. '*La* sentinelle' is the soldier (i.e. male), '*le* mannequin' is the model (i.e. female): linguistic gender and sexual identity are at odds. The *particularités* of a language are then, so far as ordinary communication is concerned, either 'superfluous' or 'harmful' (*Sit. VIII*, p. 434). They are not merely *non*-significant, but can run counter to the meaning they express. But it is precisely these elements, language as *disinformation*, or in more general terms the *practico-inert* of language, which the writer can turn to his own ends. Sartre's preoccupation is still with literature as commitment and communication, but the nature of this communication has changed radically: 'The writer's commitment aims to communicate the incommunicable (lived being-in-the-world) by using the disinformation contained in everyday language' (*Sit. VIII*, p. 454).

In 1965 Sartre defined the 'contemporary writer' as 'the *poet* who claims to be writing *prose*' (*Sit. VIII*, p. 432). In other words, the communication of contemporary prose is no longer envisaged as primarily conceptual but as indirect and allusive, as was previously the case with poetry alone. Sartre, I believe, absorbed from the *Tel Quel* group certain linguistic and aesthetic insights which encouraged him to modify his early prose/poetry distinction in favour of something more subtle which corresponded better to his own increased awareness of the 'function' of style – for example, he evolved to the point where he found Barthes's *écrivain/écrivant* distinction useful in illustrating his own conception of language as disinformation. But if Sartre adapts Barthes, it is in order to go beyond him. The key to Sartre's disagreement with *La Nouvelle Critique* lies in his view of the dialectical interdependence of *signification* and *sens* (conceptual meaning and 'sense' or 'connotation'). This view is not fully developed until *The Idiot of the Family*, but already in 1965 Sartre insists 'Without *meaning* there can be no ambiguity, the object can't come and inhabit the word' (*Sit. VIII*, p. 449) and 'Language . . . does *mean* something; and that's what has been forgotten.'[3] Sartre comes to see the literary writer as a paradoxical figure who uses the *signification* of words as a means to the evocation of their *sens*. In a real sense, then, *signification* is still primary, but even the prose artist is aiming to communicate something else. If Sartre continues to stress that 'the prose-writer has *something* to say' (*Sit. VIII*, p. 437), nevertheless the nature of that *something* appears to have undergone a radical transformation since *What is Literature?*

This something is *nothing sayable*, nothing conceptual or conceptualisable, nothing which signifies . . . Hence the phrase 'that's just literature' which means 'you're speaking to say nothing'. We must now ask ourselves what is this *nothing*, this silent unknowing that the literary object must communicate to the reader. (*Sit. VIII*, p. 437)

Sartre's nothing (*rien*) has, of course, like his nothingness (*néant*), hidden depths. His terminology in fact owes something to the vocabulary of negative theology: 'It's true that the writer has fundamentally *nothing* to say. We should understand by that that his fundamental aim is not to communicate knowledge (*un savoir*). However he does communicate . . . If the writer has *nothing* to say, it is because he must bear witness to *everything*, that is to say the singular and practical relationship between the part and the whole which constitutes being-in-the-world' (*Sit. VIII*, pp. 444–5). The writer creates through style a *singular universal* which expresses the individual's being-in-the-world, the subjective and objective dimensions of the real. This *nothing*, which is a non-conceptual totalization, dependent ultimately on the imagination, is what Sartre means by *le non-savoir* (unknowing). The task of Sartre's writer (*écrivain*) is thus defined in the 1960s and 1970s in terms almost identical with those of Jean Ricardou: 'The writer doesn't write something . . . he writes, that's all. Perhaps it's in this way that we should understand Maurice Blanchot when he suggests that the writer should feel, at the deepest level, that he has nothing *to say*.'[4]

Sartre's notion that the *vécu* (lived experience) can only be communicated through the *sens* of words not only altered his definition of the prose-writer, it encouraged him to extend the potential commitment of the poet. In 1965 he formulated his opposition between prose and poetry in terms which were more psychological than linguistic, in terms of the writer–reader relationship. He described the communication of poetry as less direct than that of prose; it reveals the author to himself, and by imaginative extension the reader to herself, but this too, in Sartre's view, involves communication through narcissism: in other words, it provides a bridge between two solitudes; the reader must identify imaginatively with the writer in order to comprehend the *sens* of the poem. Furthermore, Sartre seems prepared to recognize poetry as an essential element of *praxis*, in so far as it is complementary to prose; in the continuous process of internalization and externalization, poetry represents 'the moment of interiority . . . a stasis' (*Sit. IX*, p. 62). Such a moment of reflection has, moreover, an ethical function in so far as it involves a form of non-conceptual self-knowledge 'revealing of man to himself through *le sens*' (*Sit. IX*, p. 64). Poetry, then, like all art, is a form of *dévoilement* (revelation, disclosure), and is committed in so far as it changes the nature of our relations to the world and ourselves: 'To reveal is to change' (*Sit. II*, p. 73).

In the interview with Verstraeten, Sartre's discussion of the way language communicates is confined in the main to a psycho-linguistic level. But a psychoanalytic (and indeed a historical) dimension is also present. Sartre's understanding of the relationship of *le vécu* to *le sens* seems to have been clarified by Lacan's notion that 'the unconscious is language'.

> For me, Lacan has clarified the unconscious as a discourse which separates through language, or, if you prefer, as a counter-finality of speech: verbal formations (*ensembles*) are structured as a *practico-inert* formation through the act of speaking. These formations express or constitute intentions which determine me without being mine. (*Sit. IX*, p. 97)

Sartre is intrigued by Lacan's notion of the *inarticulable*. Desire, for Lacan, is *inarticulable*, since although I may state my desire of an object, I cannot state the unconscious forces, psychoanalytic and/or historical, which cause me to desire this and not that particular form of satisfaction. The *inarticulable* quality of desire is referred by Lacan to the unconscious. Sartre of course prefers his own notion of *le vécu* to the unconscious, and he is, by the same token, committed to the view that even the *inarticulable* is potentially communicable – communicable precisely through *le sens*, through that aspect of language which escapes our intentions in so far as it is overdetermined historically and psychoanalytically.

And it is the struggle with the inarticulable quality of desire which Sartre sees as making great artists out of his favourite writers and poets. Flaubert and Genet, Baudelaire and Mallarmé, all entertain uncomfortable relations with the symbolic order, mediated as always through the structures of family relations. Flaubert's non-valorization by an unloving mother, Genet's hostile foster-parents,

Baudelaire's mother's remarriage, and Mallarmé's mother's death conspire to produce a constellation of ill-adapted, alienated, and unhappy children unable to accept social or linguistic integration. The results are not identical: Flaubert develops a myth of the ineffable; Genet turns his feeling of exclusion from the symbolic order back against the social order: Baudelaire treads an uneasy course between rhetoric and terror, language as transparent or opaque; and Mallarmé espouses sterility. Resentment, *ennui*, and impotence are revalued in an aesthetics of scarcity and a quietist negativism. Enforced solitude is interpreted as a sign of distinction; an inability to communicate is translated as a form of spiritual elitism. In short, the *failure* of functional, instructive, easy communion, is transformed by these mystified and dissatisfied aesthetes into a nihilistic and mystifying cult of non-communication (*Sit. IX*, p. 199).

Sartre, of course, denies that it is either 'sufficient' or 'necessary'[5] to undergo family failure in order to become a post-Romantic poet. But the totality of his analyses does indicate the primacy of some kind of alienation or failure (we may think also, amongst others, of his discussion of Césaire and the Black African poets). How then is linguistic alienation transformed into poetic success? Briefly speaking, it is through the materiality of language, or what Sartre in the *Idiot* prefers to call the 'graphic configuration' of the word. The phrase is somewhat loosely used, as it refers not merely to the peculiar pictorial quality which the grapheme may have but to the 'fonction imageante' (imaging function) of words in general. In this sense it is broadly equatable with the *sens* or connotations of language. To use the terms of *L'Imaginaire*, the literary writer is one who uses the word as an analogon or image of the thing expressed. Commenting on a line from Mallarmé's *Brise Marine*, Sartre writes:

Si vous lisez: 'perdus, sans mâts, sans mâts . . .' If you read: 'lost, without masts, without masts' the poetic organization animates the word: like a cross, the *t* stands above the other letters like the mast above the ship; around it the letters are clustered – that's the hull, that's the deck: some readers, and I'm one, sense in that white letter, the vowel *a*, crushed under the circumflex accent as under a low, cloudy sky, the sail which is sagging. The negation expressed by *without* acts mainly in the universe of meaning – the boat has lost its mast, that's what we *learn*. But in the obscure world of *sense* (*sens*), the negation cannot destructure the word mast. Let's say it causes it to pale to the point of becoming the *analogon* of some kind of photographic negative. (*IF*, vol. 1, p. 929–30)

This is a good example of the *sens* working against or despite the *signi-fication*. We imagine the mast which is signified as absent. In no sense can the word *mât* be said to have, in reality, the form of a ship's mast, and, moreover, Sartre thinks our ability to imagine that this is the case depends on our knowledge that *mât* signifies a 'mast'. But the writer's art consists in making the reader adopt an 'imaging attitude' towards the word he or she is reading: 'In fact the word mast has no real or objective resemblance to the object it designates. But the art of writing consists precisely in forcing the reader . . . to find one, to make the object come down into the sign as an unreal presence' (*IF*, vol. 1, p. 930). In case our attention in the Mallarmé example should focus too exclusively on the visual aspect, Sartre reminds us that

> *Any* word, regardless of its conventional character, can have an 'imaging' function . . . in fact it's not a matter of chance resemblances between the sig-nifying material and the object signified, but rather of the felicities of a style which forces the reader to grasp the materiality of the word as an organic unity, and that unity as the very presence of the object referred to'. (*IF*, vol. 1, p. 930)

In other instances individual words may themselves evoke a succes-sion of images independent of their context. In this case, 'the graph-eme, by its physical configuration, and before any stylistic treatment, evokes resonances' (*IF*, vol. 1, p. 931). 'Le Château d'Amboise', for example, may suggest *framboise, boisé, boiserie, Ambroisie, Ambroise* (*IF*, vol. 1, p. 932). These connotations are objective in the sense that they can, potentially, be apprehended by all readers. Sartre's example in *What is Literature?* of 'Florence, femme et fleur' (*IF*, vol. 1, p. 934) belongs to this category of objective connotations. But, as in the case of *Florence*, there is always the possibility that words may have sub-jective connotations which may be of one kind for the writer and another for the reader. Of these personal connotations Sartre writes: 'They constitute, for each of us, the singular and incommunicable ground of every experience of language' (*IF*, vol. 1, p. 932). If the writer encourages these personal resonances he will create a kind of obscure 'semi-communication' (*IF*, vol. 1, p. 932) which Sartre thinks is more appropriate to the comparative narcissism of poetry than to prose. The prose writer controls and limits the personal con-notations which the poet, on the other hand, may allow to proliferate, both in his own imagination and in that of the reader. The 'incommunicability' Sartre refers to is, of course, not absolute. In the first instance, the subjective connotations of a word may be communicated indirectly through the objective connotations of other words used in conjunction with it, and secondly, the 'semi-communication' of poetry is itself accepted by the later Sartre as an indispensable means of contact between two narcissisms.

The use of the connotations or the *sens* of words (whether subjective or objective) is for Sartre a language usage which implies a preference for the imaginary and purely verbal: 'To choose the sumptuousness of names is already to prefer the universe of words to that of things' (*IF*, vol. 1, p. 934). Broadly speaking, Sartre equates awareness of the word as a *sign* (by which he means the word used to point beyond itself to a *meaning*) with the perceptual attitude, and awareness of its materiality or *sens* with the imaginative attitude (*IF*, vol. 1, p. 929). Sartre's distinction depends on a dialectic which is established first in *L'Imaginaire* and which remains the fundamental insight behind all his aesthetics: perception and imagination are radically distinct yet totally interdependent (*I*, pp. 156–8; pp. 235–56). This means that although the two aspects of words are *used* simultaneously by the writer they cannot be present simultaneously in the *reader's* mind which passes rapidly from one to the other.

Sartre, then, continues to insist on the primary role played by conceptual meaning: 'It is necessary, to make present an imaginary Calcutta clothed in all the charms of its name, to have at least a rudimentary knowledge: it's a town in India, its inhabitants are Indian' (*IF*, vol. 1, p. 934). This is the basis of Sartre's attack on what he considers the exclusive emphasis of the 'critique du signifiant'. Nonetheless, it is clear that in Flaubert's case, as in the case of Mallarmé, *signification* remains merely a means to an end which is 'the unsayable "sense" ' ('le sens indisable'). 'Form is a language which one might call parasitic since it is constituted at the expense of real language and does not cease to exploit it, by forcing it to express what it is not equipped to say to us' (*IF*, vol. 2, p. 1617). Communication of the unsayable (*indisable*) depends ultimately, then, on the imagination: 'The non-significant materiality of language can only furnish meanings (*des sens*) in the imaginary realm' (*IF*, vol. 2, p. 1616). And as Sartre made clear in *L'Imaginaire*, in imagining we become ourselves imaginary:

Certainly Flaubert transmits nothing to the realist reader except the fascinating proposition of becoming unreal in his turn. If the reader gives in to the temptation, if he becomes the *imaginary* reader of the work – he must, to grasp the *sense* behind the *meanings* (*pour saisir le sens derrière les significations*) – then all the unsayable, including the flavour of the plum-pudding, will be revealed to him allusively. (*IF*, vol. 2, p. 2003)

A further set of ideas would need to be developed before we could understand how, in Sartre's view, Flaubert is 'politically' committed in the sense of effecting change.[6] Briefly, this involves the idea of a misunderstanding between Flaubert and his contemporary reader who mistakes *Madame Bovary* for a work of realism, and is therefore tempted to give herself up imaginatively to the experience of the novel, exposing herself unwittingly to the corrosion of Flaubert's ironical nihilism. Flaubert's use of the imagination is a trap for the bourgeois public. His art is revelation (*dévoilement*) in the sense of demoralization: 'The aim of the literary enterprise is to reduce the reader to despair' (*IF*, vol. 3, p. 321). It is by the same token commitment, since, of course, 'human life begins on the other side of despair'.[7]

In conclusion then we might focus on the shift which took place in Sartre's conception of prose and poetry between 1947 and 1972. In *What is Literature?*, literature was scandal and heresy, but in a fairly narrow political sense. By 1972 it had become clear that all Sartre's literary 'heroes' – Mallarmé, Flaubert, and Genet in particular – were, like Sartre himself perhaps, hostile to their reading public. Mallarmé eschews communication, writing a form of poetic conundrum – or what Sartre calls an *objet truqué* (*Sit. IX*, p. 198) which always reduces to zero in the end – whether an absent rose, an invisible waterlily, or an abolished trinket; Flaubert creates a *simulacrum* of the real but his writing is a lure towards the terror of non-being and a radical form of nihilism; Genet buggers his readers by using apparently conventional poetic devices as a thin mask for a celebration of evil and inversion, and by playing on the gap between (linguistic) gender and sexual identity in a fashion which is literally untranslatable. All these writers use literature as an act of aggression against their readers. Non-communication is not simply a cosy language-game set out for initiates to decipher. Flaubert, Mallarmé, and Genet all bear witness to the end of the Book, to use Derrida's phrase: Flaubert's last text (*Bouvard et Pécuchet*) ends – or rather does not end – with the sight of copyists returning to their repetition of the already written; Mallarmé's Book to end all books was a constantly deferred failure; Genet (like Rimbaud and Sartre himself) simply abandoned writing.

As Sartre says of Flaubert (*IF*, vol. 2, p. 1999, and also of

Mallarmé, *Sit. IX*, p. 201), his *epoche* was so radical that it bracketed off both the world and language with it. Mallarmé's shipwreck aimed to disqualify the real entirely (*Sit. IX*, p. 2000; *IF*, vol. 3, p. 197), his refusal of communication was as thoroughgoing as Genet's nearly a century later, though it took the form of an abstention or a strike rather than a *war* - Genet's victory depends on the reader's failure.

Sartre's poets and writers give the lie to any view of him as a conventional humanist or a proponent of commitment in the narrow sense. Perhaps he too is setting a trap for the unwary reader. It would take another paper to show the way in which Sartre subverts and parodies his own literary and philosophical practice - this would include Roquentin's refusal of humanism, the parodic nature of Sartre's drama, the pastiche of Kant and Hegel in *Saint Genet*, the *Idiot of the Family* as a *roman vrai* (true novel), and what Sartre refers to as the 'self-contestation' of his autobiography, *The Words*. In all these cases, it is far less clear what is asserted and what is subverted than many of Sartre's critics would care to recognize. Sartre's fascination with the kind of poetic nihilism that ostensibly repudiates commitment might make us reconsider the comforting and facile (Derridean amongst others) dismissal of him as a fetishist of communication and the *ontophénoménologue de la libération*.

The Sartre of the 1930s and 1970s, in particular, poses a considerable threat to those for whom parricide is a constant temptation.

## Abbreviations

EN      *L'Etre et le néant*, Paris, Gallimard, 1943;
        *Being and Nothingness*, translated by Hazel E. Barnes, London, Methuen, 1957.

I       *L'Imaginaire: psychologie phénoménologique de l'imagination*, Paris, Gallimard, 1940;
        *The Psychology of Imagination*, translated by Bernard Frechtman, London, Methuen, 1972.

IF      *L'Idiot de la famille*, Paris, Gallimard, vols 1 and 2, 1971; vol. 3, 1972.

Sit. II    *Situations II*, Paris, Gallimard, 1947;
        *What is Literature?* translated by Bernard Frechtman, London, Methuen, 1950.

Sit. VIII  *Situations VIII*, Paris, Gallimard, 1972.

*Sit. IX*    *Situations IX*, Paris, Gallimard, 1972.
*Sit. X*     *Situations X*, Paris, Gallimard, 1976.

References throughout are to the French editions; all translations are my own.

## Notes

A version of this paper first appeared in *The Modern Language Review*, July 1979, vol. 74, no. 3.

1 S. Mallarmé, 'Magie' in *Oeuvres complètes*, Paris, Pléiade, Gallimard, 1951, p. 400.
2 Jean-Paul Sartre, *Critique de la raison dialectique*, Paris, Gallimard, 1960, p. 75; Preface translated as *The Problem of Method*, by Hazel E. Barnes, London, Methuen, 1964.
3 'Jean-Paul Sartre' in *Que peut la littérature?*, edited by Yves Buin, Paris, 1965, 10/18, pp. 117-18.
4 ibid., p. 94.
5 'L'engagement de Mallarmé' in *Obliques*, no. 18-19, n.d. dirige par M. Sicard, p. 190.
6 See *Sit. IX*, p. 14 and *Sit. X*, p. 112.
7 *Les Mouches*, Paris, Gallimard, 1947, Act III, Scene 2.

## · 7 ·

# On Science, Poetry, and 'the honey of being': Bachelard's Shelley

## MARY McALLESTER JONES

Gaston Bachelard died in October 1962, having retired in 1954 from the chair in the history and philosophy of science at the Sorbonne; in 1984, the centenary of his birth was celebrated not only by symposiums and conferences in France and in this country, but by an issue of postage stamps in France, which bore his portrait. An unusual accolade, surely, for a philosopher! And the response to the recent publication of *Fragments d'une poétique du feu*, the book left unfinished when he died, has shown the affection in which he is still held there, and the continuing admiration for his ability to combine in his work the separate domains of science and poetry. He has still, then, some hold on the popular imagination as 'the Dr Jeckyll of epistemology' and 'the Mr Hyde of poetry', in the phrase of one journalist. Bachelard's books continue to be widely read in France; his work on the philosophy of science is regarded as seminal, and it is an established part of the philosophy syllabus at school and university. He himself escaped the traditional forcing-ground of young French philosophers, coming to philosophy relatively late at the age of 36, as a physics and chemistry teacher. Ten years later, in 1930, he was appointed to the chair of philosophy at Dijon University, and it was here that, alongside his work on science, he began to write about poetry. In 1940, he took up his chair at the Sorbonne, and it must be remembered that his books on poetry were the work of France's leading philosopher of science. These books were not simply a way of relaxing: they too have been influential, transforming literary criticism in France, in Roland Barthes's opinion, and according to Gilbert Durand, obliging the rationalist French to take imagination seriously.[1]

How does Bachelard come to write about poetry? His interest turns from science to poetry quite unexpectedly in 1938, in the course of writing *La Psychanalyse du feu*. It is in this text that Bachelard presents for the first time his 'law of the four poetic elements', the theory of poetry that will direct his work for the next decade.[2] The dreams of all of us, the images of every poet are, he declares, determined by an affinity with earth or air, fire or water; this affinity is unconscious, it expresses values which persist in spite of the evidence of reason and experience, and it constitutes poetic truth. This notion of poetic truth is new in Bachelard's thinking, it is seminal with respect to his own work on poetic imagination, and also, as we have seen, to literary criticism in France. It does, however, pose a problem. It is not simply a question of a reversal of values, of a changing conception of human beings, formerly viewed as rational in their essence and now discovered to be, on the contrary, profoundly irrational. Such a reversal, however disconcerting, we should have to accept. Yet what occurs in *La Psychanalyse du feu* is more problematical. It is not a question of *either, or* – man is *either* rational *or* irrational – but rather of *both, and* – man is *both* rational *and* irrational. Scientific truth and poetic truth coexist.

It is scientific truth that is Bachelard's value as he begins *La Psychanalyse du feu*, his aim being 'to psychoanalyse fire', to show that fire, with all the immediate and subjective values it accumulates, is an obstacle to scientific knowledge which must be eliminated. And Bachelard never gainsays this value of objective knowledge. Indeed, he goes so far as to declare, early in the book, that 'when we turn towards ourselves, we turn away from truth' (p. 14). This statement stands, though it is in flat contradiction to the theory of poetry put forward in later chapters. The truth is and is not in us. Not *either, or*, we note, but *both, and*. This apparent illogicality, this self-contradiction in the argument of *La Psychanalyse du feu*, concentrates or exaggerates the problem of the relationship between the two aspects of Bachelard's work, on science and on poetry, and the conflicting values – rationality and irrationality – implicit in each. How are we to view his work? As a unity or as diversity, constituted by two irremediably separate parts, which have absolutely nothing to do with each other? The problem is obvious, of course, and one to which most of

Bachelard's critics have addressed themselves, some briefly, some at greater length, most choosing to regard the two aspects of his work as irreconcilably diverse. Surely this is a little too facile, too lazy? After all, Bachelard refers to poetry in his books on science and to science in his books on poetry, and more important, after 1938 he publishes books and articles on science and poetry at the same time; for example, the first chapter of *Le Rationalisme appliqué* (1949) came out as an article in 1947, when he was also preparing the two books on *La Terre* (1948). Bachelard's preoccupations are clearly concurrent, and we must not separate them.

I would like therefore to explore here the relationship between Bachelard's work on science and on poetry, and to show in particular how his work on poetry can be seen to grow out of his work on science. What unites these two aspects is his conception of the human being, and more specifically, his conception of consciousness. His books on poetry are, as a result, less concerned with practical criticism than with 'a complete theory of human imagination' (*L'Eau et les rêves*, p. 4), with 'imagination as a major force in human nature' (*La Poétique de l'espace*, p. 16), essential to 'the reality of the human being' (*Fragments d'une poétique du feu*, p. 46). Despite the many images to which he refers, Bachelard seldom examines the images of one poem or of one poet, preferring to move from image to image, from one poem – or poet – to another, and so develop his theory. I shall come back to this fragmentary character of Bachelard's practice of poetry. One of the few poets that he does linger over is Shelley, in *L'Air et les songes*, and his approach to Shelley will help us to understand how Bachelard the philosopher reads poetry, and the relationship between what he calls the reader's 'consciousness of language' (*La Terre et les rêveries de la volonté*, p. 7) and the conception of consciousness that develops early in his work and whose ground is his work on modern science.

How does Bachelard himself see the relationship between the two aspects of his work? One of the clearest and most striking formulations of his position is found in 1951, in *L'Activité rationaliste de la physique contemporaine*, where, speaking of mathematics and physics, Bachelard says this: 'As we have so often remarked in our books on the imagination, the world is conditioned by man's provocation. The world of the electron is in fact the result of provocation by reason' (p. 101). Both scientist and poet are, for Bachelard, *against* the world; both reason and imagination are engaged in a polemic with reality.

This, in his view, is the common characteristic of both science and poetry, this polemical relationship between mind and matter. Furthermore, the two aspects of his work are united by what he calls in *La Poétique de la rêverie* 'our more general philosophical thesis' (p. 5), his conception of consciousness as poetic in the etymological sense of the word, as he makes plain later in the book (p. 131), consciousness as *making*, as creating, extending, opening both the thinker and the dreamer. Bringing these two ideas together, we see that for Bachelard himself, both science and poetry are polemical and poetic. And this notion of polemics and poetics will, I believe, help us to grasp his conception of the human being and, more particularly, of the imagining consciousness.

How do these ideas of polemics and poetics, of reason, imagination, and consciousness develop? How is it that Bachelard's epistemology comes to shape his theory of poetic imagination and his approach to reading? Between 1927 and 1938 – and before his first book on poetry – he set out to develop a philosophy that can take account of the new relationship between mind and reality in twentieth-century science. Many, of course, were aware of the problem. Sir James Jeans, for instance, put it very simply like this:

an understanding of the ultimate processes of nature is forever beyond our reach; we shall never be able – even in imagination – to open the case of our watch and see how the wheels go round. The true object of scientific study can never be the realities of nature, but only our own observations of nature.[3]

Can we know only our own minds? Does the new physics mark the restoration not just of rationalism but of idealism? Bachelard rejects such a view. Rationalism and idealism, attractive though they seem, are not in his opinion philosophies adequate to modern science, because both are essentially self-sufficient, complete, closed to any development, and therefore the very antithesis of twentieth-century scientific thought, incomplete, open, endlessly progressing. Epistemology must face the facts of science, and the dominant fact for Bachelard is the progress of scientific knowledge, its 'fundamental incompleteness' (*Essai sur la connaissance approchée*, p. 13). Thus, in his thesis, Bachelard explains the creative, dynamic character of knowledge as the result of an encounter between the mind and an inexhaustible reality, which by definition resists knowledge. Between mind and reality there is not just a dialectic but a polemic, mind versus reality. In science, the most abstract of theories is always an attempt to solve a problem posed by reality, and every solution gives rise to another problem. It does indeed seem that reality is hostile to man's mind. This idea of a polemic between mind and reality underlies Bachelard's epistemology, the theory of 'approximate knowledge' first developed in 1927 in his doctoral thesis, his *Essai sur la connaissance approchée*, published in 1928.

Bachelard's epistemological model here is mathematical approximation methods, which are used to study irrationals, entities like $\pi$, for example, that cannot be reduced to whole or fractional numbers; they cannot be known exactly, and we can only approximate to their value. Approximation proceeds by relating unknown to known, irrational to rational; since the irrational is by definition finally unknowable, approximation is never complete, always open; since it is the irrational that governs every mental inflexion seeking to grasp it, we must conclude that thought is indeed ruled by an external reality. This last point must be stressed. The existence of irrationals proves that there is a reality independent of our minds; approximation demonstrates that rational processes are not wholly contingent, that they do relate to a reality outside themselves. Bachelard suggests in his thesis that there has been a counter-Copernican revolution in twentieth-century physics, that scientific thought always refers to a reality that both transcends and rules it. Approximate knowledge, that is to say 'the fundamental incompleteness' of modern scientific knowledge, is not therefore a sign of failure but an assurance of objectivity. Approximate knowledge shows too that there is no easy-going relationship between mind and reality: reality, like the mathematical irrational, resists the mind and is hostile to the mind. For Bachelard, the mind must always be *against* reality, and this polemic is indeed the sole guarantee of the objectivity of knowledge.

What we have here is surely a new conception of rationality, in which Bachelard is in effect taking us beyond rationalism, beyond sovereign reason. And from this notion of the polemical relationship between reason and reality in modern science stems his conception of the human being and of consciousness, of the imagining consciousness in particular. What is so special about this idea of polemics? First, it overcomes the problem of *either* rationalism *or* realism: reason and reality are now interdependent; mathematics, for example, exploring the possibilities of reality, and in its turn, this newly discovered reality exploring the possibilities of mathematics. And

Bachelard will give increasing importance to this last point, to the effect of knowledge on the knowing subject. This suggests the second reason why Bachelard's notion of polemics is of value, for it leads him to formulate a new view of the wholeness of human beings and of their experience: reason and reality are interdependent, imbricated, and therefore interiority and exteriority are in essence conjoined. It is this, I believe, that makes Bachelard's thought non-Bergsonian, non-Cartesian, non-Freudian, non-Husserlian, and – taking a jump and trailing my coat (very dangerous!) – non-structuralist, 'non' implying here, of course, not 'anti' but as in non-Euclidean geometry, 'beyond', 'an extension of', 'an opening of'.

Why is Bachelard's thought non-Bergsonian? In his thesis, his rejection of Bergson's epistemology is clear, and this remains a constant theme throughout his work, still present in his last book on science, *Le Matérialisme rationnel*, in 1953. For Bachelard, twentieth-century science, and microphysics especially, makes it impossible to accept Bergson's view that the aim of science is 'usefulness and practicality', that the scientist is simply 'homo faber', the tool maker who seeks to act on and control the world for practical ends. Science is on the contrary, in Bachelard's view, speculative and not utilitarian, the scientist being, as he puts it in *Le Nouvel esprit scientifique* (1934), 'homo mathematicus', 'homo aleator', exploring the possibilities of reality through mathematics, through reason (p. 55; p. 115). Reality is not something 'out there', external and separate from him and from his reason. In modern science, Bachelard declares in *Le Matérialisme rationnel*, there is no longer what he calls a 'réalisme de constatation' but a 'réalisme de construction' (p. 140): reality is not observed and recorded, but rather constructed by reason, and consequently our whole idea of the relationship between exteriority and interiority must be reconsidered. It should be emphasized here that for Bachelard this relationship is, of course, not one way but polemical, that reality in its turn constructs reason, that interiority is a function of exteriority. A major theme in all Bachelard's books on science is the effect of knowledge on the knower. Thus, science brings about 'an evolution of the mind', 'a profound human mutation'; science turns us into 'a mutating species . . . a species that needs to mutate', and we are therefore defined as being 'destined to know'.[4] These phrases are surely reminiscent of Bergson's 'creative evolution', and I think that this is where we see that Bachelard's thought is not simply anti-Bergsonian but non-Bergsonian. He takes us beyond Bergson, accepting that there is such a thing as creative evolution, yet making its motive power not the *élan vital*, the life force, but scientific thought.

For Bachelard, science has, quite clearly, an ontological dimension: what I know determines what I am, how I know determines how I am. Given the new reciprocal, polemical relationship in modern science between reason and reality, interiority and exteriority, Bachelard finds it impossible to accept Bergson's view of man as divided into two separate zones, 'moi supérieur' and 'moi profond', the world of thought and the world of the consciousness, of rational and irrational. Again, however, he does not in fact reject Bergson: he is not anti-Bergsonian but non-Bergsonian. He accepts the notion of consciousness, of the conscious subject, and that consciousness is temporal. However, in *L'Intuition de l'instant*, he takes us beyond Bergson, making consciousness and time a function of thought about reality.[5] Consciousness, Bachelard argues here, is consciousness not of duration but of the instant (p. 49), and this instant is constituted by what he terms 'nascent knowledge', by, moreover, 'consciousness of the irrational' (p. 6). This last phrase takes us back to Bachelard's conception of approximate knowledge, to his idea of reality as a mathematical irrational. For Bachelard, each instant of consciousness corresponds to a step in approximation to that irrational, and consciousness is constituted by our striving to understand and grasp a hostile, resistant reality. Consciousness and time are not, as they were for Bergson, self-sufficient, but they are in the world, *against* the world. Without the world, there is no consciousness.

Bachelard, critical though he is of Bergson, does not reject him out of hand. He takes us beyond him, out of the impasse of the isolated, individual consciousness, whose duration seems to me, whatever Bergson may say about its dynamic, organic progress, inevitably static, 'empâté de soi-même' like Sartre's 'being-in-itself', stuck forever in its own self-sufficiency.[6] Consciousness for Bachelard is consciousness of something outside itself. He propels us, then, towards Husserl, by way of Descartes, beyond Descartes in fact, and eventually beyond Husserl.

Descartes looms large in Bachelard's next major work, *Le Nouvel esprit scientifique*, published in 1934.[7] Here his explicit aim is to establish what he calls a non-Cartesian epistemology, since modern science invalidates, in his view, not only Descartes's idea of simple natures but also Descartes's method, based on enumeration and analysis. In addition, Bachelard proposes what we may call a non-Cartesian cogito. He rejects the Cartesian cogito with its solitary, unchanging self. Consciousness is not just consciousness of thinking, nor is it just consciousness of thinking about something. Consciousness for Bachelard is against a complex, hostile reality, and against its own past, too, its rational past: ideas must be endlessly rectified, for what was thought to be true is shown to be false or incomplete, imprecise. Ideas change and so, he argues, the structure of the mind must change. How can I go on saying 'I think therefore I am'? I ought instead to say 'I think therefore I evolve', 'I think against a complex reality, therefore I evolve as a complex being.' The scientist, in Bachelard's view, is made and continually remade by his thought.

This interest in what we may call the rational consciousness persists in Bachelard's work, culminating in the critique of Husserl and phenomenology that we find in his last series of books on science, published between 1949 and 1953.[8] Bachelard is attracted towards phenomenology because, with its notion of intentionality, implying the interdependence of subject and object, reason and reality, it is potentially more in keeping with his own epistemology than other theories, than rationalism or empiricism, for example. Yet he is critical of the idea of intentionality, believing it to oversimplify the relationship between mind and reality, making it too tranquil, too easy. Consciousness for Bachelard, is always *against* something, and the structure of the rational consciousness is not therefore intentional but polemical. Non-Husserlian in its last stage, non-Bergsonian and non-Cartesian earlier on, Bachelard's thinking about modern science shows his concern not just to 'open' philosophy by making plain the dialectical, polemical relationship that now obtains between reason and reality, but perhaps more important, his concern is to 'open' psychology, breaching the dykes, as it were, and letting subject and object, interiority and exteriority out of their separate confines into a new relationship, a relationship which is both polemical and poetic: reason against reality, reality against reason, reason making reality, reality making reason, and neither having existence without the other.

Let us now reconsider the relationship between Bachelard's work on science and on poetry. Given what we have discovered about his conception of rationality and of the rational consciousness, we ought surely to amend the notion that in the two aspects of his work we find conflicting, even contradictory values, rationality versus irrationality. We have seen that Bachelard wished to go beyond rationalism pure and simple, to 'open' reason, and understand the new polemical relationship between reason and reality in modern science, the new interdependence of mind and matter, subject and object, interiority and exteriority. Quite clearly, our initial assumption concerning the value of rationality was too hasty. What of irrationality? Is irrationality in fact Bachelard's chief value in his work on poetry? I believe that if we say that it is, we are again being too hasty, too simple in our conclusions. I wish to argue instead that in his work on poetry Bachelard is trying to take us beyond irrationality, to a new understanding of the imagining consciousness, of the relationship between subject and object in the images of poetry.

Bachelard's preoccupation in his books on poetry is not with the unconscious but with the imagining consciousness, which he conceives as beyond irrationality and beyond rationality, as the complement rather than the opposite of the rational consciousness. What makes me say this? The broad lines of his work suggest it, of course, with the development from a psychoanalytical to a phenomenological approach to poetic images.[9] More important though, and more revealing, is the detail of the first series of books on poetry, published between 1938 and 1948, where the influence of psychoanalysis appears to be so strong. Here, Bachelard modifies and adapts psychoanalytical concepts in terms of his own values, his own established pattern of thought. His thinking is non-Freudian rather than anti-Freudian: he tries to go beyond Freud, just as he has tried for example to go beyond Bergson. What he learns from Freud and what he is forced to admit is the existence and influence in man of the unconscious, of irrationality. Earlier, he had denied this quite categorically in *L'Intuition de l'instant* (1932), stating that 'it is thought that rules our being' (p. 71). Six years later, in *La Formation de l'esprit scientifique* (1938), Bachelard modifies and complicates this conception of the rational consciousness, influenced here by his new knowledge of psychoanalytical theory. He realizes that the obstacle to knowledge is not just resistant matter but something in the mind itself. The scientist's mind is not tabula rasa, it is instead thoroughly prejudiced, marked by preconceived ideas and values, whose origin, he now has to admit, is in the unconscious. If we pause and take stock for a moment, we see here that Bachelard's thinking is non-Freudian, that he goes beyond Freud. He does not simply study the unconscious, for this would be to divide the human being, as Bergson had done, into separate areas of experience, and this Bachelard has always refused to do. Non-Bergsonian, his thought has to be non-Freudian. What preoccupies him here is still the polemics of reason and reality, the interdependence of subject and object. Freud is simply grist to the mill of his preoccupation. Freud, I think, and then Jung, not only complicate his understanding of the relationship between man and matter, but speed him towards the discovery of what has long interested him, the point beyond rationality and beyond irrationality where subject and object merge together in what he calls the 'intermediate zone' of consciousness, which for him constitutes poetic imagination and the imagining consciousness.

Why does Bachelard turn to write about poetry? Because, as he puts it in his article 'Instant poétique et instant métaphysique', 'poetry . . . should give us both a view of the world and the secret of a soul, a being and objects at one and the same time'.[10] And why does he approach poetry through its images? Because in the image, subject and object are conjoined, inseparable. To quote L'Air et les songes, in poetic images 'subject and object are wholly and entirely relative to one another. If we separate them, we are in fact ignoring the unity of imagination' (p. 142). What is the source of poetic images? Not, for Bachelard, the unconscious, not le rêve, the night dream that reveals our instinctual depths. Here, he modifies Freud. For Bachelard, the source of poetic images lies in what he calls the 'intermediate zone' between the unconscious and the rational consciousness, in rêverie, at the threshold of rational thought, and of objective knowledge about the world, in what he also describes in L'Eau et les rêves as 'the zone of material reveries that precede contemplation' (p. 6). Poetry is for Bachelard a kind of knowledge, and according to his theory of material imagination, poetic images reveal our relationship with matter, their emotional charge is the result not of conflict with other people, as in Freudian theory, but of conflict with matter. This surely reminds us of his earlier epistemology, and we see how it shapes his theory of poetry. Imagination, like reason, is against matter, the world, reality, and his notion of the 'coefficient of adversity', for instance, makes this plain.[11] Images, for Bachelard, reveal not just the poet's consciousness of the world but his consciousness of striving to know a resistant world.

The imagining consciousness is, in Bachelard's view, polemical. Is it also poetic? Yes, and this is essential to his theory and to his practice. 'The dreamer's being is constituted by the images to which it gives rise.' Bachelard writes this in 1960, in *La Poétique de la rêverie* (p. 130), just as he had said in 1938, in *La Psychanalyse du feu*, that 'psychically, we are created by our reverie' (p. 181). The poet is made by his images. And imagination is, as he declares at the beginning of *L'Air et les songes*, 'the true experience of *openness*' (p. 7). Imagination is, so to speak, a 'taking beyond', and not, as in psychoanalytical literary criticism (one thinks of Jean Delay on Gide, for example, or Charles Mauron on Mallarmé), a 'taking back' to childhood or adolescence, an *enclosing*. Again, we see the influence of Bachelard's earlier pattern of thought on his conception of the imagining consciousness, his preoccupation with opening experience beyond the conventional confines of mind and matter, interiority and exteriority. And this preoccupation shapes not just Bachelard's theory but his practice, the way he reads poetry.

Bachelard chooses to read fragments of poems and not poems as a whole. He does this partly out of modesty and partly in a combative spirit. Modestly, he leaves aside what he refers to as 'the problem of the *composition* of a poem as a grouping of many images' because, as he explains, this involves complex cultural and historical factors and their influence on the poet which he as a philosopher of science and not, one must remember, a professional literary scholar, feels to be beyond his competence (*La Poétique de l'espace*, p. 8). But there is more to this than is apparent, for Bachelard is also taking on here those literary critics who enclose the text they read in the matrix of its cultural or historical past. He is, in fact, intolerant of literary criticism and especially of those 'dogmatic' critics, as he calls them, who approach a text with certain preconceived ideas in terms of which they interpret and evaluate it, and who as a result fail to read the text itself. The dogmatic critics he has in mind are firstly the traditional, academic literary critics in France for whom the work is the mirror of rational thought and conscious life, and secondly those who more recently had taken the psychoanalytical approach, and for whom texts are the mirror of unconscious life and the irrational. Different as they are, these critics all reduce the work to the life, forgetting that poems – and indeed all literature, all art – have been created, that they imply a fundamental break with life: 'the work of genius', Bachelard declares in *Lautréamont*, 'is the antithesis of life' (p. 102).[12] Critics also forget that literature is written, that the images of poetry are written images, that they break with images perceived in daily life and with the images of our dreams and our unconscious. The images of poetry are beyond rational and irrational: they are written language, 'an event of the logos' (*La Poétique de l'espace*, p. 7); they are 'autonomous language', and free from 'the servitude of meaning' (*Fragments d'une poétique du feu*, pp. 36, 8). With his opposition to critics who reduce the work to the life, and with the stress he lays upon reading with 'a consciousness of language' (*La Terre et les rêveries de la volonté*, p. 7), Bachelard may well appear to be something of a crypto-structuralist. Yet his insistence on reading fragments of poems at the expense of any attention to their place in the whole undermines this glimpsed affinity. And there is an awkwardness, indeed a seeming self-contradiction in his approach to the reading of poetry, for while his dislike of reductive literary criticism suggests that his own priority is the poem itself and his method that of submission to the text, his reluctance to read a poem as a whole means that this is not so, that he is instead an undisciplined and insubordinate reader. Choosing to read fragments of poems does smack of indulgent subjectivism. How does this work out in practice?

Shelley, as I have noted, is one of the few poets Bachelard lingers over, discussing him at some length in *L'Air et les songes*, in particular in the section on *Prometheus Unbound*, given below. His interest in Shelley is also one of the most enduring, his first reference to the poet being in 1942, in *L'Eau et les rêves*, his last in *La Poétique de la rêverie*, in 1960. We can only guess at the origin of his interest, especially since he did not read English easily and relied on translations of the poems.[13] His three brief references to Shelley in *L'Eau et les rêves* are made in the context of his discussion of images of Narcissus in poetry (pp. 37, 38, 42); they are typical of the images he collected 'at random', as he puts it in *Fragments d'une poétique du feu*, as he read like some botanist out collecting specimens for future study (pp. 28–9), which are preserved independently of their source – he gives the page references in the French translation for the first two, without noting which poems they are from, only indicating the source of the third (*Prometheus Unbound*) – fragments that are used not so much for themselves but, alongside many others from other writers, to illustrate his argument. Here, against psychoanalytical literary criticism, Bachelard discerns in different poets' images of Narcissus firstly a positive, 'idealising narcissism' (pp. 34–6) – Narcissus loves himself as he would wish to be, not as he is, and so creates himself – and secondly a 'cosmic narcissism' (pp. 36–45), in which there is a dialogue between natural things and nature itself, the cosmos, whether it be like that of Shelley's flower, conscious of its own beauty reflected in the beauty of nature (pp. 37, 42) or like his image of water in which is engraved that of the sky (p. 38). Paradoxically, despite limiting himself to fragments of poems, Bachelard does succeed in reading the poem itself, unlike the psychoanalytical critics he opposes, whose reading is too often a conditioned reflex and whose interpretations are limited and automatic, the text being reduced to fit a preexisting framework of ideas. In this perspective, Narcissus is and will always be a passive, negative, and neurotic figure; wherever his name occurs in literature, we know how to respond and we need not read on. This kind of criticism misses the complexity of Narcissus which Bachelard discusses, and also the variations on this theme, the different ways in which this figure is used by different writers. In practice, then, despite our initial misgivings, Bachelard does succeed in revealing the text to the reader, in making us aware not just of the words on the page before us but of their oddity, their unexpectedness.

Bachelard's first references to Shelley are in the context of his polemic with psychoanalytical criticism. In *L'Air et les songes*, he considers three of Shelley's poems in more detail, *Prometheus Unbound* explicitly against traditional academic critics who stress Shelley's ideas and life as the key to his work, and 'To a Skylark' and 'Ode to the West Wind', which show his personal pleasure in these poems. He reads 'To a Skylark' (pp. 102–4) alongside other poems about skylarks in a chapter on 'the poetics of wings', and again only looks at parts and not the whole poem, though unusually he quotes line 15 and lines 71–5 in English. He begins by stressing the 'vibrant invisibility' of skylarks which Shelley best grasps, and the 'cosmic joy' suggested by the phrase 'unbodied joy', going on to show this cosmic aspect in lines 71–5:

> What objects are the fountains
>   Of thy happy strain?
> What fields or waves or mountains?
>   What shapes of sky or plain?
> What love of thine own kind? what ignorance of pain?

For Bachelard, the skylark 'defies all metaphors of form and colour' and he supports this by paraphrasing stanzas 1–5, or more precisely the phrases 'unbodied joy', 'cloud of fire', 'the blue deep thou wingest', 'and singing still dost soar, and soaring ever singest', 'keen as are the arrows of that silver sphere'. Shelley's skylark is, he goes on to say, linking this to the first and last stanzas, a 'pure image', existing only in poetry and not in nature, representing and describing nothing. Even more strikingly, he concludes this discussion with the statement that 'a pure *poetic object* ought to absorb at one and the same time the whole subject and the whole object. Shelley's pure skylark, with its *unbodied joy*, is the sum of the subject's joy and the world's joy' (p. 104). Bachelard succeeds not only in helping us to read familiar words with fresh eyes, but in challenging us – thanks to the way his work on science has led him to understand the relationship between human beings and the world – to think about poetry as language, as breaking with everyday objects and everyday subjects, and as breaching the dykes of exteriority and interiority. Bachelard's reading of 'To a Skylark' is far more stimulating than that of F. R. Leavis, who in *Revaluation* refers to this poem as 'a mere tumbled out spate ("spontaneous overflow") of poeticalities, the place of each one of which Shelley could have filled with another without the least difficulty and without making any essential difference' (p. 215).[14] Bachelard does not read with Leavis's preconception of poetry as involving the work of 'critical intelligence', and unexpectedly perhaps, he is more attentive to the words that are there in the poem and consequently more helpful to other readers.

A comparison between the responses of Bachelard and Leavis to Shelley's 'Ode to the West Wind' is also instructive. Bachelard quotes from the poem in French, again giving only fragments – lines 1, 13, 14, 47–62 (pp. 265–6) – which are framed, too, in a chapter entitled 'the wind', by fragments from other poems by other poets, which reveal what he calls dynamic images of 'violent air', images that must be read 'dynamically' in order to share this 'cosmic wrath', otherwise they will seem, he says, derisory (pp. 256–7). And he goes on to argue that 'in dynamic imagination, everything comes to life, nothing stops. Movement creates being . . .' (p. 258). It is just this movement in Shelley's 'Ode to the West Wind' that Leavis dislikes. Familiarity with the 'sweeping movement' of the verse should not prevent us, he insists, from asking 'the obvious questions':

In what respects are the 'loose clouds' like 'decaying leaves'? The correspondence is certainly not in shape, colour or way of moving. It is only the vague general sense of windy tumult that associates the clouds and the leaves . . . What again, are those 'tangled boughs of Heaven and Ocean'? They stand for nothing that Shelley could have pointed to in the scene before him . . . In the growth of those 'tangled boughs' out of the leaves . . . we have a recognized essential trait of Shelley's: his weak grasp upon the actual. (*Revaluation*, pp. 205–6)

Leavis complains about what Shelley is not; Bachelard takes the poem as it is, paying attention to the movement of its imagery, to the wind's ambivalence, to the 'gentleness and violence, purity and frenzy' of this 'Destroyer and Preserver', and to its cosmic dimension, where, 'breath of the universe', it links the poet to the life of this cosmic force, dynamizing and vivifying him (pp. 265–6). Leavis misses this, reading Shelley through the grid of his preconception that good poetry is produced by the 'active intelligence', and complaining that in Shelley's poems 'there is nothing grasped . . . no object offered for contemplation, no realized presence to persuade or move us by what it is' (*Revaluation*, p. 210).

It would seem that Bachelard the philosopher of science takes imagination more seriously than does Leavis the teacher and critic of literature, and this may well be because of what twentieth-century science has taught him, and the way it has complicated his understanding of objects, of the relationship between subjects and objects, mind and matter, interiority and exteriority. He has learned to think beyond conventional categories, to accept in Shelley's skylark, for instance, a 'pure' image which is both subject and object. And with regard to the skylark's 'vibrant invisibility', he declares humorously – and letting his profession show – that 'in poetic space, the skylark is an invisible particle accompanied by a wave of joy . . . the philosopher, fulfilling his function by being imprudent, might propose a wave theory for skylarks' (*L'Air et les songes*, p. 101). Wave theory, with what he referred to in *Le Nouvel esprit scientifique* as 'the dualism of waves and particles' (p. 87), breaks with habits of thinking and makes us 'unlearn' our notion of objects and their reality (p. 90), bringing us 'psychological benefit' (p. 88) by disrupting our preconceptions of the permanence, place, and identity of objects. And with Heisenberg's uncertainty principle, wave theory also complicates the relationship of subject and object, in the sense that the subject's method of observation interferes with the observed object (p. 126), and also because, as Bachelard puts it, 'it is in thinking about the object that the subject is most likely to acquire new depth' (p. 170). So behind Bachelard's joke about a wave theory for skylarks is his conception of the interdependence of subject and object in modern science, and we are struck once again by all that this 'imprudent' philosopher brings to his reading of poetry from his work on science, from his conception of 'open reason'.

Shelley, Bachelard asserts, is a 'true poet' (*L'Air et les songes*, p. 145), this truth being recognized by the effect his poetry has on the reader, whose imagination is changed, *opened* by what he reads (p. 13). This would seem a dangerously subjective and impressionistic measure of truth. Again, though, our conditioned reflexes and ingrained habits of thought need to be checked, and it will be useful, at this point, to follow a longer passage in which Bachelard considers Shelley's *Prometheus Unbound* and see, quite simply, if his approach works, if it helps us to read the poem. Why *Prometheus Unbound?* Bachelard had referred to Prometheus in *La Psychanalyse du feu*, inventing in chapter one the notion of the 'Prometheus complex' against that of the Oedipus complex, persuaded that human beings are driven not by sexual instincts but by the need and desire to know, by a 'will to intellectuality', the Prometheus complex expressing, he says, 'all those tendencies that drive us to *know* as much as and more than our fathers' (p. 26). Discussing in *L'Air et les songes* Shelley's account of the Prometheus story, Bachelard writes against those who prejudge Shelley's poetry, as for example T. S. Eliot does in 'The Use of Poetry and the Use of Criticism', taking it to be didactic and concerned with abstractions.[15] His choice of *Prometheus Unbound* is polemical, then. How does he read it? Bachelard's text is given below, in my own translation:

Shelley must have loved all nature, and in his celebration of river and sea, he surpasses other poets. His tragic life has bound him forever to the destiny of water. For us, though, it is the *air* that marks his work most profoundly, and if we were allowed only one adjective with which to describe a poet's work, then there would probably be little disagreement that Shelley's poetry is *aerial*. Yet however apt this adjective may be, it remains inadequate. We wish to prove that Shelley is, materially and dynamically, a poet of the aerial substance. The beings of the air, such as wind, perfume, and light, beings that have no form, all act *directly* on Shelley:

> The wind, the light, the air, the smell of a flower affects me with violent emotions.[16]

If we reflect upon Shelley's work, we shall see that, in some men, the soul responds to the *violence of gentleness*, sensitive as it is to the weight of all things weightless; we understand too how souls like this are dynamized by their very sublimation.

Shelley's poetic reverie bears the stamp of that *oneiric sincerity* which is, we would argue, decisive in poetry, and we shall in due course offer both direct and indirect proof of this. Let us now establish the terms of our discussion and take an image in which the 'oneiric wing' is obvious:

> Whence come you so wild and so fleet,
> For sandals of lightning are on your feet,
> And your wings are soft and swift as thought.[17]

The images here shift very slightly, detaching the wings from the sandals of lightning, yet this shift cannot destroy the unity of the image; the image is indeed one and indivisible, and what is soft and swift is the movement, and not the wing or the wing's feathers that some dreamer's hand caresses. Once again, we must insist that an image like this does not admit of any allegorical interpretation; it is as a movement of the imagination that our enraptured soul must understand it. Indeed, we would go as far as to say that this image is an action of the soul, that we shall understand if we are willing to *undertake* it. Elsewhere, we read that:

> An antelope
> In the suspended impulse of its lightness,
> Were less ethereally light.[18]

Shelley presents us with a hieroglyph that the imagination of forms would have great difficulty in deciphering. It is dynamic imagination that provides the key here: 'suspended impulse' is, in point of fact, oneiric flight. Only a poet can explain another poet. Alongside this 'suspended impulse' that leaves the imprint of flight in us, we might place these three lines from Rilke:

> There, where no path was ever made
> We flew.
> The arc is still imprinted on our minds.[19]

Now that we have seen something of what is fundamental and distinctive in Shelley, let us make a more detailed study of the deepest sources of his poems. Take for instance his *Prometheus Unbound*. We shall very soon see that this is an *aerial Prometheus*. If the Titan is bound to the mountain top, it is so that he may receive the very life of the air. He strains towards the heights with *all the strength* of his chains. He possesses to perfection the dynamics of his *aspirations*.

It is very probable that when Shelley, with all his humanitarian aspirations, dreamed his clear dreams of a happier human race, he saw in Prometheus a being who *raises* man to stand and confront Destiny, and the very gods themselves. All Shelley's demands for social justice are present and active in his work. Nevertheless, the imagination – whether we are talking about its resources or its movements – is always completely independent of any social commitment. Indeed, we are convinced that the real poetic force of *Prometheus Unbound* has absolutely nothing to do with any kind of social symbolism. The imagination is, in some spirits, more cosmic than social. This in our opinion is true of Shelley. Gods and demi-gods are not so much people – clear images, more or less, of human beings – but rather *psychic forces* which will play their part in a Cosmos possessing a truly psychic destiny. Let no one hasten to say at this point that these characters must therefore be *abstractions*: instead, this *force of psychic elevation*, this supreme example of the Promethean force, is preeminently concrete. It corresponds to a psychic *operation* with which Shelley was very familiar, and which he wanted to convey to his reader.

Let us remember first of all that *Prometheus Unbound* was written 'upon the mountainous ruins of the Baths of Caracalla, among the flowery glades' and facing 'dizzy arches suspended in the air' (preface). Any *terrestrial* would see columns here: an aerial can only see 'arches *suspended in the air*'. More accurately still, it is not the *shape* of the arches that Shelley looks at, but, if we may be allowed to use the word, their *dizziness*. The native land where Shelley dwells with heart and soul is the aerial realm, the land of the highest places. The drama of this land of his comes from this very dizziness, from this vertigo which is provoked so that it can be overcome and our victory savoured. Thus, man pulls at his chains in order to know the momentum of his eventual liberation. Yet let us make no mistake about it, the positive operation here is liberation. It is this liberation that makes clear the primacy of the intuition of air, which comes before the solid, terrestrial intuition of the chain. The real meaning of Promethean dynamism is to be found in this vanquished vertigo, in liberty's shaking chains.

In fact, even in the preface to *Prometheus Unbound*, Shelley makes it perfectly clear that we must interpret his Promethean images in a strictly psychological sense:

> The imagery which I have employed will be found, in many instances, to have been drawn from the operations of the human mind, or from those external actions by which they are expressed. This is unusual in modern poetry, although Dante and Shakespeare are full of instances of the same kind: Dante indeed more than any other poet, and with greater success.

Thus, *Prometheus Unbound* is placed under the aegis of Dante, that most verticalizing of poets, exploring as he does the two verticals of Heaven and Hell. For Shelley, every image is an *operation*, an operation of the human mind; the image has a spiritual, inner principle, even though it is thought to be the mere reflection of the external world. So, when Shelley tells us that 'poetry is a mimetic art', we must understand that poetry imitates what it does not see: human life in its innermost depths. It imitates forces rather than movements. The life we see and the movements we make can be described quite adequately in prose. Poetry alone can bring to light the hidden forces of our mental and spiritual life. Poetry is, in Schopenhauer's sense of the word, the phenomenon of these psychic forces. Any truly poetic image will have something about it that makes it resemble a *mental operation*. Understanding a poet in Shelley's sense does not therefore entail a kind of Condillacian analysis of the 'operations of the human mind', as a hasty reading of the preface to *Prometheus Unbound* would lead us to think. The poet's task is to set images in motion with his light touch, and so ascertain that in them the human mind is operating humanly, that these are human images, humanizing cosmic forces. We are led, then, to the cosmology of the human. Instead of living out naïve anthropomorphism, man is restored to profound and fundamental forces.

Now, mental life is characterized by its predominant operation: it desires to grow, to rise up. Its instinct is to seek the *heights*. Thus for Shelley poetic images are all operators, *elevation operators*, in fact. To put it another way, poetic images are operations of the human mind in so far as they give us lightness and height, and raise us up. They have only one reference axis: the vertical axis. They are essentially aerial. If a single image in a poem fails to fulfil this function of conferring lightness, then the poem is brought to the ground, and man returns to slavery bruised by his chains. With all the spontaneity of genius, Shelley's poetics always manages to avoid any such accidental heaviness, composing a sweet, harmonious nosegay of all the flowers of ascension. Shelley can, it seems, with one careful finger, measure the force which lies in every bud and frond, and raise it above the earth. Reading him, we understand Masson-Oursel's perceptive words: 'the summits of mental life are very much like tactisms'.[20] We *touch* the growing heights. It is in this region of the summits of mental life that Shelley's dynamic images operate.

It is not hard to understand that images which are so clearly polarized in the direction of height can easily acquire social, moral, and Promethean values. Yet these values are not sought after, they are not something that the poet is aiming at. Coming before any kind of social metaphor, the dynamic image reveals that it is a primary psychic value. Love for mankind sets us above our own being and offers no more than a little further assistance to one whose constant desire is always to live above his own being, at the summit of being. Thus, imaginary levitation is very ready to receive all the metaphors of human greatness; however, the psychic realism of levitation has its own driving force, which is in effect internal. This is indeed the dynamic realism of an aerial psyche.

> *L'Air et les songes. Essair sur l'imagination du mouvement*, Paris, Corti, 1943, pp. 49–53.[21]

Again, Bachelard's reading may seem undisciplined and impressionistic, hopping as it does between fragments – from Shelley's letter to lines 89–91, Act IV of *Prometheus Unbound*; from lines 75–7 of *Epipsychidion* to a Rilke poem, then back to the preface of *Prometheus Unbound* – and holding everything together by his notion that Shelley's imagination obeys the element of air. Subjective though his approach may be, Bachelard's insights coincide remarkably with the statistics given by Richard Harter Fogle in his study *The Imagery of Keats and Shelley*, which suggests through an image-count the importance of motor imagery in Shelley (pp. 33–5) and the link between his rich visual imagery and sensations of swiftness (pp. 94–100); 'the insatiable eye of Shelley', he notes, 'seeks always to pierce through, to go beyond physical possibility into the realm of the supernatural' (p. 46).[22] Fogle points up the ill-founded critical generalization that Shelley's poetry 'celebrates "a world of ideal abstractions" ' (p. 31), a view which his disciplined, orderly study of Shelley's imagery shows to be without foundation. This critical commonplace is also undermined by the scholarly work on Shelley by Harold Bloom and P.M.S. Dawson, all three supporting Bachelard to a remarkable degree – unwittingly – in his assertion that in Shelley imagination takes precedence over social commitment.[23] To quote Dawson: 'The world must be transformed in imagination before it can be changed politically, and it is here that the poet can exert an influence over "opinion". This imaginative re-creation of existence is both the subject and the intended effect of *Prometheus Unbound*' (p. 109).

For Bachelard, then, Shelley is 'a poet of the aerial substance', whose Prometheus is 'aerial', and certainly rereading the poem with a Bachelardian eye, one becomes very much aware of this aspect of Shelley's imagery. But what does it indicate? How are we to interpret it? There appears again to be a contradiction in Bachelard's approach: his use of the word 'oneiric' and his reference to 'the deepest sources' of Shelley's poems seem to indicate a psychoanalytical reading, while this is undermined by his emphasis on poetic images as 'operations of the human mind', which raise us up to 'the summits of mental life', to 'the summit of being'. The problem lies with Bachelard's idiosyncratic use of 'oneiric', not as a synonym for 'unconscious' but as a way of distinguishing between *rêve* and *rêverie*, as in fact the adjective for *rêverie*, that intermediate zone between consciousness and the unconscious, which as we have noted 'precedes contemplation'. He does not wish to cut off human beings from the world and isolate them in the unconscious. For Bachelard, on the contrary, Shelley's images not only liberate but take us beyond ourselves. Here, his reading differs from Fogle's: Shelley does not take us 'into the realm of the supernatural', he leads us instead 'to the cosmology of the human'. To quote *L'Eau et les rêves*: 'imagination . . . is a faculty of superhumanity. Man is man in proportion as he is superman. Man should be defined by the group of tendencies that drive him to go beyond the *human condition*' (p. 23). But how can we go beyond ourselves?

If we pause and reflect, we discern here again the stamp of Bachelard's conception of human consciousness as polemical and poetic: just as science has for him an ontological dimension, so too does poetry, and the reading of poetry. Hence my earlier suggestion that Bachelard's thought should be viewed as non-structuralist, as 'opening' structuralism. When we read, we are in language, in 'linguistic space' (*La Poétique de l'espace*, p. 11); more precisely, we are against new language, 'new' because it is not ours and because it is unexpected, even odd, 'an explosion of language' (*La Terre et les rêveries de la volonté*, p. 7), 'a violating of language' (*Fragments d'une poétique du feu*, p. 39). And this consciousness of new language does not decentre us but rather it changes us: 'if, examining a literary image, we are conscious of language', Bachelard writes, 'we receive from it a new psychic dynamism' (*La Terre et les rêveries de la volonté*, p. 7). He is persuaded that, as he says in *Lautréamont*, 'the poet must create his reader' (p. 103), that 'the chief function of poetry is to transform us' (p. 105). The reader, in a state of 'open imagination', must 'continue the writer's images' (*La Terre et les rêveries du repos*, p. 92), opening himself to something beyond himself, to 'imagination which is offered' (*Fragments d'une poétique du feu*, p. 37). If Bachelard writes about the images of poetry in a way that seems rambling and impressionistic, it is in large measure because he seeks to 'continue' these images, because reading is valued not just for its revelations about someone else but for the possibilities it releases in the reader. And Bachelard is not simply a reader: he writes what he reads, for us and for himself. He describes himself reading 'pen in hand' (*L'Air et les songes*, p. 283), and enjoins us to do the same, either copying out the poem we read or in our own way 'continuing' the writer's images. Why read like this? Reading 'pen in hand' means that we are doubly exposed to language, first to language that is not our own, that is different, and then to language which is at one and the same time ours and not ours, language which did not exist before our encounter with this new linguistic object, yet which does not simply repeat that object but in its own way 'continues' it. Writing what we read helps us to understand ourselves, to grasp something of our own complexity, playing as it does between the poles of subject and object, and so breaching the dykes of the internal and external worlds.

Bachelard the philosopher brings to his reading of Shelley ideas formed in and growing out of his work on twentieth-century science, and this is particularly clear when he 'continues' *Prometheus Unbound*, interpreting Shelley's phrase 'operations of the human mind' in his own terms, as restoring man 'to profound and fundamental forces' through the interdependence of the human and the cosmic: man is restored to himself by his polemics with the world, 'restored' not in the sense of recovering identity but of discovering the difference that is an ontological necessity. Bachelard the reader guessed – humorously – that heaven must be an enormous library, and his reader's prayer is well known: 'give us this day our daily need' (*La Poétique de la rêverie*, p. 23). We smile, but recognize that he is serious, for without this need, we shall not seek the sustaining 'other', and we shall starve. Bachelard the philosopher and reader of Shelley's *Prometheus Unbound* chose in old age to return to 'the central figure' of Prometheus in his unfinished 'La Poétique du feu', published at last in 1988. The different figures of Prometheus in mythology and literature suggest to him 'a *going beyond the self*' (*Fragments d'une poétique du feu*, p. 115), and he notes that for Jung, Prometheus represents consciousness (pp. 126–7). Perhaps this is what drew him, instinctively, towards this particular poem. Bachelard restates his own view of consciousness in this last book, finding new metaphors for it. Consciousness is not as Bergson conceived it, he reaffirms; it is discontinuity, it is 'kaleidoscopic consciousness', rich and ever-changing (p. 32). And his fragmentary way of reading poetry is described here quite explicitly as being 'systematic' (p. 105), a way of recovering, against life, that fragmentary, 'kaleidoscopic consciousness'. A last metaphor expresses very strikingly Bachelard's view of the two aspects of his work, on science and on poetry, not as *either* the same *or* different, but as *both* the same *and* different, as a sustaining, nourishing discontinuity:

the human being is a hive of beings. It is distant thoughts and unruly images that are the honey of being. (*Fragments d'une poétique du feu*, p. 47)

# Notes

A germinal form of this chapter appeared in the *Journal of the British Society for Phenomenology*, vol. 12, no. 1, January 1981, as 'Polemics and Poetics: Bachelard's Conception of the Imagining Consciousness'.

1 Roland Barthes, 'Criticism as Language', *Time's Literary Supplement*, 27 Sept., 1963: 'Gaston Bachelard . . . founded a whole critical school which is indeed so prolific that present-day French criticism in its most flourishing aspect can be said to be Bachelardian in inspiration . . .' (p. 739); Gilbert Durand, *Les Structures anthropologiques de l'imaginaire*, Paris, Presses Universitaires de France, 1963, passim.

2 *L'Eau et les rêves. Essai sur l'imagination de la matière*, Paris, Corti, 1942; *L'Air et les songes. Essai sur l'imagination du mouvement*, Paris, Corti, 1943; *La Terre et les rêveries de la volonté*, Paris, Corti, 1948; *La Terre et les rêveries du repos*, Paris, Corti, 1948.

3 *Physics and Philosophy*, Cambridge, Cambridge University Press, 1942, pp. 175–6.

4 *La Philosophie du non. Essai d'une philosophie d'un nouvel esprit scientifique*, Paris, PUF, 1940, p. 9; p. 144; *La Formation de l'esprit scientifique. Contribution à une psychanalyse de la connaissance objective*, Paris, Vrin, 1938, p. 15; *L'Activité rationaliste de la physique contemporaine*, Paris, PUF, 1951, p. 223.

5 *L'Intuition de l'instant*, Paris, Stock, 1932; edition used: Paris, Gonthier, 1966.

6 *L'Etre et le néant*, Paris, Gallimard, 1943, p. 32; *Being and Nothingness*, translated by Hazel E. Barnes, London, Methuen and Co., 1957, pp. lxii–lxiii, where the phrase is in fact omitted by the translator.

7 *Le Nouvel esprit scientifique*, Paris, PUF, 1934.

8 *Le Rationalisme appliqué*, Paris, PUF, 1949; *L'Activité rationaliste de la physique contemporaine*, Paris, PUF, 1951; *Le Matérialisme rationnel*, Paris, PUF, 1953.

9 For the latter, see *La Poétique de l'espace*, Paris, PUF, 1957; *La Poétique de la rêverie*, Paris, PUF, 1960; *La Flamme d'une chandelle*, Paris, PUF, 1961.

10 Originally published in *Messages*, t.1, cahier 2, 1939; now included in *L'Intuition de l'instant*, Paris, Gonthier, 1966, pp. 101–11, quotation from p. 103; also in *Le Droit de rêver*, pp. 224–32 (see note 3).

11 *L'Eau et les rêves*, p. 213; *La Terre et les rêveries de la volonté*, p. 29, 52–3, 62; Sartre borrowed this idea from Bachelard in *L'Etre et le néant*, pp. 389, 561–2, 564; see translation (note 8), pp. 324, 481–2, 484.

12 *Lautréamont*, Paris, Corti, 1939.

13 Both John G. Clark in 'Bachelard devant la poésie anglaise' and Paul Ginestier in 'Bachelard et ses lectures anglaises' draw attention to the fact that Bachelard's interest in English poetry coincides with the Occu-

pation; for both articles, see *Revue de littérature comparée*, avril–juin, 1984.

14 F.R. Leavis, *Revaluation: Tradition and Development in English Poetry*, London, Chatto & Windus, 1936.

15 T. S. Eliot, 'The Use of Poetry and the Use of Criticism', 1933, in *Selected Prose of T.S. Eliot*, edited and with an introduction by Frank Kermode, London, Faber & Faber, 1975, pp. 81–6.

16 Bachelard's footnote attributes this quotation to Louis Cazamian, *Etudes de psychologie littéraire*. Cazamian in fact quotes (in French) from a letter from Shelley to Claire Clairmont, written at Pisa on 16 January 1821. I quote here from this letter, published in *The Letters of Percy Bysshe Shelley*, edited by Roger Ingpen, London, C. Bell and Sons Ltd., 1914, p. 843.

17 *Prometheus Unbound*. Bachelard quotes Shelley in the French translation by Rabbe, without referring to the specific poem.

18 *Epipsychidion*. Again, Bachelard gives only the page reference to the Rabbe translation.

19 My translation. Bachelard's footnote: Rilke, *Poems*, translated into French by Lou Albert-Lasard (VI).

20 My translation. Bachelard's footnote: Masson-Oursel, *Le Fait métaphysique*, p. 49.

21 Bachelard continues to discuss Shelley on pp. 53–65; I omit these here for the sake of brevity and because he makes much the same points. A full translation of this book is now available as: *Air and Dreams: An Essay on the Imagination of Movement*, translated by Edith Farrell and C. Frederick Farrell, Dallas, Texas, Dallas Institute of Humanities and Culture Publications.

22 Richard Harter Fogle, *The Imagery of Keats and Shelley: A Comparative Study*, Chapel Hill, University of North Carolina Press, 1949.

23 Harold Bloom, *Shelley's Mythmaking*, New Haven, Yale University Press, 1959; P.M.S. Dawson, *The Unacknowledged Legislator: Shelley and Politics*, Oxford, Clarendon Press, 1980.

## · 8 ·

# Philosophy's Refuge:
# Adorno in Beckett

## JAY BERNSTEIN

*'Ah the old questions, the old answers,*
*there's nothing like them!'*
Samuel Beckett

1. Beckett's *Endgame* is too central to Adorno's thought to elaborate its place in a short compass:

The essay on *Endgame*, 'Trying to Understand Endgame', presents it as revealing the final history (*Endgeschichte*) of the human subject. The essay, while characterizing the truth content of the play, cannot itself sustain that content, for the truth contents of works of art cannot (now) be discursively redeemed. For us, for now, authentic artworks, such as *Endgame*, can grasp our age more accurately, more acutely, more perspicuously than can analytic thought. But that this is so requires philosophical elaboration; such an elaboration is the work accomplished by *Aesthetic Theory*, which was, of course, to be dedicated to Beckett. *Aesthetic Theory*, then, is the tracing of the possibility of art being the saying of what philosophy cannot, can no longer, say.[1]

The subject matter of aesthetics ... is defined negatively as its undefinability. That is why art needs philosophy to interpret it. Philosophy says what art cannot say, although it is art alone which is able to say it: by not saying it. (*AT*, p. 107)

This articulation of the relationship between art and philosophy is not without precedent; to register, or at least to begin to register the particulars of Adorno's employment of it is the governing intention of what follows.

2. A first approximation: Art's way of saying by not saying can be projected through art's constitution as an autonomous realm of awareness in Kant's critical system. That constitution is a product of a double isolation: first, the diremption of questions of moral value from questions of truth and falsity – the fact/value distinction; and second, the separation of artistic worth from moral worth – the inscribing of art within the autonomous domain of the 'aesthetic'. This latter separation is perspicuously represented in the Kantian dictum that works of art are purposeful in themselves while lacking any positive, practical (ethical) end over and above their complexion. These exclusions mark the silencing of art. However, even in Kant, art is defined not only by means of the exclusion of cognition and moral worth, but equally through the *approximation* and *analogy* in aesthetic judgments of taste or judgment in a concept and the requirement of universality. Kant, we might say, models his account of aesthetic judgment on what is excluded from it.

Because a double logic of exclusion *and* approximation and analogy is operative here one might be tempted to say that taste (in Kant) represents an anamnesis and an adumbration of some substantial rationality of which it is a cipher; that as excluded from the work of conceptual judgment and autonomous moral legislation the pleasure represented in judgments of taste is the (violently) repressed, whose repression is the condition for the specious purity of truth and moral worth; and then we had better say, too, that aesthetic pleasure has suffering (via exclusion and repression) as its condition. And perhaps here we should raise the question of the efficacy and thoroughness of Kant's double logic, that is, the question of whether what is excluded is wholly excluded, of whether it can, conceptually, remain excluded? How is what occurs here different than what occurs in theories of language which begin by instituting a distinction between literal and metaphorical discourse?

All these are thoughts and questions which Adorno does or could raise: but for his inaugural interrogation of these matters we need to look elsewhere. Adorno contends that while Kant's theory is philosophically false, it is socially and historically true. In modernity art's forms become autonomous from the discursive and normative rationality governing non-artistic practices. Crudely, that autonomy is required in virtue of, on the one hand, the demand by capitalist economies to be autonomous from non-economic values, hence permitting the reduction of all use objects to exchange equivalences; and, on the other hand, the formal and historical *a prioris* governing artistic practices themselves, which presumptively require those practices, insofar as they do stay out of the market place of mass art, to recognize the formal and technical exigencies peculiar to each specific practice. But these exigencies turn out in each case to instigate a normative practice, a praxis, within their respective object domains, producing, hence, non-discursive, value-impregnated truth claims.

Thus, to say that art is consigned to an autonomous realm is to say that art's own forms have no non-artistic validity. But this is to say that artistic production, insofar as it remains true to its forms, can sustain only artistic – 'aesthetic' – significances. So the explanation of the thesis that the truth claims of art are unredeemable is that art's forms are autonomous from the discursive and normative forms of non-artistic domains, and since the autonomy of art's forms is a condition for their 'truth' production, then *a fortiori* art's truth claims are unredeemable in terms external to art itself. In, for example, Gadamerian terms, this is to claim that the differentiation infecting artistic reception equally infects artistic production, and it infects by stripping art's *forms* of their previous discursive and teleological significances.

3. A second approximation: Because art's praxis has become autonomized, consigned to a realm outside the centre(s) of societal production and reproduction, its praxis is a pseudo-praxis, a praxis which transforms without external societal effects. Nonetheless, art's very restriction to an autonomous domain entails that its forms can, although harassed, provide a reminder and a clue as to what non-dominating or normatively constituted praxis might be like. Because art works are clues and reminders inscribing more than mere logical possibilities, they possess truth contents making truth claims.

Art works talk like the good fairies in tales: if you want the unconditioned, it will be bestowed to you, but only *unkenntlich*, indecipherably. By contrast, the truth of discursive knowledge, while unveiled, is precisely for that reason unattainable. (*AT*, p. 183)

What, minimally, Adorno is here claiming is that the only conception of discursive rationality we have at our disposal is instrumental rationality, the rationality of Weberian rationalization. Adorno ties this rationality to commodity production which reduces qualitatively distinct individuals to exchange equivalences. Knowledge in accordance with this regime is unveiled because it tolerates no alterity. In its universality this regime of knowledge and reason has become unreason, its promise of freedom domination.

Art, on the other hand, figures what it would be like to comprehend individuals without dominating them. The claim that this is what occurs in art depends, again, upon Adorno's contention that there is a fundamental social truth underlying Kant's account of aesthetic judgment. Works of art do unify their diverse elements by means of their forms; but the operation of these forms is *less than* the unity accomplished through conceptual synthesis. Conceptual synthesis, as identity thinking, represses the non-identical, the sensuous complexity and individuality of any particular item. Art forms, techniques, and modes of ordering, as residues of earlier practices stripped of normative authority and discursive validity, as (now) autonomously 'aesthetic' forms, can only insist that the elements and materials upon which they work are susceptible to another sort of integration. Art objects are 'unique', their uniqueness (non-identity) lying in their non-conceptual form of unification. Art forms, then, synthesize without dominating; their work of unification mimicking or analogous to conceptual unification and teleological synthesis without, however, ever attaining to their level of explicitness. Because art works are not conceptual wholes, they are not redeemable through ordinary discursive forms; because their work of unification is an analogue of conceptual unification and teleological (practical/normative) synthesis, they claim for themselves cognitive and ethical attention.

Art works are impossible objects: if aesthetic praxis were really transformative, then art works would be 'true', that is, art objects would be worldly objects, not purposeless but purposeful; if, on the other hand, they were mere objects or artefacts, they would be just things or meaningless but purposeful. Works are meaningful, they enact a synthesis, but not discursively true; they are purposeful but without a practical purpose. Their meaning is a semblance of truth without domination; their purposelessness an image of use value that cannot be exchanged. Their purposelessness is their form of resistance to exchange – a form that is harassed and subject to defeat.

Their non-conceptual form is their form of resistance to identity thinking – a form that is harassed by the desire for meaning, e.g. in engaged or committed art, and by the will to interpretation. The autonomy of art is the plus, the surplus, the excess, the non-identical which allows identity thinking to continue unharassed. Art is the remainder, the result of the exclusions which allowed an autonomous economy to centre itself without the encumbrances of the claims of sensuousness or teleology (the submersion of use value by exchange value), and is equally the periphery forever threatening and threatened by the centre. In this way the Kantian thought that aesthetic awareness mimics the unifying work of conceptual judgment without, however, actually bringing the art object under a concept, becomes both a conception of artistic practice, a conception of how artistic form is to deal with its raw materials, and a statement about the socio-historical predicament of art rather than an *a priori* truth about it.

4. Now an obvious critique of Adorno at this juncture would be to claim that art's forms are not sufficiently autonomous from the dominant modes of societal reproduction for them to avoid complicity with what they deny. Adorno agrees and goes further:

> art is part and parcel of the process of the disenchantment of the world . . . It is inextricably entwined with rationalization. What means and productive methods art has at its disposal are all derived from this nexus. *(AT*, p. 80)

Art's practices and progress, even when they are regarded as autonomous, especially when they are regarded as autonomous, cannot be altogether detached from the logic of Enlightenment. Even the idea of 'autonomy' evokes the ideological figure of the autonomous subject, the free subject, the constitutive and truth-making subject: the subject of domination. And art's forms and techniques, too, are but a version of the liberation of technique, of a growth in the forces of production. Yet form remains art's resistance to, and distance from, empirical reality, art 'mobilizes technology in a different direction than domination does' (ibid.). Artists must submerge their autonomy in the autonomy of their forms; for all that artists are still the makers and producers of works. This approaches what can be regarded as the riddle of art.

A metaphysics of art today has to centre on the question of how something spiritual like art can be man-made or, as they say in philosophy, merely pos-

# JAY BERNSTEIN

ited, while at the same time being true. . . . To ask how an artefact can be true is to pose the question of how illusion – the illusion of truth – can be redeemed. Truth content cannot be an artefact. Therefore every act of making in art is an endless endeavour to articulate what is not makeable, namely spirit. (*AT*, p. 191)

Art's attentiveness to the demands of form in its 'endless endeavour to articulate what is not makeable' images the conditions necessary for art to be something that does not fit into empirical reality, for art to be non-identical; only what does not fit into empirical reality can be true. 'Art,' Adorno says, 'is rationality criticizing itself without being able to overcome itself' (*AT*, p. 81).

Art is both part of the disenchantment of the world and a critique of disenchantment; either way, art is historical, as are its truths. Because of this, art's resistance to empirical reality is only ever temporary; its not fitting into empirical reality, which is its determinate negation of society, is not a permanent achievement of the work itself, but depends equally on its conditions of reception. Reception, the will to interpretation, together with changes elsewhere tend to neutralize works, depriving them of their critical edge. 'Neutralisation is the social price art pays for its autonomy' (*AT*, p. 325).

Without form hyper-Fichtean positing is unavoidable, squandering the difference between art and artefact, truth and domination. Yet form is no longer sufficient to guarantee authenticity or autonomy; after all, art's autonomy is its *lack* of purpose or point (in extra-artistic terms), and its forms harbour complicity and resistance in equal measure.

. . . in modernist arts the achievement of the autonomy of the object is a *problem* – the artistic problem. Autonomy is no longer provided by the conventions of an art, for the modernist artist has continuously to question the conventions upon which his art has depended; nor is it furthered by any position the artist can adopt towards anything but his art.[2]

5. *Endgame* is set in a shelter (or ark, perhaps) after the disaster, let's say a nuclear war or the flood; certainly, for Adorno, after Auschwitz. Toward the end of the play Clov, after announcing that there is no more pain-killer, takes down the picture (painting), the pain-killer, the remnant of art, the opaque ark of meaning, which has hung face to the wall since the beginning of the play, and hangs up the alarm-clock in its place.

> Hamm: What are you doing?
> Clov: Winding up.
> Hamm: Look at the earth.
> Clov: Again!
> Hamm: Since it's calling to you.

Let us, for present purposes, ignore the questions of time and history here, that winding up is both finishing and, in this context, beginning; and let us ignore too the question of the 'alarm' (isn't it too late for alarms, or is this one set to wake the dead?). Let us focus.

Art, or philosophy, or any form of practice is bound to be inadequate, an inappropriate response to the now infinite disaster. As Adorno succinctly puts it, there 'is simply no conceivable standpoint from which the disaster might be named or articulated' (*AT*, p. 354). But we are always standing somewhere, talking; so winding up, having done with art and meaning is less easy than it appears: the habit of meaning is hard to break. Maybe, but who are we to say, the task of ending meaning is infinite too (maybe that is the disaster – too), an uncompleteable task; perhaps we can be stopped, but not finish. But things are worse than this, truly, for there are these *others*: lovers, fathers, mothers, sons, the earth, which, dominated, disfigured, deformed as they are – more – 'corpsed', 'zero' as they are, call to us, still lay claim to us. Or do they?

How can art stop being a pain-killer yet be appropriate to what makes all response inappropriate and still, still authenticate the call of the things of this unworldly world? How can it make a promise that is not complicit with what has undone all promises or kept them too well?

Perhaps this is just wrong, perhaps I am making too much of an idle line of dialogue; perhaps nothing calls us, claims us that could not be shown to be culpable, another lie or curse or promise, another harbinger or dove of meaning – which in this situation is in a way true. But this is just Beckett's artistic problem: to authenticate alterity, excess, the non-identical, in such a way that recuperation, his meaning it, promising it, and our interpreting it, is impossible. Only in this way can the idea of determinate negation be sustained, can the unreason of all our reasoning and interpreting (meaning) be demonstrated, and the reason of aesthetic 'irrationality' be vindicated.

6. Readings of Beckett tend to either overshoot or undershoot this

target; that this is Beckett's target, I shall come to later. Here is Stanley Cavell overshooting:

These are the endgames of suffering with which we begin: I win, my suffering ends, either when I learn perfectly that suffering is punishment, that is to say, that I deserve it, that I am perfectly sinful; or when I win the competition of suffering itself. These exhaust the strategies of suffering used in the shelter. To get out, these ways of winning have to be brought to an end; suffering has to stop being *used*, has to stop *meaning* anything, and become the simple fact of life. Where it is a game, it is a losing game; where existence is interpreted, sheltered, it is lost. . . .

Solitude, emptiness, nothingness, meaninglessness, silence – these are not the *givens* of Beckett's characters but their goal, their new heroic undertaking. To say that Beckett's message is that the world *is* meaningless, etc. is as ironically and dead wrong as to say it of Kierkegaard or Nietzsche or Rilke, for whom emptiness or perfect singleness are not states – not here and now – but infinite tasks. Achieving them will require passing the edge of madness, maybe passing over, and certainly passing through horror, bearing the nausea Zarathustra knows or the vision of oneself as a puppet ('the husk, the wire, even the face that's all outside') as in Rilke's fourth *Duino Elegy* – not protesting one's emptiness, but *seeing* what one is filled with. Then the angel may appear, then nature, then things, then others, then, if ever, the fullness of time; then, if ever, the achievement of the ordinary, the faith to be plain, or not to be. . . . We *have* to talk, whether we have something to say or not; and the less we want to say and want to hear the more willfully we talk and are subjected to talk. How did Pascal put it? 'All the evil in the world comes from our inability to sit quietly in a room.' To keep still.[3]

This recruits Beckett to Cavell's own, in its own way challenging, ethical comprehension of Wittgenstein's rejection of theory, the attempt to make the facts of life, what we do, although always too much or too little, suffice, urging us to acknowledge the sufficiency of our ways of going on or failing to do so. Although Beckett (and/or Hamm) does strive to undo theological meaning, strives to make the world un-created, so that it can stop being God's world and become (again, at last) ours,[4] and further, strives to thwart the fetishes of sense or meaning which resound in all those progeny of theological meaning that go by the name of philosophy, it would nonetheless be false to claim that *we* could ever be in a position to just acknowledge the facts of life, that that could ever do the trick for us, letting the angel appear. This, typically, de-historicizes our predicament, and Beckett's, too much. It is no accident, I think, that Cavell so quickly lets the shelter become *the* ark, forgetting, or taking insufficient note of the fact that it is (also) a bomb shelter, the writing figuratively after the bomb, literally after Auschwitz – if the difference between that figure and that fact can register, be 'rationally' grasped, make any difference. The thought that if we could just sit still, just stop theorizing, even if this is not 'just' but an infinite task, appears in the light of present history to be a case of misplaced concreteness, as if the task of silence, solitude, meaninglessness might be a better bet (option, plan, programme) than the games of meaning. In saying this I do not mean to oppose therapeutic undoing to, say, revolution; but simply wish to note how much more and differently intractable our position is as it manifests itself in Beckett than in Cavell's account, and further note how much more circumspect Beckett is about the outcome or how it might be achieved. If there is a Utopian moment in Beckett, and I will agree that there is, it is not named or nameable. You cannot get there from here.

7. Here is Adorno apparently undershooting:

Through its own organized meaninglessness, the plot must approach that which transpired in the truth content of dramaturgy generally. . . . The interpretation of *Endgame* therefore cannot chase the chimera of expressing its meaning with the help of philosophical mediation. Understanding it can mean nothing other than understanding its incomprehensibility, or concretely reconstructing its meaning structure – that it has none.[5]

Like Cavell, Adorno recognizes that the work of the play is to undo meaning, that meaninglessness is a goal of sorts. Hence Adorno's strategy of pointing to Beckett's use of parody to undo the conventions of the unity of time, place, and action; his parody of the philosophemes of existential literature, his dehydration of the dialectic of master and slave, etc. All of this might lead to the suggestion that, say, the meaning of the play is that there is no meaning. But that, surely, is too facile, too close to the easy rejection of meaning, the existential angst or celebration of meaninglessness; the play sets out to undo. That kind of meaninglessness will not do, if for no other reason than it leaves out of account the work of the play itself.

Adorno does not undershoot in this way, but the suspicion that he does derives from his unwillingness, shall we say, to interpret the play (as Cavell does, for example). Some of the frustration and disorientation one encounters in reading 'Trying to Understand *End-*

*game'* orginates in Adorno's curious combining of a studied elaboration of certain key elements in the play's construction while simultaneously maintaining an equally studied silence as to the play's overall meaning. Although on first reading one experiences this practice of elaboration and silence as an oblique interpretation of the play requiring decipherment, further reading confirms the simple duality of the practice. Adorno is silent and not oblique about the play's meaning.

> Achieving an adequate interpretive understanding of a [modernist – JMB] work means demystifying certain enigmatic dimensions without trying to shed light on its constitutive enigma. (*AT*, p. 177)

8. It is Adorno's silence that requires decipherment; and whatever that silence does signify, it is not meaninglessness.

> Beckett's plays are absurd not for their absence of meaning – if they had no meaning they would be irrelevant rather than absurd – but because they put meaning on the agenda, tracing its history. His work is dominated by the obsession with positive nothingness and by an equally obsessive concern with meaninglessness in its historical genesis. We deserve the emptiness we live in, but no positive meaning can be attached to this emptiness. (*AT*, pp. 220–1)

By 'positive nothingness' Adorno intends, I take it, that nothingness that is *achieved* through the negation and cancellation of previous modes and strategies of bestowing meaning on experience. This nothingness is a historical accomplishment, slightly more accessible than the telos of the infinite task Cavell recommends. But one must not be seduced by this accomplishment into thinking its end is itself an answer, a meaning. Rather, as Adorno puts it, it puts meaning on the agenda. And we must say here that the last 'it' refers to the play as a whole.

'Look at the earth . . . Since it's calling to you.' And so, too, is Beckett's play. The calling is, to be sure, a call to meaning, but as such, as it appears and calls it is equally the play's resistance to meaning. The call is meaning being put on the agenda; the resistance is the meaning we are trying to leave behind. The play works if these two meanings can be separated and their difference sustained.

Beckett's play resists meaning while placing it on the agenda through being a work claiming us, calling to us *beyond* our capacity to interpret or redeem its call. Its suggestion of meaning is achieved negatively, through its cancellation of positive meaning while remaining indefeasibly *a work*. Its Utopian suggestion of a reconciliation between masters and slaves, fathers and sons, man and nature is not said; its appearance is a consequence of the artistic rigour of its negations. Each of Beckett's later reductions continue this path: the more stringent, minimal, negative the work, the more authentic the hypnotic suggestion of meaning becomes. Meaning can stay on the agenda just so long as it is not for us.

The mark of authenticity of works of art is the fact that their illusion shines forth in such a way that it cannot possibly be prevaricated, and yet discursive judgment is unable to spell out its truth. (*AT*, p. 191)

9. Beckett's reflection on his play's meaning comes in the 'play within a play', in Hamm's story which is told centrally about two-thirds of the way through the play, and whose eventual, deferred completion coincides with the play's end; indeed, in some oblique way Hamm's ability to end his story seems to be a condition for the play's ending. I read this story as, of course, part of Hamm's attempt at self-understanding and self-justification; but more, as a parodic inversion of some familiar narratives of belief and salvation, *and* as an elliptical allegory of the place of art (stories, narrative, plays, etc.) in a world without meaning.

The story, told throughout in a 'narrative tone', concerns a man coming to Hamm to secure aid for his starving son. It is Christmas Eve, the son has been asleep three days, the father requests some bread. Hamm's first response is to challenge the man: imagine your son getting better, what then? 'I lost patience. (Violently) Use your head, can't you, use your head, you're on earth, there's no cure for that.'[6] One can 'cure' hunger, but not the human condition, meaninglessness. Hamm continues: the man has touched a chord in him; he offers to take him into his service, there the man could die in peace and comfort. Here perhaps we are to imagine the man prevaricating briefly; then he asks Hamm if he would consent to take the child in too.

It was the moment I was waiting for. (Pause.) Would I consent to take in the child . . . (Pause.) I can see him still, down on his knees, his hands flat on the ground, glaring at me with his mad eyes, in defiance of my wishes. (Pause. Normal tone.) I'll soon have done with this story.

It is not until his final monologue, his final reckoning, which ends the play, that Hamm does complete the story, as if returning to a task long left incomplete. After contriving a short elegiac poem, itself perhaps a commentary on the play, Hamm suddenly returns to the story:

If he could have his child with him . . . (Pause.) It was the moment I was waiting for. (Pause.) You don't want to abandon him? You want him to bloom while you are withering? Be there to solace your last million last moments? (Pause.) He doesn't realize, all he knows is hunger, and cold, and death to crown it all. But you! You ought to know what the earth is like, nowadays. Oh, I put him before his responsibilities! (Pause. Normal tone.) Well, there we are, there I am, that's enough.

10. It has been suggested that the play can end at this juncture because the story has allowed Hamm 'to reveal his deep sense of not having been cared for . . . and his deep resentment that such care could ever exist for anyone else: the father in his story must surely be a false altruist, as the narrator's arguments about responsibility prove'.[7] This won't do, most evidently because it is quite unclear that the play does 'end': Clov is not gone, Hamm's parents, perhaps, are not dead (And even if dead, is *he* done with them? What is it to be done with a parent? Their physical death may make our dealings with them less cumbersome, but not necessarily easier); the conclusion, Hamm's final words, 'Old stancher! . . . you remain' are both false (Clov is still there) and a decisive echo of Hamm's first speech. It all may begin again. Worse, such an 'ending' would imply that we could have done with this world, with meaning and being, merely through an expression of resentment and disappointment. Endings, as traditionally understood, require a metaphysical substantiality which modernist art in general, and the whole movement of Beckett's play in particular, of necessity, must refuse.[8]

11. In his first speech we find Hamm saying: 'Enough, it is time it ended, in the refuge too.' All is ended outside the refuge, outside the ark of art. But how are things to be ended in the refuge? In what sense would it remain, still, a refuge? It is these questions which circulate around Hamm's narrative, providing it with its thematic and structural significance.

Hamm's story/parable/chronicle/autobiographical tale is, we've said, an (in)version of a host of New Testament tales (especially *John*

4:46–53). Most emphatically, however, it parodies, repeats, inverts, comments upon *Genesis* 22. We tend to read that story through Kierkegaardian eyes, as a tale of the utter alterity of God, of his excessiveness, of the demand for a teleological suspension of the ethical, and of the groundlessness of faith. The Bible appears less circumspect in attributing a motive to Abraham: 'But the angel of the Lord called to him from heaven and said, "Abraham! Abraham!" And he said, "Here am I." He said, "Do not lay your hand on the boy, or do anything to him; for now I know that you fear God, seeing you have not withheld your son, your only son, from me." ' These gods, the fearful and the loving, they always asked too much and gave too little, or gave more than we could bear. Even here, excess and domination mingle, obedience and meaning coalesce; non-identity quickly recuperated, by an angel no less. Why should Hamm demand less than an angel . . . or a god? (There is a slight problem here in that the Hebrew of the time did not distinguish fear from obedience, so that perhaps no motive is being attributed to Abraham. I find this conjecture implausible; if they did not distinguish fear from obedience, how can we in our reading of the story? Could we ever fully detach this story from the game of threats, tests, and promises in which it is embedded?)

In this new parable of excess, this riddle of the non-identical, Hamm, this (new, last) God-king-master-father-son-self-subject, finds the father's excessive behaviour intolerable. We should not, however, be tempted by an easy psychologism here, be tempted to say that Hamm attempts to negate the father's love or benevolence or altruism, for we have tried love and fear, sacrifice and suffering, benevolence and altruism, these dogs of meaning. Beckett is careful to extinguish all motive from the story. This is a parable of the non-identical, of what cannot be interpreted, conceptualized, explained, or understood. Hamm, like a good god or critic, provides temptations, strategies for containing, denying, controlling this excess, this truth beyond illusion, this illusion beyond prevarication. How could this narrative of excess end? *End* and still be excessive? Of course, the narrative does not end; we do not know what the father did, and hence are prohibited from conjecturing an explanation, a *reason* for his choice. The inadequacy, the hopelessness of Hamm's conclusion is clear.

But you! You ought to know what the earth is like, nowadays. Oh, I put him before his responsibilities.

What appears here is a luminous incommensurability.

12. The assumption governing the belief that modernist art is now the organon for philosophy is that philosophy is irrevocably conceptual in its praxis, and conceptual praxis is (necessarily) abstract: identity thinking. Philosophy, then, cannot avoid complicity with domination. Its attempts to avoid complicity – ellipsis, parataxis, fragmentation, examples – do not suspend complicity so much as provide a reminder of it. Art's artefactuality and its reliance on non-conceptual techniques open a space between it and empirical existence. That space is not indelible. Further, the meaning of that space as a determinate negation of empirical existence is not something art can say without forfeiting its title as art. Philosophy can continue only by becoming non-philosophy, through the sub-ordination of its praxis to the praxis of art. Adorno continues the praxis that was philosophy, but it is not philosophy that he practises. The title *Aesthetic Theory* marks the incommensurability of the work with itself, the impossibility and the necessity of its content.

13. *Coda*. Works of art are

after-images of prehistorical shudders in an age of reification, bringing back the terror of the primal world against a background of reified objects . . . Even if mankind once upon a time, in a condition of helplessness vis-a-vis nature, really feared the shudder that was gripping it, the opposite fear of the dissipation of that shudder is equally keen and legitimate. Enlightenment is always accompanied by the fear that truth, which set Enlightenment in motion, is going to be sacrificed in its progress. Thrown back upon itself, enlightenment moves farther and farther away from its goal, which is some kind of objective certainty. Hence under the strain of its ideal of truth, enlightenment is forced to retain what it tends to discard in the name of truth. (*AT*, p. 118)

Aesthetic transcendence and disenchantment achieve unison in the speechlessness that characterizes Beckett's work. (*AT*, p. 117)

. . . no more pain-killer.

# Notes

1 References in the text to Adorno's *Aesthetic Theory* (*AT*) will be to C. Lenhardt's translation, London, Routledge & Kegan Paul, 1984. Some

slight modifications in the translation have been made where necessary. *Aesthetische Theorie*, edited by Gretel Adorno and Rolf Tiedemann, was published posthumously in Frankfurt am Main by Suhrkamp Verlag, 1970.

2 This is not Adorno, but Stanley Cavell, 'Ending the Waiting Game', in his *Must We Mean What We Say?*, Cambridge, Cambridge University Press, 1976, p. 116.

3 ibid., pp. 151, 156, 161.

4 See ibid., pp. 140–1.

5 'Trying to Understand *Endgame*', translated by Michael T. Jones, *New German Critique*, Spring 1982. 'Versuch, das Endspiel zu verstehen', in *Noten zur Literatur II*, Frankfurt am Main, Suhrkamp Verlag, 1961.

6 Samuel Beckett, *Endgame*, London, Faber & Faber, 1956, p. 37. For the next two quotes see pp. 37 and 52 respectively.

7 Kristin Morrison, *Canters and Chronicles*, London, University of Chicago Press, 1983, p. 39.

8 'What the early Lukacs called the discharge of meaning was supposed to be the ability of a work of art to reach its inner destination and therefore come to an end, much like an old person who dies after having savoured life to its full extent. Today this is denied works of art. They can no more die than can the hunter Gracchus. This manifests itself directly as an expression of horror. The unity of art works cannot be what it must be, i.e. a unity of a manifold. By synthesizing of the many, unity inflicts damage on them, hence also on itself. Works of art then are deficient, regardless of whether they are immediate entities or mediated totalities' (*AT*, p. 212).

# Index

Abraham 56, 189

Abraham, N. 104; and Maria
Torok's *Cryptonomie: le verbier de
l'homme aux loups* 104; and
Torok's *L'écorce et le noyeau* 109n

absence 80; dialectic of 80; and
presence 80

abyss the, 52, 76–7; *see also mise-en-abîme*

action 132

Adorno, T. 5–6, 177–91; *Aesthetic
Theory* 6, 177, 187, 190, 191n;
'Trying to Understand *Endgame*'
177, 185–6

aesthetics 39, 67n, 71–2, 177–80;
*see also* Kant

*ahnend* 62

alienation 147; and language 142–3;
and self-expression 142

alterity 55–6, 80–1, 91n; of the
night 81

anamnesis 178; and hypomnesis
103

*Angst* 15–16; and *Gelassenheit* 15–16

anteriority 49–50, 60–2; of the
poem 50, 60–1; as *préssentiment*
61–2

*aporia* 78

approximation 178; mathematical

157; *see also* knowledge

Aristotle 29

art 6, 30, 37, 41, 43–5, 47, 177,
179, 180, 182, 183, 188, 190;
committed 181; metaphysics of
181; modernist 190; and morals
178; and philosophy 177, 183,
189; as protection 43; and
representation 43; work of art as
absence 45–8; *see also il y a,*
praxis

Auschwitz 182, 185

Austin, J.L. 97

authentic: Being 24; Being-
towards-death 8–10, 12–13, 21–2;
Being-a-whole 14, 23; existence
10

authenticity 13, 16, 21–2, 52–3, 56;
and death 53; of erring 52; and
inauthenticity 13–14, 22; *see also*
Being

auto-eroticism 73

Bachelard, G. 5–6, 153–76;
*L'Activité rationaliste de la
physique contemporaine* 155; *L'Air
et les songes* 155, 162–5, 168–71,
173; *L'Eau et les rêves* 155, 162,
164, 173; *Essai sur la connaissance*

Index

Hyginus 20

idealism 135, 156; *see also il y a*
identity: non-identity 183, 189;
    thinking 181, 190
*il y a*, the, 4, 42–6, 55–8, 64, 69n;
    and art 43; and the existent 45;
    and idealism 42; and the neuter
    49; relationship to the night 42–
    4, 46; *see also* Levinas
image 67n–68n, 91n
imagination 141, 145, 148, 154,
    155, 162–3, 167–8, 169–70, 172–
    3; 'dynamic' 166; the imaginary
    149; and perception 141, 149;
    and reason 155, 156; *see also*
    poetry
individual, the 142–3; and
    domination 180
infinity: 'good' and 'bad' 106
information: theory of 92n
inspiration 50–2; as time of the
    poem 51
interiority: and exteriority 158–9,
    160–1, 167, 174
introjection 102, 104; and
    incorporation 102, 103–4, 106; as
    psychological term 102

Jahn, G.R.: 'The Role of the
    Ending in Leo Tolstoi's "The
    Death of Ivan Il'ch"' 34n
Jung, C.G. 174

Kafka, F. 50
Kant, I. 1, 4, 89, 126, 127, 134,
    151, 181; aesthetic judgement
    180; critical system of 178;
    Derrida on 'transcendental
    illusion' 127; *Schematismuslehre*
    83; 'transcendental illusion' 127–8
Kaufmann, W. 14–16, 18
Kelkel, A. 38–40, 58
Kierkegaard, S. 1–2, 5, 184, 189;
    *Concluding Unscientific Postscript* 2

Klossowski, P. 7–9
knowledge 156, 158, 180;
    Bachelard's 'approximate
    knowledge' 157, 159; discursive
    179; objectivity of 157, 162; *see
    also* reason, science
Krell, D. 90
Kristeva, J. 5, 112–37;
    'L'Engendrement de la formule'
    112; 'genotext' 113, 136;
    'intertextuality' 117; 'Objet ou
    complément' 123–5; 'productivity
    called text' 119

Lacan, J. 134, 146; and
    consciousness 126; *Écrits* 126;
    notion of inarticulable 146
Lacoue-Labarthe, P.: *Mimesis* 69n
Land, N. 4
language 1, 73, 134, 141, 146, 155,
    173, 178; alienating power of
    142–3, 147, 149; circle of 73;
    essence of 2; limits of 2; and
    linguistic space 173; materiality
    of 141, 147, 149; meta- 72–3;
    outside 141; of poem 49–50, 72;
    poetic 44, 48–9, 51; and Sartre's
    *practico-inert* 143–4; and silence
    63; and speech 142, 143; and
    thought 142; of tradition 63
Laporte, R. 41
law 63; astro-physical 83
Leavis, F.R.: *Revaluation* 166–7; on
    Shelley 166–7
Levinas, E. 4, 18, 32n, 37–69; and
    absence of the gods 48; and
    death 18; and the 'dire' (saying)
    58; 'Énigme et Phénomène' 54,
    69n; and ethical relation 57; and
    ethics 55, 58, 69n; *Existence and
    Existents* 42–5; the face of the
    Other 18; and the *il y a* 4, 42–6,
    55–8, 64, 102; and insomnia 42–
    4, 46; and inspiration 50, 60; and
    neutrality 47–8, 58; and the

*Compiled by Jamie Brassett and Sharon Bowes*